"Building on her work in Intercultural Therapy and Supervision, Dilek explores how culture, race, and diversity shape group therapy. Drawing on four decades of clinical and teaching experience, she weaves insights, reflections, and theory to create inclusive, culturally responsive group spaces centred on the client's voice. A thoughtful and engaging contribution—highly recommended."

Ravind Jeawon, *BBS, PDipICPsy, MIACP, Psychotherapist, Practice Manager, Clinical Supervisor*

"British group analysts have long awaited a reframing of group-analytic theory, and Dilek Güngör has answered the call. Centring on the historically excluded "other," she highlights overlooked voices and intercultural dimensions. By challenging colourblind narratives, her work offers an inclusive space for practitioners and clients to engage with group dynamics, providing a corrective and comprehensive approach."

Charles Brown, *Psychoanalytic psychotherapist and supervisor*

"This book offers a timely exploration of group psychotherapy in intercultural contexts. Clear and accessible, it speaks to bilingual readers and those for whom English is not a first language, blending theory and clinical insight into a valuable resource on identity, belonging, and dialogue across cultures."

Ayten Şare, *Senior Group Analytic Psychotherapist and Clinical Supervisor, UKCP Reg*

"This book invites readers into a meaningful conversation on group therapy across cultures. Through reflective insight and clinical experience, the author explores how identity, belonging, and dialogue take shape in groups. Warm in tone yet rigorous in scholarship, it is a valuable resource for practitioners working in diverse settings."

Sega Habtom, *Senior Counsellor, BACP Reg., Working at Nafsiyat-Intercultural Therapy Centre*

The Art of Reflective Practice in Intercultural Group Therapy

The Art of Reflective Practice in Intercultural Group Therapy proposes a relational, practice-based, and ethically reflective model for working with culturally diverse groups in therapeutic settings.

Most existing texts on intercultural therapy tend to focus on individual work, often overlooking the complexities unique to group contexts. This book aims to address that gap by exploring how cultural difference influences group dynamics, therapeutic processes, and clinical outcomes. It also considers what arises when patients from diverse cultural backgrounds come together in a group setting, attending to the internal experiences of both the group members and the therapist. Rooted in group analytic traditions and drawing on the foundational work of S.H. Foulkes and Jafar Kareem, this book places intercultural sensitivity, lived experience, and cultural narratives at the centre of group analytic practice.

This book is aimed at therapists, counsellors, nurses, students, and practitioners working with groups or individuals – especially those from diverse cultural backgrounds. It offers practical, accessible guidance for addressing the complex dynamics of cultural diversity in therapeutic settings.

Dilek Güngör, UKCP- and Nafsiyat-registered psychotherapist, group analyst, and clinical supervisor, integrates her multicultural heritage and personal experiences into her therapeutic practice and writings on intercultural group work.

The Art of Reflective Practice in Intercultural Group Therapy

A Group-Analytic Perspective

Dilek Güngör

Routledge
Taylor & Francis Group
LONDON AND NEW YORK

Designed cover image: © Dilek Güngör, Flower in Vase (1993)

First published 2026
by Routledge
4 Park Square, Milton Park, Abingdon, Oxon OX14 4RN

and by Routledge
605 Third Avenue, New York, NY 10158

Routledge is an imprint of the Taylor & Francis Group, an informa business

British Library Cataloguing in Publication Data
A catalogue record for this book is available from the British Library

Library of Congress Cataloging-in-Publication Data
A catalog record has been requested for this book

ISBN: 978-1-041-21191-4 (hbk)
ISBN: 978-1-041-21189-1 (pbk)
ISBN: 978-1-003-72601-2 (ebk)

DOI: 10.4324/9781003726012

Typeset in Sabon
by Taylor & Francis Books

To my son, Umut Ulaş Er, whose childhood I had to watch from afar, yet whose presence I now hold close, trusting that he always felt my love; and to my patients worldwide, whose courage has shaped my journey.

Contents

About the Author

In this book, Dilek Güngör explores the world of intercultural group therapy through theory, clinical cases, and the therapist's personal reflections. The book reveals the challenges and insights of working across cultures, while questioning the limits of mainstream healthcare for marginalised communities. More than a guide, it invites therapists and students to reflect, write, and engage deeply, thereby opening new paths for understanding, connection, and culturally responsive practice.

The author is a psychoanalytic and intercultural psychotherapist, group analyst, and clinical supervisor, who has been registered with the UK Council for Psychotherapy (UKCP) since 1996. She trained at Goldsmiths, University of London, and at the Institute of Group Analysis. Her multicultural heritage and personal journey, as well as the significant challenges that she has faced, inform her therapeutic approach. She has held senior roles at the Nafsiyat Intercultural Therapy Centre, the Women's Therapy Centre, and other statutory and voluntary organisations. In addition, she has contributed to key publications, including *Intercultural Therapy: Challenges, Insights and Developments* (edited by Baffour Ababio and Roland Littlewood, Routledge, 2019) and *Intercultural Supervision in Therapeutic Practice: Dialogues, Perspectives and Reflections* (edited by Baffour Ababio, Routledge, 2023).

Foreword

Writing about intercultural therapy has historically been concerned with the individual setting. From the outset, the work of Jafar Kareem and his colleagues at Nafsiyat focused on what happens when migration, race, class, faith, and culture enter the analytic relationship between therapist and patient. That work remains vital.

This book carries that inheritance into the group setting. Dilek Güngör shows how the group is not simply a gathering of individuals, but a place where cultural histories, exclusions, and possibilities of connection are lived out in the open. In doing so, she extends the reach of intercultural therapy and breaks new ground that has been left untouched for too long.

Her writing is rooted in experience – nursing, community development, mental health, psychotherapy, exile, and analysis. She already knew something of marginalisation, as aspects of her Kurdish identity were pushed to the edge of public and cultural life in Türkiye (formerly Turkey) long before she came to Britain. These are not side notes. They shape the way she listens and the way she writes.

Language is central here. Turkish is her mother tongue. English is the language in which she works and has written this book. She has also written in Turkish. The constant negotiation between the two – what is lost, what can be carried across, what changes in translation – is part of her practice. There is the risk of being misunderstood, of nuance slipping away, of speaking with an accent heard before the words. None of this is incidental. It threads through her work and her understanding of what is at stake in intercultural therapy.

The style is distinctive. Reflective. Sometimes autobiographical. Open, unhurried, often free-flowing. She writes in a way that invites readers to pause with her, to recognise themselves in the material, and to think alongside her rather than to be instructed. Her writing is accessible, but never superficial.

What she describes is demanding work. Group therapy is never simple, and in intercultural contexts the complexity deepens. She writes of silences that weigh heavily, of fear and suspicion, of exclusion felt and enacted. She does not cover over these realities. She shows how staying with them allows meaning to emerge, slowly, unevenly, but with substance.

The book also includes what is all too often absent from the literature: the voices of Black and minoritised therapists. Where are their accounts, their clinical insights, their perspectives? Why do they appear so rarely, while other voices – White voices – are heard again and again?

As a concept, interculturality predates Nafsiyat. What Kareem and his colleagues did was to give it a distinctive shape within psychotherapy – psychoanalytic and intercultural, carrying migration, race, class, language, and faith into the centre of their work. It is from this shaping that Güngör builds, extending it into the life of the group. Her achievement lies in showing how Nafsiyat's intercultural tradition can live within group practice, carrying its psychoanalytic and cultural attentiveness into the shared life of the group.

The book will be helpful to many. Trainees who are beginning to notice cultural dynamics in groups but lack words for them. Practitioners who have long sat with these tensions and want to see them named and worked with in writing. Supervisors who need to hold intercultural awareness and group process together. It also offers a perspective that refuses reduction to procedure – one that applies as much to management as to clinical practice.

I commend *The Art of Reflective Practice in Intercultural Group Therapy: A Group-Analytic Perspective* – a book written with honesty and openness, grounded in a long personal journey, and alive to the realities of group life.

It does not tell the reader what to do. Instead, it reminds us how thinking and listening can be held.

Baffour Ababio
Intercultural psychoanalytic psychotherapist and Clinical Director at Nafsiyat Intercultural Therapy Centre, London; Editor of *Intercultural Supervision in Therapeutic Practice: Dialogues, Perspectives and Reflections* (Routledge, 2023)

Preface

This preface introduces the key themes explored throughout the book. It begins by tracing my personal and professional journey, highlighting the challenges I faced as a political writer and how these experiences shaped my relationship with writing. It then critically reflects on dominant models in group therapy – particularly those of Farhad Dalal, Irvin Yalom, and Otto Kernberg – and their frequent neglect of the lived realities of marginalised patients. The preface concludes by outlining the book's central aim: to prioritise intercultural sensitivity, challenge mainstream assumptions, and advocate for more inclusive therapeutic practice.

From an early age, writing was my sanctuary – a way to process thoughts and emotions. I am deeply grateful to my tutor and supervisor at the University of London, Professor Diane Waller, whose encouragement transformed the act of writing into both an intellectual and personal pursuit. Yet my relationship with writing was profoundly shaped by trauma. As a political activist advocating for women's rights – a cause seen as threatening to the system – I was arrested and spent nearly two years in prison. To avoid a 15-year sentence, I denied authorship of my articles, which focused on women's rights and the pervasive dominance of men, even within left-wing politics. This left a lasting mark, making it difficult to write freely for many years.

These experiences strengthened my commitment to justice and deepened my respect for human resilience. They also planted the earliest seeds of my therapeutic journey, shaping my sensitivity to pain, my endurance and my awareness of the complexities of human care. My work in intercultural therapy continued to evolve, often prompting me to question whether my experiences could contribute meaningfully to a field dominated by conventional narratives. Through dialogue with colleagues and patients, alongside training in group analytic psychotherapy, I recognised the value of both my story and those of my patients. These reflections inspired me to write a book that challenges established models and offers fresh, practice-based insights. As a minority psychotherapist and group analyst, I have faced moments of self-doubt, questioning the strength of my voice. Yet, as this work unfolded, its purpose became clear: this book is not only a personal testament but also a contribution to intercultural group therapy, especially for those whose voices are often under-represented – patients from working-class backgrounds, Black and other minority ethnic groups, and individuals with limited education or literacy.

With over 30 years of experience as a psychotherapist and a lifetime of involvement in nursing and human care, my clinical work is informed by a comprehensive understanding of care, healing, and human complexity. This extensive background enriches the insights shared throughout the book, grounding theoretical perspectives in practical wisdom gained from diverse settings and populations. While detailed clinical examples are presented in later chapters, this foundational experience underpins the reflective and critical approach adopted here.

Acknowledgements

I extend my deepest gratitude to all my patients, whose courage and determination have profoundly shaped my understanding of resilience. Their trust in sharing their individual journeys of growth and recovery has been a continual source of inspiration.

I am particularly grateful to my group analyst, the late Tom Hamrogue, and to the group members who challenged me to engage with the complexities of culture shock and group dynamics. Although the group was predominantly composed of White European patients, I was the only one whose background, accent, and appearance stood out from the majority, which often brought issues of difference to the surface. Tom's consistent and thoughtful presence enabled me to transform these challenges into opportunities for growth and deeper self-awareness. His theoretical and clinical insights continue to inform my understanding of group and intercultural therapy. While Tom supported me, he did not simply offer comfort – he also challenged me, helping to sharpen my awareness and deepen my understanding. Before joining the group, I worked with my individual therapist, Parizad Bathai. Through her I was meaningfully shaped in both my professional and personal development, which provided a strong foundation for my therapeutic work. I am also deeply grateful to Roderick Cameron, with whom I had therapy for many years. Leaving the group felt like parting from family – a profound loss I explored through further analysis. These relationships have been crucial to both my personal and professional development.

I greatly appreciate the support I received during the writing process. I am particularly appreciative of Baffour Ababio for his generosity and encouragement, my colleague and friend Gita Patel, and the late Evonne Cameron-Phillips, whose wisdom enriched our peer supervision and continues to inspire me.

I am especially indebted to Jane Cook, a nurse, colleague, and the Chairperson of Nafsiyat, whom I have known since 1994 and with whom I had the opportunity to work in support of homeless people and refugees. Her compassion and dedication have been a meaningful source of inspiration in my work. My 32 years at the Nafsiyat Intercultural Therapy Centre have been the most rewarding of my career. Engaging with colleagues and patients from diverse backgrounds has continually enriched my understanding of intercultural therapy and has naturally deepened my commitment to the field. These experiences shaped this book and continue to shape my practice. To all those who have influenced my path, directly or indirectly, I offer my deepest gratitude. This book reflects the many voices, challenges, and moments of growth I have encountered along the way.

Background to the Book

This book explores the complex nature of therapeutic and large group dynamics through a framework grounded in theory, informed by clinical experience, and shaped by broader social realities. I share my personal perspective on the experiences, challenges, and insights that underpin my approach to therapy. I practise as a progressive psychotherapist, guided by principles of social justice, equality, and respect for diverse perspectives, while firmly opposing all forms of fascist ideology.

My mother tongue is Turkish. My paternal heritage is Kurdish-Kurmanji, and my maternal roots lie in Yörük (Nomadic Turkmen) ancestry. Socio-political pressures obscured my Kurdish identity during childhood; I only recognised its importance in adulthood. While I do not explore this in detail here, it remains a significant part of who I am and continues to inform both my worldview and my clinical work.

I arrived in the United Kingdom in 1988 under difficult circumstances and later became a British citizen. Despite having attended an English grammar school in Türkiye, life in the UK came as a profound culture shock. The language, attitudes, and lifestyle were alien to me. I felt overwhelmed but managed to maintain a composed exterior – a skill honed during my time as a hospital theatre nurse.

A chance encounter at the Medical Foundation for the Care of Victims of Torture (now Freedom from Torture) introduced me to therapy. It marked a turning point that led to years of individual and group analysis. I chose to face emotional pain without medication, trusting in the power of talking therapies.

My group therapy journey is rooted in both personal and family experiences. Over the years, I have worked in nursing, education, community development, and mental health. My first job in the UK was as a domestic cleaner – an experience that taught me humility and attention to detail, and inspired a metaphor that continues to guide my therapeutic work. I think of myself as a 'mind cleaner' – someone who helps people to clear emotional and psychological clutter. This journey has also been shaped by the quiet reality of exile; building a life and starting a family away from my homeland has deepened my understanding of resilience, belonging, and the emotional complexities often encountered in group therapy.

At first, I hesitated to include personal information in this book, yet I recognised that it adds valuable context for readers, especially given the limited literature on intercultural therapy. Sharing felt risky. But as I read more and stopped comparing my work to others, I embraced the challenge. With support from friends and colleagues, I now share my insights with confidence, showing that this work is possible. If I can do it, others can too.

I once believed that analytic therapists should remain anonymous. Over time, I have come to see that the question is not whether to disclose, but how and why. When done thoughtfully, personal sharing can deepen therapeutic understanding (Casement, 1985). One of the freedoms that comes with age is the ability to speak more openly, without fear of judgement. I also believe that group therapists, by nature, are social people, which can make thoughtful disclosure in therapy both possible and meaningful.

Although Freud emphasised neutrality, he occasionally disclosed personal material when it served a theoretical purpose. In *The Interpretation of Dreams*, his analysis of the 'Irma's injection' dream provides one such example (Freud, 1900). I take this further – not to centre myself, but to ground theory in lived experience. Sabina Spielrein and Anna Freud also integrated personal elements into their work. Spielrein drew on her own analysis and emotional struggles to shape early psychoanalytic thought (Clarke, 2001; Jung, 1961), while Anna Freud, in her focus on child analysis, openly acknowledged the challenges she faced in practice (Young-Bruehl, 1988).

While the 'blank screen' model remains dominant in analytic traditions, I challenge its rigid application, particularly for patients from Black and ethnic minority backgrounds (Comas-Díaz, 1994; Constantine and Sue, 2006). In my view, authenticity and thoughtful self-disclosure enhance therapeutic work by addressing cultural complexity and fostering trust. In that spirit, I share my experiences in this book to enrich the therapeutic dialogue and affirm that people from marginalised backgrounds can engage in and contribute to analytic work, especially if an intercultural framework is offered.

This book explores intercultural group therapy through theory, clinical practice, and personal reflection. It encourages therapists to engage critically with group dynamics and cultural tensions by fostering a reflective stance. In particular, I hope that analytic therapists will feel invited to consider and share their own assumptions, uncertainties, and missteps – not as failures, but as opportunities for learning. It is through such honest reflection that our clinical work can deepen and evolve. In a profession rooted in human connection, authenticity is essential. Therapists who recognise uncertainty and learn from mistakes build stronger relationships. Clinical errors are inevitable; what matters most is our response.

Each chapter in this volume blends theoretical ideas with real-world clinical examples to illustrate how cultural awareness and sensitivity can strengthen therapeutic work. Themes include group dynamics, race and identity, supervision, and the impact of immigration.

Although intercultural therapy has analytic roots, these are often overlooked. Much of the literature focuses on individual therapy, leaving group settings underexplored. This book builds on S.H. Foulkes's group-analytic model and is informed by the important contributions of Jafar Kareem, Roland Littlewood, and Lennox Thomas in the field of intercultural therapy. It offers a distinct perspective by centring cultural narratives, lived experience, and intercultural sensitivity within group settings – a continuum that informs this book's reflective approach and clinical insights. I write primarily as a clinician. My clinical practice often leads the way, with theory following naturally – whether aligning with existing models or evolving through lived experience.

My writing may feel free-flowing – I welcome that. I do not strive for perfection as a writer or a therapist. Writing allows me to reflect and invite dialogue. Spoken words fade; written words endure.

I do not write to instruct with certainty but to offer experience as a resource, recognising that psychotherapy is not about perfection, but about engagement, reflection, and growth. I hope that this book will encourage others – especially those from under-represented backgrounds – to share their voices. I have observed that some White, Western therapists publish entire books centred on a single patient. Meanwhile, many Black and ethnic minority therapists – despite their depth of insight – hesitate to share. Their silence is shaped by systemic and personal barriers. I hope that this book will address that imbalance.

Finell (1985) reminds us that therapists may unconsciously use narcissistic defences, such as splitting, denial and, projection, if they haven't undergone rigorous personal analysis. This is particularly relevant to my own worldview, which emphasises critical self-reflection, awareness of positionality, and ongoing personal and professional growth. In intercultural work, recognising one's assumptions and blind spots is not optional; it is essential for ethical and effective practice. Intercultural group therapy, while grounded in psychoanalytic and group analytic traditions, expands them by placing cultural, racial, and social diversity at the centre. It responds to the marginalisation of patients' lived experiences in many mainstream models, especially those from under-represented communities. This approach invites therapists to develop openness to difference and to reflect critically on identity and power. It helps to build therapeutic spaces that acknowledge complexity and foster deeper connections with others.

References

Casement, P., 1985. *On Learning from the Patient*. London: Tavistock Publications.

Clarke, J., 2001. *In Search of Jung: Historical and Philosophical Enquiries*. London: Routledge.

Comas-Díaz, L., 1994. 'Women of Color and Psychotherapy', *Psychotherapy: Theory, Research, Practice, Training*, 31(4), pp. 597–606.

Constantine, M.G. and Sue, D.W., 2006. 'Factors Contributing to Optimal Human Functioning in People of Color in the United States', *The Counseling Psychologist*, 34(2), pp. 228–244.
Finell, J.S., 1985. 'Narcissistic Personality Disorders and the Therapeutic Relationship', *Psychoanalytic Psychology*, 2(1), pp. 17–30.
Freud, S., 1900. *The Interpretation of Dreams*. London: Hogarth Press.
Jung, C.G., 1961. *Memories, Dreams, Reflections*. London: Collins.
Young-Bruehl, E., 1988. *Anna Freud: A Biography*. New Haven, CT: Yale University Press.

Why I Chose This Title

The title of this book, *The Art of Reflective Practice in Intercultural Group Therapy: A Group-Analytic Perspective*, captures the aim of this book: to approach group psychotherapeutic work with cultural sensitivity and awareness. The word 'art' reflects the relational and flexible nature of intercultural group psychotherapy, resisting rigid methods and allowing space for context and nuance.

Grounded in group-analytic principles, the intercultural model offers a richer, more inclusive framework for all patient groups. It draws attention to the way in which cultural narratives, power relations, and unconscious processes – including those shaped by race and racism – subtly influence group life.

Bringing together theoretical reflection, clinical experience, and cultural awareness, this book presents a comprehensive group-analytic approach, carefully crafted with patience and respect for complexity. The front cover features an oil painting that I produced in 1993, at the start of my group therapy training. Rather than the human figures typically seen on books about group therapy, I chose a colourful bouquet of flowers to reflect the warmth, vibrancy, and diversity of intercultural group work. The bouquet also symbolises the group itself – different flowers coming together to form something greater than the sum of their parts, just as individuals in therapy create a group.

Note on Terminology

Throughout the book, I use the term 'patient' rather than 'client'. This choice reflects my belief that therapy is a gradual process, requiring patience, understanding, and persistence. Transformation unfolds slowly, and the term 'patient' reminds us of the care, attention, and time that is essential to the therapeutic journey.

Note on Confidentiality

To safeguard patients' privacy and to uphold the highest ethical standards, all identifying details – including names, locations, and specific time frames – have been intentionally altered. Clinical examples and stories have been fictionalised or are presented as composites: while inspired by real cases and group work, details have been changed and characters created or combined to prevent public identification. This approach preserves confidentiality while maintaining the integrity of the work and keeping the reader's focus on the therapeutic process and its insights.

References to certain real organisations (e.g. Nafsiyat) and individuals (such as teachers and supervisors) have been retained with respect and appreciation. These exceptions have been included with care and do not compromise the confidentiality of any patients or therapeutic work.

List of Abbreviations

BBC	British Broadcasting Corporation
CBT	Cognitive Behavioural Therapy
CEO	Chief Executive Officer
ESOL	English for Speakers of Other Languages
FGM	Female Genital Mutilation
GP	General Practitioner
IAPT	Improving Access to Psychological Therapies
IOPC	Independent Office for Police Conduct
NHS	National Health Service
PTSD	Post-Traumatic Stress Disorder
UKCP	UK Council for Psychotherapy
UNFPA	United Nations Population Fund
UNHCR	United Nations High Commissioner for Refugees
WHO	World Health Organization

Introduction

This introduction critically examines how key figures in the psychodynamic and group therapy literature engage with cultural and group processes. While Jafar Kareem's work offers a foundational understanding of cultural identity in therapeutic contexts, his focus remains primarily on the individual experience. Nevertheless, his contributions provide a vital conceptual lens through which group dynamics can be more deeply understood and contextualised.

In contrast, although the approaches of Farhad Dalal, Irvin Yalom, Nancy McWilliams, and Otto Kernberg offer valuable insights, they tend to prioritise either the individual or the group without fully addressing the sociopolitical, cultural, and systemic forces that shape therapeutic encounters. Using Kareem's framework as the foundation, this introduction explores the strengths and limitations of these theorists' models in the context of culturally diverse group therapy.

A notable exception to the general neglect of race in the group therapy literature is Farhad Dalal's *Race, Colour and the Processes of Racialization*, which offers a rigorous examination of unconscious racial dynamics and institutional exclusion. Dalal challenges therapists to confront the way in which race and power operate within groups, linking these processes to wider societal structures (Dalal, 2006). However, his framework pays limited attention to the way in which race intersects with class, education, and economic marginalisation – particularly in the lives of working-class, uneducated, or illiterate patients from Black and other ethnic minority backgrounds. This omission reflects a wider gap in the field, where those most in need of culturally competent care are often overlooked. A more explicit engagement with these intersecting dimensions could enhance the inclusivity of his model and bring it closer to the lived realities of many patients.

While Dalal refers to working-class experience and poverty in some of his other writings, these themes are not consistently developed within his group therapy framework. Moreover, the relative scarcity of clinical case studies limits the demonstration of how his theoretical ideas translate into practice. A more sustained focus on the interplay between race, class, education, and economic marginalisation would strengthen his contribution and more effectively address the complex realities faced by disadvantaged patients.

DOI: 10.4324/9781003726012-1

A persistent assumption within analytic psychotherapy is that it primarily suits educated, middle-class patients. This belief is reinforced by dominant models such as Irvin Yalom's *The Theory and Practice of Group Psychotherapy*, which is rooted in White, middle-class experience and often universalises psychological processes. While Yalom's focus on the 'here and now' remains clinically powerful, it can overlook the profound impact of historical oppression, trauma, and future uncertainty – factors that deeply shape the emotional lives of marginalised patients (Yalom, 2005). Moreover, many of Yalom's works primarily involve middle-class patients, reflecting this limited scope. In intercultural group therapy, the 'here and now' cannot be separated from the wider sociopolitical context in which patients live. To engage diverse patient groups more meaningfully, group therapy models must integrate awareness of history, migration, systemic inequality, and intersecting identities. Moving beyond universal assumptions not only enriches clinical understanding but also promotes greater cultural responsiveness.

Otto Kernberg's object relations approach, with its focus on transference and personality organisation, offers a valuable framework for understanding individual psychology (Kernberg, 1984, 1998). Yet, when contrasted with the needs of intercultural group therapy, its limitations become evident. The model pays little attention to sociocultural dynamics such as cultural identity, displacement, or collective trauma. In a group context, this absence risks pathologising difference by neglecting the broader forces that shape patient experience. To remain relevant in diverse therapeutic settings, Kernberg's framework would need to expand beyond the individual level, integrating social and cultural dimensions that acknowledge how identity, history, and belonging influence both personality and group interaction.

Garland, Jones, and Kolodny's *The Group Therapy Experience* (2010) offers a comprehensive introduction to group processes, covering stages, roles, and therapeutic factors. While clinically useful, it pays limited attention to cultural, racial, or social power dynamics, reflecting a more generalised approach. Similarly, Schwartz and Tschinkel's *Interpersonal Process in Therapy Groups* (1988) emphasises interpersonal dynamics but does not extensively address culture, race, or identity. Both texts largely overlook the sociopolitical factors that shape the group experiences of marginalised populations.

In light of these limitations across the literature, this book adopts a different starting point. It is grounded primarily in Foulkes' group analytic tradition, offering a relational and culturally responsive approach. Foulkes' experience as a refugee, together with his conceptualisation of the group as a dynamic network, provides a strong foundation for examining issues of race, class, migration, and exclusion. His concept of the 'matrix' – a shared unconscious network that shapes group dynamics – offers a valuable framework for understanding cultural enactments within groups. By integrating Kareem's insights into individual cultural identity (Kareem and Littlewood, 1992) with

Foulkes' principles, this book advances a culturally sensitive model of group therapy that is explored here more fully than in previous discussions.

Although early group analysis was often practised with educated, middle-class populations, later group analysts have made efforts to broaden its reach. When I joined the Institute of Group Analysis in 1993 for my personal analysis, both the patients and the analysts were predominantly White and middle class. During my supervision training in 2007, led by Dr Harold Behr, I again found myself among mostly White, middle-class therapists – an experience I found challenging. I was fortunate to have Dr Behr as my clinical supervisor; his support was a source of strength throughout my training.

Today, the institute is becoming more diverse, with a growing number of Black and ethnic minority students entering the programme. However, representation remains limited, and structural inequalities persist. True inclusivity requires a sustained commitment to addressing systemic barriers. Issues of race, culture, and minority experience should not be confined to a single lecture or a passing reference; instead, they need to be embedded as ongoing concerns throughout the training programme.

I argue that analytic intercultural group therapy can be highly effective for marginalised populations, provided that therapists are interculturally competent and engage openly with issues of power, difference, and exclusion. This involves acknowledging the significance of patients' cultural narratives and maintaining continuous self-reflection. A reflective, iterative approach – alternating between stepping back to reflect and forward to engage – deepens therapy and enhances cultural sensitivity. For patients from ethnic minority backgrounds, the therapeutic work often carries an additional layer, as they bring not only personal dynamics but also the impact of cultural displacement, discrimination, or marginalisation. Recognising these dual dimensions of experience allows therapy to address complexity without diminishing the significance of challenges faced by other patients. Some may argue that a humanistic approach is more suitable for ethnic minority patients. Yet many of these patients do not wish to cover up their difficulties; they want to reach the roots of their struggles. Group analytic therapy, with its focus on unconscious processes, relationships, and the influence of social context, offers the depth needed to work through these issues in ways that other approaches may not fully address.

Following the closure of the Goldsmiths Group Analytic Unit as a result of funding constraints, formal group analytic training opportunities have been limited. In this context, the Institute of Group Analysis, although still somewhat restricted, is increasingly offering training in group analytic practice for minority students.

Nancy McWilliams (2011) has made a significant contribution to contemporary psychodynamic thought, particularly through her focus on the therapeutic relationship, therapist subjectivity, and cultural awareness. She emphasises the therapist's inner world and self-reflection as central to clinical work. Her writing advances understanding of personality, defences, and the unconscious, while recognising the influence of social context. However, her work focuses mainly on individual therapy and offers limited guidance for group settings. I chose McWilliams because her relational and culturally aware approach provides a vital foundation for exploring culture and unconscious dynamics, which I extend here into group therapy – where interpersonal and collective processes make cultural enactments more visible.

However, McWilliams' contributions, while invaluable for individual therapy, leave questions about how her relational and cultural sensitivity might unfold within a group setting. In groups, the therapist's subjectivity interacts not with a single patient but with multiple subjectivities, each shaped by different cultural narratives. This shift from the dyadic to the collective highlights the limitations of applying her framework directly to group therapy. For instance, McWilliams' insights into personality organisation and defences are highly valuable in individual work, yet within groups such dynamics often surface collectively and are intensified through multiple interactions. Likewise, the therapist's inner responses – so central in her thinking – become even more complex when shaped simultaneously by several cultural narratives. Her emphasis on self-reflection and cultural awareness therefore provides an important foundation; however, without explicit attention to group processes, issues such as collective identity, cultural enactments, and sociopolitical forces risk being overlooked. Integrating McWilliams' relational depth with group analytic principles creates a richer, more culturally responsive approach – one that attends both to the inner world of the therapist and to the unfolding dynamics within the group.

Patrick Casement (1985, 2006) similarly emphasises the therapist's inner world and ongoing self-reflection, both of which are central to intercultural competence. While his approach offers useful clinical insights, it remains rooted in Western psychoanalytic traditions and does not directly engage with the sociopolitical and cultural complexities that therapists face in diverse clinical settings. Nonetheless, aspects of Casement's thinking – especially learning from the patient – resonate with the reflective, relational stance advocated here. His emphasis on openness to what emerges in the therapeutic encounter can also be extended into the group setting, where the therapist is confronted not only with a single transference but with multiple and, at times, conflicting projections. In such contexts, the principle of 'learning from the patient' acquires an added dimension: it requires the therapist to learn not only from individuals but also from the collective expressions of the group. While Casement does not himself elaborate this group dimension, his reflective orientation provides a valuable foundation for thinking about intercultural group therapy.

Throughout this book, theory and lived experience are interwoven to demonstrate how reflective practice can be expanded and applied in culturally diverse group therapy. Grounded in clinical examples, the book aims to provide a practical and accessible framework for understanding complex identity and power dynamics in therapy. It emphasises that such work does not only involve understanding others but also the practitioner's personal journey, and this requires humility, openness, and a willingness to learn from every encounter.

The idea that our humanity extends beyond cultural and national boundaries has long been recognised, notably by the French philosopher Michel de Montaigne ([1580] 2003), who questioned the limits of fixed identities and emphasised a broader kinship with the world. This perspective aligns with the ethos of intercultural therapy. While cultural identities shape the way in which we see ourselves and others, they do not erase the deeper threads that connect us. Recognising these shared experiences allows for more meaningful encounters, grounded in empathy and mutual respect. In therapy – particularly intercultural therapy – the capacity to see the humanity in others, beyond labels and assumptions, forms the foundation for genuine understanding and transformation.

References

Casement, P., 1985. *On Learning from the Patient*. London: Routledge.

Casement, P., 2006. *OnLearning from the Patient*. 2nd edn. London: Routledge.

Dalal, F., 2002. *Race, Colour and the Processes of Racialisation: New Perspectives from Group Analysis, Psychoanalysis and Sociology*. Hove: Brunner-Routledge.

Foulkes, S.H., 1948. *Introduction to Group-Analytic Psychotherapy: Studies in the Social Integration of Individuals*. London: Hogarth Press.

Garland, B., Jones, K., and Kolodny, R., 2010. *The Group Therapy Experience*. London: Sage.

Kareem, J. and Littlewood, R., 1992. *Intercultural Therapy: Themes, Interpretaions and Practice*. Oxford: Blackwell Scientific Publications.

Kernberg, O.F., 1984. *Severe Personality Disorders: Psychotherapeutic Strategies*. New Haven, CT: Yale University Press.

Kernberg, O.F., 1998. *Ideology, Conflict, and Leadership in Groups and Organizations*. New Haven, CT: Yale University Press.

McWilliams, N., 2011. *Psychoanalytic Diagnosis: Understanding Personality Structure in the Clinical Process*. 2nd edn. New York: Guilford Press.

Montaigne, M.de [1580] 2003. *Essays*. Trans. M.A. Screech. London: Penguin Classics.

Schwartz, H. and Tschinkel, T., 1988. *Interpersonal Process in Therapy Groups*. New York: Guilford Press.

Yalom, I.D., 2005. *The Theory and Practice of Group Psychotherapy*. 5th edn. New York: Basic Books.

Chapter 1

Understanding Group Dynamics in Therapy and Social Life

Groups – whether political, activity-based, or support-focused – shape both individual and collective experience. Human beings are inherently social; life gains meaning through relationships. Our early interactions, whether nurturing or neglectful, shape our worldview and behaviour, setting the tone for how we relate to others.

In societies where community and group connections are central, a sense of belonging is vital for emotional and psychological development. We learn emotional and behavioural patterns through these early group experiences. Healthy groups nurture wellbeing, offering support, understanding, and validation. In contrast, dysfunctional groups may reinforce harmful roles, perpetuate trauma, and hinder growth. A child's first group – whether family or community – forms the lens through which they see themselves and the world. When these formative experiences are wounding, individuals may later turn to group therapy as a space for healing and transformation.

Although loneliness is sometimes romanticised, human existence is fundamentally relational. Even in individualistic societies, isolation is ultimately unsustainable. The COVID-19 pandemic starkly revealed the importance of meaningful relationships and reaffirmed the role of group dynamics in therapy as a vital source of support during times of crisis and uncertainty.

Balancing individuality with group belonging is particularly complex in Turkish and Kurdish cultures, where family and communal ties hold significant influence. Group therapy offers a space to explore and renegotiate these dynamics, allowing individuals to reflect on how their sense of self and belonging has been shaped by broader cultural and familial systems.

Financial Barriers and Group Therapy

Financial constraints often limit access to therapy. Group therapy, however, presents a more accessible and cost-effective alternative. As awareness grows within ethnic minority communities, it becomes a crucial means of overcoming the cultural and financial barriers that might otherwise deter individuals from seeking support.

DOI: 10.4324/9781003726012-2

Understanding group dynamics is essential not only in therapy but also in everyday life – within families, workplaces, and communities. These interactions reveal the underlying patterns that shape relationships, offering insights into behaviours that can either hinder or support personal and collective growth.

Overview of Therapeutic Groups

Karl Marx (1845), philosopher and social theorist, argued that human identity is formed through social relations rather than in isolation. This idea underpins group therapy, where an individual's experience is inseparable from the collective's dynamics. It highlights not only abstract notions of humanity but also the concrete structures and relationships that shape how we perceive ourselves and others.

Building on Marx's idea of social relations, early 20th-century thinkers such as Sigmund Freud (1921) and Georg Simmel (1972) explored the way in which individual psychology is shaped by group dynamics. Simmel's studies of small groups provided a foundation for understanding collective behaviour, while Freud's *Group Psychology and the Analysis of the Ego* (1921) highlighted unconscious processes that emerge when people gather. However, Freud's theories have been criticised for assuming that Western psychological experiences apply universally and for overlooking cultural differences. Fanon (1952) emphasised how colonialism and racial oppression shape the mind in ways that Freud's Eurocentric model did not consider, and Said (1978) argued that Western assumptions in psychological theories risk imposing 'universal' categories that ignore cultural and historical particularities. These insights helped to lay the groundwork for group therapy, which situates individuals within their social contexts and emphasises shared experiences, mutual support, and the co-construction of emotional growth.

These foundational ideas shaped the emergence of group therapy as a vital therapeutic method. In therapeutic groups, individuals are not viewed as isolated entities but as products of their social contexts. Within the group, members uncover and express vulnerabilities that might otherwise remain hidden. Through shared experiences and mutual support, individuals build emotional resilience and reconnect with both themselves and others.

Since its early development in the 20th century, group therapy has steadily grown in significance. Sharing thoughts, emotions, and experiences within a supportive collective offers considerable psychological, emotional, and physical benefits. It provides a space to confront difficulties, reframe self-perceptions, and foster personal growth.

As Montaigne ([1580] 2003) insightfully noted: 'There is nothing more difficult and more useful than for a person to express themselves. I am always rearranging myself because I am always expressing myself.' Group therapy facilitates such 'rearrangement' through relational expression, creating fertile ground for healing and transformation.

In the early 20th century, Joseph Pratt brought together tuberculosis patients for educational and support purposes, laying the groundwork for group-based therapeutic interaction. In the decades that followed, principles of group dynamics and psychodrama were further developed in psychiatric settings, shaping contemporary group psychotherapy practices. Some of this work, however, has been critiqued for reflecting predominantly middle-class Western perspectives, raising questions about cultural applicability.

When I worked as a nurse in a tuberculosis hospital in Türkiye (formerly Turkey), I facilitated support groups for patients without knowing that there was an established theory behind such work – I simply followed my instincts. It was reassuring to learn that there was a theoretical foundation for what I was intuitively practising.

Evolution of Group Therapy in the 20th Century

Group therapy evolved significantly throughout the 20th century, shaped by contributors from diverse cultural and intellectual backgrounds. One of the most influential figures in analytic group therapy was S.H. Foulkes, who, after fleeing Nazi Germany, began to develop his approach during the 1940s in England. Working alongside sociologists such as Norbert Elias, Foulkes integrated psychoanalytic theory with a sociological understanding of group dynamics, laying the foundations of group analysis. While not explicitly Marxist, his approach reflected themes that align with Marxist thought – particularly the emphasis on social structures and power dynamics, which continue to shape the way in which group members relate to one another in therapeutic settings. These insights remain deeply relevant in the 21st century and resonate strongly with my own intellectual, professional, and personal framework.

Although Foulkes did not identify with Marxism, his attention to social and relational structures echoes central concerns in Marxist theory. Similar themes can be found in the work of Farhad Dalal (2002), who foregrounds race, class, and institutional power in group analytic practice. While their perspectives differ – Foulkes through psychoanalytic group analysis and Dalal through a more critical sociopolitical lens – both underscore the importance of recognising how broader social forces shape therapeutic processes. This shared emphasis on power and context enriches our understanding of group therapy as embedded within wider cultural and historical frameworks.

Foulkes' clinical impact during World War II was profound. At Northfield Military Hospital, his work with soldiers helped to establish what would later be known as the 'therapeutic community' model. He was instrumental in the development of two major strands of group therapy: psychoanalytic group therapy, rooted in Freudian theory, and the Tavistock model, shaped by W.R. Bion (1961). Bion, drawing heavily on Melanie Klein's theories of unconscious processes and object relations, focused on individuals' emotional experiences within the group container. Klein's work on internal psychic structures and early anxieties offered a way to understand the unconscious dynamics that emerge in group settings. In contrast, Foulkes viewed the group itself as a relational matrix – an interactive system – through which psychological change unfolds (Foulkes, 1964, 1982).

Despite their lasting influence, both Bion's and Foulkes' theories have been critiqued for focusing predominantly on psychodynamic and abstract processes. Bion's group theory, in particular, tends to universalise unconscious dynamics while neglecting sociopolitical realities such as race, class, and culture (Fanon, 1952; Fernando, 1991). This absence limits the models' relevance to diverse populations and underscores the importance of integrating a sociocultural perspective into contemporary group therapy. Without this, historical and structural traumas – especially those affecting marginalised communities – remain overlooked (Fernando, 1991; Said, 1978).

After the war, Foulkes continued his work at the Maudsley Hospital in South London, where he further developed his theories and the clinical practice of group analysis (Foulkes, 1975; Hoggett, 2009; Gabbard, 2010). His legacy was commemorated at the 21st Foulkes Conference in 1997, where group analyst Bryan Boswood emphasised Foulkes' commitment to exploring how social power and collective pressures shape individual personality development – a theme central to his career. Despite some resistance within the wider therapeutic community, these insights have had a profound and lasting impact on the field.

I had the opportunity to attend the conference in 1997 and observed how Foulkes' ideas continue to inspire rich, interdisciplinary dialogue among practitioners, scholars, and trainees. His emphasis on group dynamics, social context, and shared meaning-making remains central to current discussions shaping the future of group therapy.

As my own work is closely aligned with that of Foulkes, I am particularly drawn to his enduring commitment to the study and practice of group therapy. His extensive writings have influenced generations of therapists. Foulkes died suddenly from a coronary thrombosis on 8 July 1976, aged 77, while leading a seminar and surrounded by his colleagues – an apt ending to a life dedicated to understanding the emotional and relational complexities of therapeutic groups (de Mijolla, 2005).

Integrating Diverse Influences into My Work

My approach to group work is informed by a broad range of influences, including the foundational insights of Foulkes as well as perspectives from European and African analysts, supervisors, and various schools of thought. While my work is grounded in these established traditions, it continuously evolves to address the shifting needs of contemporary society. I believe that every psychotherapist brings a unique blend of their own culture, personality, and knowledge to their practice, thereby enriching the therapeutic process. Even within the same institution or training model, therapists inevitably develop distinctive approaches, each adding depth and complexity to the work.

Some of the ideas I developed were initially met with scepticism but were gradually embraced by colleagues and institutions – sometimes even adopted as their own. Their eventual acceptance was largely due to their proven effectiveness for patients.

Throughout most of my career, I have worked in institutional settings, engaging in intensive face-to-face clinical work with patients. These environments offered meaningful opportunities both to contribute to and to critically challenge established practices. I chose these institutions because they provided a platform from which to effect broader change within the field. Although private practice was always a secondary option, I have now stepped away from institutional roles to focus fully on a smaller private practice, as well as my writing and painting.

Personal recognition has never been my primary concern. What matters most is the wider dissemination of sound ideas and the promotion of effective clinical practice. From my perspective, the collective growth of the therapeutic community holds greater value than individual acknowledgement.

While I do not claim to present entirely new concepts, my work offers a distinctive focus on intercultural issues – topics that are often overlooked or inadequately addressed in group settings, yet are crucial to contemporary therapeutic practice. My approach is consistently shaped by the perspectives of my patients, ensuring that their lived experiences inform the therapeutic process. Although the ideas I explore are grounded in well-established theory, I maintain that they remain essential to contemporary practice, and consequently have been further developed by others in the field.

A core principle of my work is that therapy must engage directly with issues such as racism, cultural discrimination, class, gender, and sexual orientation, while also fostering psychological resilience. I reject the assumption, still found in some institutions, that analytic therapy is unsuitable for refugees or individuals with limited formal education. My clinical experience has consistently proved otherwise. Addressing psychological processes in isolation is not enough; therapists must also confront the wider societal and structural forces that shape their patients' lives. Intercultural therapy is not a diluted form of analytic work; rather, it is a more robust model. By integrating cultural, historical, and sociopolitical dimensions, it transcends traditional Western analytic frameworks and offers a deeper, more relevant form of therapeutic care.

References

Bion, W.R., 1961. *Experiences in Groups and Other Papers*. London: Tavistock Publications.

Casement, P., 1985. *On Learning from the Patient*. London: Routledge.

Casement, P., 2006. *Learning from Life: Becoming a Psychoanalyst*. London: Routledge.
Clarke, A.C., 2000. *2001: A Space Odyssey*. New York: ROC.
Comas-Díaz, L. and Greene, B., 1994. *Women of Color: Integrating Ethnic and Gender Identities in Psychotherapy*. New York: Guilford Press.
Constantine, M.G. and Sue, D.W., 2006. *Addressing Racism: Facilitating Cultural Competence in Mental Health and Educational Settings*. Hoboken, NJ: Wiley.
Dalal, F., 2002. *Race, Colour and the Processes of Racialization: New Perspectives from Group Analysis, Psychoanalysis and Sociology*. Hove: Brunner-Routledge.
Dalal, F., 2006. 'Racism: Processes of Detachment, Dehumanization, and Hatred', *The Psychoanalytic Quarterly*, 75(1), pp. 131–161. Available at doi:10.1002/j.2167-4086.2006.tb00035.x.
De Mijolla, A. (ed.) 2005. *International Dictionary of Psychoanalysis*. 3 vols. Detroit, MI: Thomson Gale/Macmillan Reference USA.
Fanon, F., 1952. *Black Skin, White Masks*. Translated by C.L. Markmann. London: Pluto Press.
Fernando, S., 1991. *Mental Health, Race and Culture*. London: Mind Publications.
Finell, J.S., 1985. 'Narcissistic Problems in Analysts', *International Journal of Psychoanalysis*, 66(4), pp. 433–445.
Foulkes, S.H., 1964. *Therapeutic Group Analysis: Principles and Practice*. London: George Allen & Unwin.
Foulkes, S.H., 1975. *Group-Analytic Psychotherapy: Method and Principles*. London: Gordon and Breach Science Publishers.
Foulkes, S.H., 1982. *Group Psychotherapy: The Psychoanalytic Approach*. New York: Basic Books.
Freud, S., 1900. *The Interpretation of Dreams*. Translated by A.A. Brill. Ware: Wordsworth Editions.
Freud, S., 1921. *Group Psychology and the Analysis of the Ego*. Translated by J. Strachey. London: Hogarth Press.
Gabbard, G.O., 2010. *Long-Term Psychodynamic Psychotherapy: A Basic Text*. Arlington, VA: American Psychiatric Publishing.
Garland, J.A., Jones, H.E., and Kolodny, R.L., 2010. *The Group Therapy Experience*. 4th edn. New York: Basic Books.
Hoggett, P., 2009. *Researching Beneath the Surface: Psycho-Social Research Methods in Practice*. Edited by S. Clarke and P. Hoggett. London: Routledge.
Kareem, J. and Littlewood, R., 1992. *Intercultural Therapy: Themes, Interpretations and Practice*. Oxford: Blackwell Scientific Publications.
Kernberg, O.F., 1984. *Severe Personality Disorders: Psychotherapeutic Strategies*. New Haven, CT: Yale University Press.
Kernberg, O.F., 1998. *Aggression in Personality Disorders and Perversions*. New Haven, CT: Yale University Press.
Marx, K., 1845. 'Theses on Feuerbach', in K. Marx and F. Engels, *Collected Works*, vol. 5. London: Lawrence & Wishart. Available at https://www.marxists.org/archive/marx/works/1845/theses/ (accessed 24 September 2025).
McWilliams, N., 2004. *Psychoanalytic Psychotherapy: A Practitioner's Guide*. New York: Guilford Press.
Montaigne, M.de. [1580] 2003. *Essays*. Translated by M.A. Screech. London: Penguin Classics.
Said, E.W., 1978. *Orientalism*. New York: Pantheon Books.

Schwartz, L. and Tschinkel, P., 1988. *Interpersonal Process in Therapy Groups*. New York: McGraw-Hill.
Simmel, G., 1972. *Georg Simmel on Individuality and Social Forms*. Edited by D.N. Levine. Chicago: University of Chicago Press.
Yalom, I.D., 2005. *The Theory and Practice of Group Psychotherapy*. 5th edn. New York: Basic Books.
Young-Bruehl, E., 1988. *Anna Freud: A Biography*. New York: Summit Books.

Chapter 2

Whose Therapy Is It? Power, Culture, and Belonging in Clinical Practice

Who defines the therapeutic space – and whose realities does it serve? In culturally diverse groups shaped by systemic inequality, this question becomes vital.

Group therapy provides a unique and practical setting where cultural, social, and relational dynamics come to life. Groups typically comprise between seven and nine participants who do not know each other beforehand, are carefully selected by the group therapist, and meet for 90 minutes at an agreed time and place to ensure psychological safety and clear boundaries. Following Foulkes' approach, with input from Jafar Kareem, the group functions as a social and emotional matrix: participants influence each other in the here and now, while the therapist maintains free-floating attention, observing and reflecting without directing the process (Foulkes, 1964; Kareem and Littlewood, 1992).

Unlike individual therapy, the group dynamic allows participants to witness, mirror, and challenge one another's experiences, fostering connection, belonging, and shared understanding. Emotions that often feel isolating – such as shame or internalised guilt – become shared experiences, promoting self-awareness and insight. Naturally, tensions, differences, and unconscious dynamics emerge; when facilitated thoughtfully, these provide rich material for both personal and collective growth. In this way, the group acts as a microcosm of broader society, reflecting cultural, social, and relational complexities while offering opportunities for healing through dialogue, empathy, and mutual recognition.

A defining feature of group therapy is that participants, as patients, can give feedback, challenge one another, and provide support to fellow members. All participants are regarded as equals and are free to respond and engage, in contrast to individual therapy where the therapist primarily guides and monitors interactions. These principles of collective exploration and mutual influence are central to group analytic therapy, which was introduced by Foulkes in the 1940s. He emphasised that therapy is conducted by the group, of the group, and includes the conductor, thereby giving rise to the term group analytic psychotherapy (Foulkes, 1975).

Within the context of cultural complexity, systemic inequality, and the challenges of addressing race and identity, group therapy provides a unique

DOI: 10.4324/9781003726012-3

and practical setting in which these dynamics come to life. It allows participants to explore personal struggles collectively and to develop shared understanding under careful facilitation by the therapist.

As group therapy mirrors broader societal dynamics, it often brings challenges related to race, identity, and systemic inequality to the surface. Therapists working in culturally diverse groups must manage these realities thoughtfully, balancing ethical responsibility with cultural attunement to create a safe and inclusive environment. This chapter explores how these challenges emerge in group settings and outlines strategies – such as active listening, structured reflection, and culturally responsive facilitation – for managing them effectively, thereby fostering trust, inclusion, and meaningful therapeutic growth.

Racism and discrimination deeply impact the lives of Black and ethnic minority patients in the United Kingdom. Reflecting on my own experiences has been both painful and challenging – not only in recognising racism in others but also in confronting my own internalised biases (Thomas and Sillen, 1972).

In Europe, conversations about race are frequently reduced to black-and-white terms, obscuring the rich diversity of communities comprising Turkish, Kurdish, Latin American, Asian, Iranian, Armenian, Bulgarian, Irish, Welsh, or Scottish peoples. Many Turkish-speaking individuals, for example, resist being categorised as either Black or White. My own identity has been interpreted differently by others – I am sometimes mistaken for Latin American, French, or Greek – revealing how societal biases influence perception, including within therapeutic spaces.

An accent can also be a source of discrimination. I can recall an incident that took place when I was working for the health authority in which a medical practice refused to share information with me, yet readily cooperated when a colleague with a standard English accent made the same request. This episodes highlights the way in which language and accent serve as subtle markers of exclusion – even in professional environments.

Some psychotherapists argue that racism is a political issue and therefore lies outside the scope of therapy. However, therapists inevitably bring their own fears and biases into the room, shaped by personal histories and societal influences. Avoiding conversations about racism risks reinforcing the very inequalities that therapy seeks to address.

Intercultural therapy acknowledges the barriers faced by ethnic minority patients across therapeutic modalities. These obstacles often stem from models rooted in Western European traditions, which may not reflect patients' lived realities. A universalist approach tends to overlook the cultural, social, and historical dimensions that shape psychological wellbeing.

In healthcare settings, general practitioners may misinterpret symptoms in ethnic minority patients, resulting in misdiagnoses – such as schizophrenia or psychosis – when psychotherapy may be more appropriate (Kareem and Littlewood, 1992). Such errors often stem from a lack of cultural competence and contribute to the mistrust that many minority patients feel towards mental health services. Conversely, professionals may overcompensate in their efforts to demonstrate cultural awareness, misattributing issues to cultural difference. For instance, a therapist working with a Turkish patient experiencing domestic violence might mistakenly link the problem to cultural norms rather than recognising it as an individual or relational issue. Overgeneralisation can be equally harmful, obscuring the patient's experience and impeding effective support.

The most respectful and effective approach is simple: if a therapist does not understand something, they should ask. Open, curious, and non-judgemental questioning creates space for the patient's voice to emerge without assumptions. Genuine cultural understanding arises from this relational stance – not from presumed expertise.

Racial dynamics in therapy are complex. A Black patient may feel that their difference is either exaggerated or dismissed by a White therapist; a White patient may question the credibility of a minority therapist. Therapists from Black and minority backgrounds may also encounter direct racism from their patients. At the same time, systemic racism can shape how Black patients relate to therapists from their own communities. Even when patient and therapist share the same ethnic background, wider societal racism and internalised prejudices can influence the therapeutic relationship. For example, a Black patient may experience mistrust, ambivalence, or hesitation towards a Black therapist as a result of these unconscious effects (Kareem and Littlewood, 1992).

These dynamics are closely connected to internalised racism, which occurs when marginalised individuals absorb negative stereotypes imposed by the dominant culture. Internalised racism fosters self-doubt, self-rejection, and the idealisation of dominant traits. Such beliefs damage not only individuals but also weaken solidarity and perpetuate systemic oppression (Kareem and Littlewood, 1992). In therapy, internalised racism may surface as shame, silence, or resistance – especially when cultural identity is explored. Therapists must be able to name and work through these dynamics if they are to offer meaningful and effective support.

Addressing internalised racism requires psychological insight as well as systemic change – dismantling structural inequalities and creating environments that empower marginalised identities. When conducted in a genuinely intercultural manner, group therapy becomes a powerful space for this work. Patients confront personal struggles while also witnessing and challenging the broader societal forces that shape their experiences. The collective nature of group therapy promotes shared understanding, solidarity, and the redefinition of identity beyond imposed societal narratives.

Mainstream mental health services often fail to provide culturally sensitive, safe, and accessible spaces for minority patients. Many struggle to make sense of their experiences within systems that pathologise or disregard their cultural and social realities. Intercultural therapy, in contrast, makes psychotherapy more accessible and relevant – particularly for Black and ethnic minority patients. Intercultural therapy views mental health through the lenses of race, ethnicity, and culture, integrating individual experience with social context. It recognises that cultural factors shape psychological life and seeks to balance clinical observation with patients' lived realities. Jafar Kareem (1930–1992), founder of the London-based Nafsiyat Intercultural Therapy Centre, challenged the emphasis on 'inner psychic reality' in traditional psychotherapy. He argued that sociopolitical and economic conditions must be addressed in therapeutic work. Recognising these external forces allows for a deeper understanding of how systemic inequalities generate emotional distress.

Therapists working interculturally must adapt their methods to reflect the diverse cultural frameworks of their patients, rather than imposing fixed models. This responsiveness enhances engagement, deepens trust, and fosters a more inclusive therapeutic process (Sue and Sue, 2016). Such adaptations do not move away from analytic work; they deepen it, making it more attuned to the patient's unique cultural context.

This raises broader questions: what do we mean by culture, identity, and group dynamics? Culture is often invisible – embedded in daily interactions and reinforced through unspoken rules. Groups quickly detect and respond to deviations from these norms, shaping what is considered acceptable or unacceptable (Rack, 1982; Herskovits, 1955). Additionally, culture is variable. For example, the societal culture in Türkiye (formerly Turkey) 30 years ago was very different from what it is today. Human psychology exerts considerable effort to adapt to this changing culture.

Language plays a central role in cultural identity. A Turkish saying captures this: 'A person has as many personalities as they have languages.' Language reflects cultural influences, revealing class and regional distinctions. Migrants adapt to new languages while retaining accents and expressions from their native tongues. This adaptation goes beyond vocabulary – affecting values, social codes, and ways of thinking. For example, the Turkish phonetic alphabet and absence of gendered pronouns highlight how language shapes perception and thought.

Linguistic and cultural shifts often create tensions, particularly between public and family languages. In educational settings, pressure to conform to dominant linguistic norms can generate anxiety and self-doubt. People internalise these societal expectations, which then shape their emotions, behaviours, and interactions.

In group therapy, recognising cultural nuances is essential. While identifying shared experiences can foster connection, overemphasising similarities at the expense of differences – such as race, ethnicity, gender, class, or sexual orientation – can marginalise some members. In predominantly White, middle-class groups, individuals from Black, Asian, African, or LGBTQ+ communities may feel unseen, misunderstood, or excluded. This alienation can lead to emotional withdrawal or disengagement. Although it may seem easier to focus on what unites the group, genuine therapeutic work requires courage to explore what sets members apart. Addressing these differences – even uncomfortable ones – fosters deeper understanding and creates a more inclusive therapeutic space.

Some therapists, unaware of their own cultural assumptions, may impose rigid frameworks that reinforce exclusion. Cultural awareness is crucial to ensure that all group members feel seen and heard. Culturally sensitive therapy honours diverse perspectives, enriching the therapeutic process. Intercultural group therapy brings together individuals from varied backgrounds to explore how cultural identity shapes thoughts, emotions, and relationships. Group interactions reflect broader societal dynamics, making it vital for therapists to facilitate open dialogue around biases, assumptions, and norms.

Power dynamics shaped by ethnicity, class, gender, and age must be addressed. Therapeutic relationships inevitably mirror wider cultural assumptions, affecting how members engage. Ageism – whether directed against younger or older members – can influence who is heard, taken seriously, or sidelined. Exploring these dynamics enhances self-awareness, enabling individuals to recognise their own biases and stereotypes, which is essential for creating a truly inclusive group environment.

In intercultural analytic group therapy, emotional experiences are closely linked to cultural identity. Open dialogue allows members to work through emotional blocks, develop healthier coping strategies, and challenge internalised narratives. Communication extends beyond words – non-verbal cues such as body language and silence are equally important. Therapists must stay attuned to these subtleties to support meaningful, inclusive communication. For instance, Black and minority patients may respond with silence at times – not because they lack something to say, but because the environment feels unsafe or unreceptive. In this context, silence becomes a form of self-protection amid implicit or unacknowledged power dynamics.

Cultural competence is not a fixed goal but an ongoing process involving self-reflection, humility, and learning from lived experience as much as theory. Engagement with marginalised communities offers invaluable insights. This approach encourages self-reflection for therapists and group members alike, prompting examination of their assumptions and biases. Creating a safe space in which to discuss racism, discrimination, and inequality is crucial. Avoiding these topics only reinforces existing power imbalances. Even therapists from minority backgrounds may struggle to fully understand the experiences of White Western patients. Bridging such gaps requires curiosity, humility, and a commitment to lifelong learning. The Nafsiyat Training Team, led by Baffour Ababio, emphasises that sociopolitical awareness is vital for genuine cultural competence. Embracing diversity strengthens therapeutic relationships and broadens perspectives. This approach is grounded in psychoanalytic theory – especially Melanie Klein's concepts of projection and introjection as defences

(Klein, 1946), later extended by Wilfred Bion in group contexts (Bion, 1961). When explored safely, these mechanisms open gateways to deeper insight and emotional growth.

In group therapy, the therapist facilitates reflection and dialogue, helping individuals to balance past experiences with present concerns. By providing consistency and psychological safety, therapists enable patients to challenge unhelpful beliefs, explore difficult emotions, and make sense of complex social identities. While the focus remains on the here and now, past experiences and unconscious attitudes inevitably shape current interactions. Clinical examples in later chapters will illustrate these complexities.

Group members hold multiple roles – as interpreters of their experiences, advisers to one another, and witnesses to each other's journeys. Meaningful engagement requires self-examination, which can be challenging; patients often more easily recognise difficulties in others than in themselves. Within a supportive group, these psychoanalytic dynamics unfold gradually, allowing fears, biases, and unprocessed emotions to surface. This process is fundamental to genuine transformation. The aim is not short-term relief but lasting change through greater awareness, emotional insight, and authentic relational engagement. Group therapy can be likened to a shared meal: nourishing when inclusive, but alienating when voices are ignored or dominant narratives go unchallenged. The therapist's role is to ensure that all members can contribute and benefit, and that diverse perspectives are both valued and meaningfully integrated.

Facilitating group therapy involves more than gathering participants. It requires managing complex dynamics, nurturing emotional development, and maintaining psychological safety. Professional training, supervision, and personal group analysis experience are essential. A skilled therapist draws on clinical knowledge, patience, insight, authenticity, and cultural sensitivity. Group therapists face unique challenges: their interventions are visible to all, deepening trust but demanding emotional resilience. Within this shared space, participants learn to listen, express themselves, and reshape their narratives. Witnessing emotions in real time strengthens connection and deepens self-awareness.

Intercultural analytic group therapy also embraces a feminine perspective, recognising that healing men can contribute to women's wellbeing. Mixed-gender groups foster mutual understanding, while women-only groups provide the safety often necessary for trauma recovery.

Discomfort is inherent in group therapy, yet over time members can grow stronger through its therapeutic potential. Addressing unhelpful behaviours helps to break down internal barriers and encourages genuine change (Foulkes, 1991). Some members may resist or withdraw when emotions become overwhelming, making inclusion and a sense of belonging essential for sustained engagement.

Despite its effectiveness, group therapy is often undervalued and mistakenly seen as a cheaper alternative to individual therapy. In reality, it is a distinct and powerful modality that promotes collaboration within a democratic space, where the therapist facilitates rather than dominates.

Group therapy reveals hidden dimensions of personal and social identity. Members act as role models, demonstrating trust and resilience. Often, how we see ourselves differs from how others perceive us – a realisation that can be unsettling but ultimately transformative. Group feedback offers meaningful insights that deepen self-awareness and support emotional growth.

Group versus Individual Therapy: Key Differences

Group therapy requires skilled therapists to manage group dynamics and cultures, working with the collective rather than focusing solely on individual experience, as emphasised by Foulkes (1984). Destructive forces within the group can be transformed into growth-promoting elements, as explored by Nitsun (1996) in *The Anti-Group: Destructive Forces in the Group and Their Creative Potential.*

Unlike individual therapy, which is based on a one-to-one relationship, group therapy involves between three and nine participants and typically has a duration of 90 minutes. In my experience, when co-facilitated, therapists must maintain mutual respect and adopt a cohesive, collaborative approach.

While individual therapy often positions the therapist as a 'witness' or a 'mirror', group therapy fosters collaboration, allowing feedback and support to emerge organically from the group. According to Bateman and Holmes (1995) and Schlapobersky (2016), this group dynamic more closely mirrors real-life social interactions. In groups, the therapist holds a dual role: both observer and participant. Members contribute perspectives, promoting collective learning and deeper insight. Repetitive or disruptive behaviours are explored within the group, fostering patience and mutual understanding.

Emotions such as guilt and shame are processed collectively in group therapy. This shared experience can diffuse transference across participants and reduce irrational self-blame. By contrast, these emotions are addressed privately within the therapist-patient dyad in individual therapy.

Group therapy benefits from member diversity. Often, minimal therapist intervention is needed, as the group itself becomes a therapeutic resource. Cultural sensitivity and active listening are vital to maintaining a healthy dynamic. Each group forms its own distinct culture, shaped by its members, requiring the therapist to remain self-reflective, often through supervision or peer consultation.

In addition to being more cost-effective than individual therapy, group therapy is unique in fostering shared learning, collaboration, and emotional support. Therapeutic processes such as receiving feedback from multiple perspectives, learning through group dynamics, and benefiting from the group's collective energy can only be fully realised in a group setting. These advantages make group therapy a powerful and invaluable healing modality.

The Role of Intellectual and Cultural Influences in Shaping Therapeutic Practice

The foundations of my therapeutic identity have been shaped not only by clinical experience but also through interdisciplinary influences and the challenge of integrating diverse perspectives. While supervision from various mentors has played a central role in this development (as discussed in Chapter 4 in this volume), insights drawn from literature, art, and philosophy have been equally significant. Thinkers and artists such as Pablo Neruda, Frida Kahlo, Fyodor Dostoevsky, Alexandre Dumas, and Leo Tolstoy continue to inspire my approach, emphasising creativity, emotional depth, and the complexity of the human condition. Their work serves as a reminder that therapeutic practice must engage with the full range of human experience, often extending beyond psychological theory alone.

Early in my career, I encountered challenges from fellow professionals representing differing theoretical orientations. Although sometimes difficult, these encounters encouraged me to critically examine my own assumptions and to synthesise varying viewpoints. Such experiences were essential in broadening my understanding of therapeutic work and fostering an approach that remains flexible and responsive to the realities of clinical practice.

A particularly revealing moment arose during supervision with a British psychoanalyst affiliated with the organisation in which I was employed. She questioned whether therapy was appropriate for a Peruvian patient who was facing profound social, economic, and emotional challenges. Her perspective reflected a broader bias present within certain analytic traditions – one that often assumes that therapy may be unsuitable for refugees or individuals from disadvantaged backgrounds. Such views risk overlooking the fact that many refugees and marginalised individuals, despite significant external hardships, engage in therapy with openness and a genuine commitment to change – provided that treatment is culturally sensitive and appropriate. Their engagement offers valuable opportunities for therapeutic growth and challenges assumptions that psychoanalytic work is only relevant for those with particular privileges. In these organisations, supervisors were assigned to me, and I was expected to work with them even if I disagreed with their views. Rather than avoiding these challenges, I chose to engage by questioning and discussing concerns openly.

Conversely, when therapy fails to address the cultural and psychological needs of these individuals, some disengage or drop out – not necessarily due to resistance, but because the therapy itself does not serve them effectively. In such cases, practitioners may interpret withdrawal as a sign of unreadiness or conclude that the therapeutic model is inappropriate. While these interpretations are often made with good intentions, they risk failing to recognise the limitations of the therapeutic framework and may inadvertently place undue responsibility on the patient, rather than prompting reflection on the therapy provided.

I hold that therapy should be accessible to all individuals, including those who have experienced significant trauma, irrespective of educational or socio-economic background. People who have faced profound adversity often approach therapy with openness to self-reflection and personal growth. This underscores the importance of an intercultural therapeutic approach – one that is sensitive to cultural differences and responsive to the resilience and agency of those navigating complex life circumstances.

For therapy to continue evolving, practitioners and institutions must engage in ongoing self-examination, acknowledging and addressing implicit biases that may influence clinical work. Cultivating an atmosphere of respect, curiosity, and inclusivity is essential. Prioritising therapeutic approaches that respond to the specific needs of diverse populations ensures that patients receive both understanding and competent care. Institutional initiatives, such as working groups focused on diversity and inclusion, can meaningfully contribute to this evolution by incorporating a broad range of perspectives, thereby enhancing accessibility and effectiveness.

Challenges in Health Institutions and Therapy Centres

Intercultural therapy requires a deep understanding of the cultural concept of the person, which shapes how individuals experience distress and healing within their social contexts (Kirmayer, 2007). This perspective challenges clinicians to move beyond universal assumptions about mental health and to engage with each patient's unique cultural reality. Building on this, Kirmayer (2012) argues that cultural competence should not be viewed as a fixed skill set but as an ongoing process of critical self-reflection, humility, and openness to complexity in clinical practice. Together, these insights emphasise the importance of therapists remaining adaptable and culturally responsive, fostering therapeutic environments that genuinely meet the needs of diverse populations.

Throughout my experience in health institutions and therapy centres, I have observed systemic challenges that influence the delivery of psychological care. Common remarks heard during professional discussions include:

- 'We receive highly traumatised patients with multiple issues.'
- 'Are they suitable for therapy?'
- 'They lack insight.'
- 'Let's refer them elsewhere.'
- 'Let's send them back to their community; they can manage.'

Such statements reveal a reluctance to engage with patients whose difficulties are perceived as complex or overwhelming. This hesitancy often excludes those most in need of care, reinforcing systemic barriers and limiting access to psychological support. The implicit assumption appears to be that some patients fall outside the scope of therapeutic help – raising important ethical and professional concerns about responsibility and inclusion in mental health services.

This raises an important question: who decides which factors make a patient 'heavy' or 'unworkable'? Excluding people with complex trauma, multiple diagnoses, or limited insight risks neglecting those who might benefit most from ongoing therapy. The role of mental health professionals is not to avoid complexity but to engage with it sensitively – adapting methods to meet patients within their psychological and cultural realities, and collaborating as a team when needed.

Addressing these challenges demands a commitment to ethical and compassionate practice. Anthropological perspectives, such as those of Das (2007), emphasise that trauma is not merely an individual psychological event but is deeply rooted in social, cultural, and structural contexts, underscoring the need to understand patients within their broader social worlds. Working with individuals in acute distress requires not only theoretical knowledge and clinical skills but also emotional resilience. Complexity should be recognised as an inherent part of therapeutic work, necessitating ongoing learning, reflective supervision, and robust institutional support.

To ensure that therapy is truly inclusive and effective, professionals and organisations must confront systemic biases and regard cultural competence as an ongoing process of self-reflection and responsiveness to diversity (Kirmayer, 2012). Developing frameworks that support – rather than marginalise – those experiencing profound psychological hardship is essential. By fostering a culture of responsibility, openness, and curiosity, mental health services can engage meaningfully with complexity and respond with the seriousness and care it requires.

Strengthening Emotional Muscles: The Role of Professional Responsibility, Compassion, and Clinical Flexibility in Therapy

Therapists, much like engineers, rely on foundational principles to support psychological stability. Yet therapy is far from a mechanical process; rather, it involves engaging with the emotional complexities of human relationships. To work effectively in this context, therapists must cultivate both technical competence and emotional resilience. Ongoing development through rigorous training and clinical supervision is essential, enabling practitioners to refine their approach while remaining grounded in ethical and professional integrity (Behr, 1996). Behr emphasises that effective supervision is not merely a hierarchical exercise but a collaborative process of 'paravision' – a peer-informed model that fosters shared responsibility and reflective practice. This approach values humility, openness, and mutual learning as key to professional growth and emotional strength.

Montaigne ([1580] 2003) observed that written testimonies are often valued more highly than spoken ones. In therapy, however, we engage not with fixed accounts but with evolving human experience. Unlike machines, people require emotional presence and relational responsiveness. The therapist's task is to offer support while maintaining emotional boundaries, ensuring that their own pain does not become entangled with the patient's. Achieving this balance requires self-reflection, supervision, and a strong sense of professional responsibility (Fernando, 2010).

Therapy is most effective when the patient's emotions and narrative take precedence over rigid theoretical frameworks. While theory provides valuable structure, over-reliance on predefined models can constrain the therapeutic process. Drawing on diverse perspectives encourages creativity and flexibility, allowing practitioners to respond more effectively to each patient's unique needs (Moodley and Palmer, 2006).

The willingness to question rigidity is essential in therapeutic work. Clinical decisions should emerge from direct engagement with the patient rather than being driven solely by theoretical assumptions. For example, a patient was denied treatment based on a referral letter, without being offered an initial consultation. I challenged this and advocated for a face-to-face assessment. Through an intercultural therapeutic approach, the patient regained confidence and eventually discontinued antidepressant medication. This experience underscored the importance of direct engagement and the risks of excluding patients prematurely (Tribe and Morrissey, 2004).

Therapy alone, however, may not be sufficient in complex cases. Collaborative work with psychiatrists, social workers, link workers, community nurses, and even physiotherapists – since many patients present with psychosomatic complaints – is often necessary to provide comprehensive care. A multidisciplinary approach enhances outcomes and ensures that patients receive the holistic support they need (Sue and Sue, 2012).

Compassion and life experience are invaluable in therapy. Therapists who have faced personal challenges often develop emotional resilience, which strengthens their ability to support others. At the same time, it is essential to separate one's own pain from that of the patient; without this, therapeutic boundaries can become blurred.

Effective therapy requires both formal training and lived experience. When working with individuals who have experienced trauma, therapists must provide structured, compassionate care that fosters safety and trust. Combining theoretical knowledge with emotional insight enables therapists to help patients to develop their own emotional resilience.

Ultimately, strengthening emotional muscles is not simply a personal task; rather, it is a professional responsibility. It requires continuous learning, cultural humility, and a commitment to relational depth across difference (Fernando, 2010; Moodley and Palmer, 2006).

An Overview of Psychoeducation Groups: Psychoeducation and the Value of 'Wellbeing Groups' in Marginalised Communities

I facilitate psychoeducation groups for individuals who are uncertain about therapy or have a limited understanding of what it entails. These groups are especially valuable within marginalised communities, where therapy is often misunderstood or met with suspicion. In some cultures, psychological treatment is still associated with being 'mad', a label that reinforces stigma and discourages people from seeking help. Yet madness is not an absolute truth; rather, it is a social construct that is defined and judged differently across time, cultures, and contexts. When patients express fear of being called 'mad', I often ask, 'What is wrong with being mad?' By inviting reflection, we can move away from seeing madness as a weakness and instead approach it with greater compassion, patience, and openness (Priebe et al., 2012).

These psychoeducation groups help to reduce psychological, economic, and social pressures on the wider healthcare system. They offer a safe space for participants to explore emotions and challenges, alleviating anxiety and preparing them for possible therapeutic engagement. Sessions typically have a duration of 60 to 75 minutes, providing a structured and contained environment. Participants are encouraged to reflect and decide – without pressure – whether short- or long-term therapy may be suitable (Public Health England, 2015).

The group setting fosters mutual support, guided by the therapist through an intercultural lens that honours cultural diversity and difference. Such sessions provide a meaningful introduction to therapy for those hesitant to engage, particularly in communities where psychological treatment is stigmatised or perceived as relevant only to severe illness (Baskin et al., 2021).

In my practice, I refer to these psychoeducation groups as 'wellbeing groups' to encourage a more accessible and culturally sensitive understanding of therapy. They provide a non-threatening environment where participants can learn about the structure, purpose, and potential benefits of therapy without immediately confronting deep trauma. The aims of these groups include:

1 Understanding the group therapist's role;
2 Recognising the importance of trained psychotherapists;
3 Differentiating therapy from everyday conversations;
4 Emphasising boundaries, trust, and confidentiality;
5 Promoting self-awareness and understanding one's impact on others;
6 Fostering belonging and openness to difference; and
7 Encouraging personal growth and a willingness to learn.

By offering a supportive, structured space, these groups enable individuals to explore their emotional needs at their own pace and make informed decisions about whether – and how – to engage in therapy.

Assessing Patients Before Group Therapy: The Role of the First Meeting

In intercultural analytic therapy, the initial meeting holds particular significance. As my late mother remarked, 'Guests are welcomed by their appearance and attire, and farewelled by their feelings and thoughts.' This reminds us that while first impressions matter, it is emotional resonance that leaves a lasting impact. Similarly, early perceptions shape expectations, but meaningful engagement determines the depth of connection.

The assessment session serves as a microcosm of the therapeutic journey. A patient's outward presentation – how they speak, behave, or express themselves – may not fully reflect their inner world. Therapists must attend both to what is said and what remains unspoken. Sensitivity, patience, and clinical curiosity are essential for recognising emotional pain or resistance that may be difficult to articulate.

Cultural competence is crucial for building trust. In intercultural contexts, therapists must respect diverse worldviews, communication styles, and belief systems. This includes awareness of cultural taboos, varied expressions of distress, and differing expectations of therapy. Cultural sensitivity should not be mistaken for mere comfort or reassurance; rather, it aims to support patients in exploring deeper emotional roots.

The initial session offers space for mutual assessment. While some practitioners prefer extended evaluations, I usually limit this to one or two sessions, encouraging patients to engage with the group process rather than focusing solely on the therapist. Early orientation to group dynamics supports participation from the outset.

At this stage, the therapist assesses the patient's suitability for group therapy, while the patient considers their comfort with the therapeutic framework. Clear boundaries and realistic expectations help to reduce anxiety and foster openness. Even if therapy does not continue, the session offers a valuable opportunity for patients to voice concerns and consider future support options.

Regardless of the outcome, patients should leave feeling respected, contained, and with a clear understanding of the next steps. If group therapy is not recommended, this should be communicated sensitively to avoid feelings of rejection. The priority remains to guide patients towards the most appropriate form of support.

A well-conducted assessment promotes patient agency by enabling informed decisions. It provides clarity, direction, and engagement, even if therapy is not the immediate outcome.

Structure and Methods of the Assessment Session

While some therapists use pre-session forms or telephone assessments, face-to-face meetings remain indispensable. Observing body language, tone, and emotional expression offers a more complete understanding of the patient. The session typically unfolds in three phases:

1. Introduction: Clarifying the therapist's role and the purpose of the session.
2. Exploration: Using open-ended questions to invite the patient to share experiences and expectations.

3 Conclusion: Supporting reflection on the appropriateness of therapy and outlining next steps.

Key questions include:

- Why are you seeking therapy?
- What do you hope to achieve?
- Why now?
- How do you express your emotions?

In some cultures – such as Turkish and many Asian communities – emotional distress often presents as physical symptoms (e.g. stomach ache, headache, chest pain, general discomfort) rather than through emotional language. This somatisation is well documented in cross-cultural psychiatry (Kleinman, 1980; Tseng, 2001), making recognition of these patterns essential for accurate assessment and engagement. Assessment also explores core aspects of the patient's life – family dynamics, personality, childhood experiences, social and cultural background, and underlying fears or anxieties. These factors provide essential context for tailoring therapy.

Exploring the meaning of a patient's name can open powerful conversations, especially among Black and ethnic minority patients – although I have also found it meaningful with White patients. Names often carry deep personal and cultural significance. For instance, a Turkish patient named Yeter ('enough') explained that, as the seventh daughter, her name reflected her parents' wish to stop having baby girls. This experience had profoundly shaped her sense of worth and identity. Such insights can shed light on longstanding emotional patterns.

Similarly, my own name, Dilek ('wish' or 'desire'), carries a unique emotional tone. I was welcomed with joy. This sense of being wanted, even in difficult circumstances, gave me strength. Perhaps this feeling of being cherished contributed to my resilience.

The Group Therapist's Role: Dynamics, Leadership, and Challenges

The group therapist's role extends beyond facilitating discussion. It involves managing group dynamics while fostering a safe and supportive environment. Emotional sensitivity, cultural awareness, and clinical adaptability are essential to shaping a meaningful therapeutic experience. Drawing on the work of Foulkes, the founder of group analysis, the therapist is seen not as a directive leader but as a participant-observer who supports the group's emerging culture and unconscious communication.

Jafar Kareem's contributions further emphasise the importance of cultural context, particularly within intercultural therapeutic settings. His concept of 'cultural concordance' challenges therapists to consider how cultural identity, language, and worldview influence the therapeutic alliance. Leadership, in this view, is about containment and attunement – creating a holding space where difference can be acknowledged and transformation can unfold.

The assessment session lays the groundwork for this process. It enables both patient and therapist to evaluate whether group therapy is suitable. Unlike individual therapists – who may sometimes overlook the potential of group work – group analysts tend to consider both individual and collective therapeutic paths. This distinction reflects a common challenge: some individual therapists struggle to imagine how their patients might benefit from a group setting. Within institutions, this can lead to subtle tensions or competition between individual and group therapists. My training in both approaches has helped me to recognise their respective strengths and to encourage constructive dialogue between them.

Establishing the Group Process

Foulkes (1964) provides the foundational theory of group therapy, highlighting how the therapist's presence shapes the group's emotional atmosphere and the relational dynamics within it. His work focuses on the collective processes that support emotional resilience and healthier interpersonal patterns.

Building on this, Fernando (2010), Thomas (1992), Kareem and Littlewood (1992), and Ababio (2019) offer valuable insights from intercultural and individual therapeutic perspectives. Their emphasis on cultural humility, responsiveness to difference, and sensitivity to individual backgrounds enriches the group context, helping to address diverse identities and complex cultural dynamics.

In my practice, I integrate these perspectives by combining Foulkes' group therapy framework with the intercultural awareness and clinical adaptability advocated by Fernando, Kareem, Littlewood, and Ababio. This allows me to create a therapeutic space that honours both the collective emotional processes of the group and the unique cultural experiences of each member.

Cultural Sensitivity and Group Dynamics

Each group member brings distinct cultural narratives, communication styles, and relational expectations. Some express themselves openly; others may rely on indirect or nuanced forms of communication. The therapist's ability to attune to these differences fosters trust and inclusion (Sue and Sue, 2016).

Disruptive behaviour may point to unresolved emotional pain or unconscious resistance. In such cases, the therapist assesses the situation carefully and often seeks supervision. After thoughtful exploration, the therapist may support the patient in recognising that the group is no longer the most appropriate setting for their development. This collaborative process respects both patient autonomy and group wellbeing.

For example, a male patient who repeatedly interrupted others began to disrupt group cohesion. Through exploration and supervision, he came to recognise that stepping back would better support both his personal growth and the group's process. His decision to leave allowed the group to maintain a more stable atmosphere. During this period, the group remained containing and tolerant, which helped to preserve stability even while managing the disruption. Meanwhile, the patient continued his reflection through individual therapy.

Group therapy also offers a space to explore emotional injuries shaped by culture, migration, and trauma. Patients are encouraged to reflect on how past experiences can influence current relationships and coping strategies. In intercultural settings, paying attention to these dynamics is essential for meaningful engagement and therapeutic progress (Constantine and Sue, 2006; Dalal, 2015).

Institutional Power and External Pressures

Beyond the interpersonal and cultural complexities within groups, institutional forces also shape therapy practice. At times, institutional power subtly overrides clinical judgement. There have been occasions when, despite my reservations about the therapeutic readiness of a particular group or context, I have been asked to set up a group due to external funding requirements. These requests, often driven by funders' expectations rather than clinical needs, reveal how therapy can become shaped by organisational agendas. While collaboration with institutions is important, such pressures can compromise the integrity of the therapeutic process. This raises critical questions about ownership and whose interests are ultimately being served – those of the patients, the therapists, or the institutions funding the work. Organisations rely on external funding and, unfortunately, they may ask therapists who are not even trained in group therapy to take on multiple roles. Workers become unhappy, and the quality of work may suffer.

While institutional forces may shape the context in which therapy occurs, the group itself remains a vital space for both patients and therapists to engage deeply with interpersonal and cultural complexities.

The Group as a Training Ground

Group therapy is transformative not only for patients but also for trainee therapists. Through observation and participation, trainees gain direct experience in managing group dynamics, emotional processes, and therapeutic boundaries.

This immersive involvement supports the development of emotional intelligence and reflexivity – qualities essential to becoming a grounded professional. The group becomes a microcosm of broader social patterns, offering critical insight into communication, power relations, and cultural dynamics (Dalal, 2015).

Trainees apply psychodynamic and intercultural concepts in real time, deepening both theoretical and practical understanding.

Working in supervised groups strengthens professional identity. Trainees learn to balance empathy with appropriate boundaries, manage countertransference, and develop their therapeutic stance. This process fosters confidence and cultivates a resilient sense of self (Sue and Sue, 2016).

Although some trainees discontinue their personal group therapy shortly after qualifying, it is advisable to remain involved for at least one to two years. This period allows time to process endings, experience loss, and consolidate learning. Continued engagement deepens emotional resilience and supports ongoing professional growth.

Some trainees may initially believe that they have no personal issues to address – an omnipotent stance that can hinder their development. However, it is vital that they work through their own unresolved emotional experiences before beginning clinical practice.

Cultivating Group Culture

Group culture develops organically through shared interaction. The therapist facilitates this process by modelling openness and encouraging emotional risk-taking, rather than directing the group's content. When honesty, empathy, and constructive challenges are supported, the group becomes a safe space for change.

A strong group culture fosters trust and deepens therapeutic work (Foulkes, 1975). Members feel psychologically secure enough to explore personal themes, challenge one another respectfully, and engage in a collective process of transformation.

In intercultural or minority group contexts, cultivating culture requires greater attentiveness. Power imbalances, historical trauma, and dominant cultural norms shape the group's emotional climate. Dalal (2002) emphasises the importance of addressing these dynamics through critical reflection. Other minority theorists echo this view, advocating culturally responsive practices that confront unconscious bias and affirm diverse identities (Sue and Sue, 2016; Constantine and Sue, 2006). A therapist attuned to these dynamics strengthens group cohesion and supports more inclusive outcomes. Each session is unique, shaped by the group's evolving dynamics and the individual contributions of its members.

The clinical section of this book examines how group culture unfolds in practice and how these dynamics are managed within real therapeutic settings.

Interpreting Fears and Context

Although it is not always possible to identify the precise origins of an individual's fears, therapeutic work can support the development of emotional resilience by engaging with subjective experience and personal narratives (Casement, 1990; Schlapobersky, 2016). Group therapy offers a space in which such fears may be expressed, contained, and reconsidered. Over time, patients may begin to recognise unconscious patterns and emotional responses shaped by family dynamics, cultural histories, and broader social structures.

Dalal (2002) draws attention to the ways in which racialisation and cultural legacies influence the unconscious, offering valuable insights into how background and identity shape emotional experience within therapeutic settings. Engaging with unresolved emotions in this context can contribute to the development of more coherent internal dialogues, which in turn may support healthier relationships and psychosocial functioning (Sandler et al., 1992).

Family Dynamics and Cultural Scripts

Reflections on familial roles – shaped by attachment, cultural scripts, and intergenerational expectations – often emerge in group settings. These reflections help to clarify how earlier relational dynamics inform current behaviours, emotional regulation, and interpersonal styles (Comas-Díaz, 1994; Sue and Sue, 2016). Lennox Thomas (1992), in particular, emphasises the importance of family narratives within cultural contexts, highlighting how these shape emotional patterns and influence interpersonal dynamics. As patients develop greater awareness, they may begin to interrupt harmful patterns and relate to others with increased honesty and care.

Family Structure and Psychoanalytic History-Taking

Family structure – including birth order and sibling relationships – can shape interpersonal expectations, competition, alliances, and modes of emotional regulation. Winnicott (1965) described psychoanalysis as an extended form of history-taking, one that explores personal narratives to uncover unconscious dynamics. Seemingly simple questions such as 'What was your childhood like?' or 'Can you share some family memories?' can help to reveal formative experiences influencing current behaviour Thomas, L. (1995).

Systemic Perspectives on Family Patterns

Systemic theorists such as Bowen (1978) emphasise the intergenerational transmission of emotional roles, while Minuchin (1974) draws attention to how family boundaries and hierarchies affect individual development. These frameworks are pertinent in group therapy where unresolved familial dynamics may be unconsciously re-enacted. Recognising such patterns enables attuned therapeutic interventions that can help to reshape entrenched relational behaviours.

Ending the Session

Clear and thoughtful communication at the end of sessions helps to preserve the therapeutic frame. In line with Casement's (1990) and Lemma's (2003) emphasis on reflective practice, the therapist supports patients in managing feelings of sorrow, anxiety, anger, guilt, or relief, while maintaining a sense of safety and continuity. Questions such as 'What are your thoughts on continuing therapy?' or 'Did this session meet your expectations?' invite reflection and help patients to actively process their experiences.

Some patients may require additional time to decide whether to continue therapy; others may choose to end it. As Holmes (1996) highlights, the therapist respects each patient's autonomy without imposing expectations, offering containment and understanding, as Murdin (2000) recommends, even when the session concludes.

Short-Term versus Long-Term Dynamics in Intercultural Group Therapy

Short-term therapy tends to address immediate relief and urgent needs, while long-term work supports deeper transformation and sustained self-discovery. For lasting wellbeing, long-term therapy enables more substantial growth (Sommers-Flanagan and Sommers-Flanagan, 2018). It is also associated with reduced reliance on emergency services and medication, benefiting both individuals and healthcare systems (McDermut et al., 2001).

Short-term, closed groups evolve as members enter and exit together. The therapist must manage these transitions in harmony with the group's rhythm, while acknowledging the emotional weight of endings. Group therapy naturally invites emotional investment; endings often evoke grief, reflecting human experiences of separation and loss (Yalom, 2005; Bion, 1961).

Short-term groups are more common in public mental health settings due to limited resources. While accessible and focused, their introduction requires sensitivity to avoid reinforcing stigma or confidentiality concerns. Safety, inclusivity, and trust remain central (Corey, 2016).

Although I value long-term work for its depth, short-term models are often employed in under-resourced systems to broaden access and meet procedural targets. Long-term therapy allows patients to explore relational patterns, develop deeper self-awareness, and process complex or longstanding issues. It supports sustained trust, the integration of new insights, and the gradual transformation of behaviour and coping strategies, enabling more enduring change. In contrast, short-term therapy prioritises immediate problem-solving and symptom relief, offering practical benefits for those with time or resource constraints. While it can be effective for focused issues, it may not allow the same depth of exploration or relational insight as longer-term work. However, in large healthcare organisations, the emphasis on efficiency and targets can reduce therapy to a box ticking exercise, limiting flexibility, depth, and the opportunity for sustained therapeutic change (Miller, 2006; Day and Schoenrade, 1997).

Supporting Transitions and Preparing for Ending

A vital role for the therapist is to prepare group members well in advance for the ending of therapy. This involves open conversations about the emotional impact of separation, framing the ending as a natural stage rather than an abrupt loss. Such preparation fosters emotional readiness (Yalom and Leszcz, 2020).

To help to manage grief, therapists may invite members to reflect on the group experience and insights gained. This supports a sense of closure and recognition. Emphasising coping strategies developed during therapy reinforces progress and encourages a confident transition beyond the group (Schiller and Morgan, 1996).

Regular self-reflection also benefits therapists, especially when working with emotionally charged themes such as separation and loss. Clinical supervision provides a space to process these experiences, sustain emotional presence, and build resilience (Falender and Shafranske, 2004). Reflective practice protects therapists from absorbing group dynamics in ways that could compromise clinical effectiveness (Yalom and Leszcz, 2020).

In intercultural contexts, supervision is particularly important. Patel (2024) highlights the value of intercultural supervision in managing cultural nuances around endings, enabling sensitive interventions. Güngör (2024) emphasises the role of reflective supervision in supporting the therapist's emotional responses, preventing burnout, and sustaining therapeutic effectiveness during difficult conclusions.

Dealing with Separation, Loss, and Institutional Challenges

John Bowlby's attachment theory, developed through studies of infant-caregiver relationships, offers valuable insights into how group members experience separation and loss at the end of therapy. Bowlby (1980) described how early attachment bonds shape later responses to separation, which may emerge as grief, anxiety, or fears of abandonment. These attachment-based patterns help to explain the intensity of emotions projected onto therapists during endings, underscoring the need for sensitive and containing interventions (Gelso and Hayes, 1998; Yalom and Leszcz, 2020).

As therapy draws to a close, members may experience grief, sorrow, or anger. These emotions are often projected not only onto the therapist – reflecting unmet childhood needs for love, protection, and validation – but also outwardly onto organisations or systemic authorities, reflecting perceived neglect or inequity. Ethnic minority patients' anger may reflect profound frustration that their needs are neglected or underserved due to financial constraints. This externalised anger highlights systemic failures and the painful reality that economic limitations translate into inadequate care for marginalised groups. Therapists must recognise and contain these complex responses while maintaining firm therapeutic boundaries (Gelso and Hayes, 1998). Güngör (2024) emphasises the critical need for therapists to remain emotionally grounded in these moments, especially within intercultural groups where endings may trigger deep wounds related to displacement, cultural loss, and systemic injustice.

Even in so-called long-term therapy – which often lasts no more than two years and is deemed long only in comparison to 12-week group programmes – endings may evoke profound sorrow. Economic constraints within public mental health services frequently limit the duration of therapy. While short-term therapy may be cost-effective, it rarely allows sufficient time to address deeper emotional wounds (Corey, 2016). Patients from marginalised groups are frequently directed towards programmes that are receive inadequate funding, such as cognitive behavioural therapy (CBT) and Improving Access to Psychological Therapies (IAPT), which have been shown to have limited effectiveness for Black and ethnic minority patients.

Ideally, there would be no need for separate centres for Black and ethnic minority patients, as all patients could be fully supported within mainstream statutory health services. Unfortunately, this remains unlikely, as these services are often not fully accessible or culturally responsive. Consequently, patients frequently rely on specialised organisations, which are under-resourced and unable to meet demand due to funding constraints. Funders provide limited resources yet expect these organisations to deliver an enormous amount of work. As a result, patients are sometimes referred to more intensive interventions, such as intercultural-analytic therapy. Although clinically appropriate, such interventions rarely receive sustained funding, leaving patients to navigate fragmented care pathways and disrupted support, despite the commitment of organisations such as Nafsiyat to culturally sensitive care.

Patel (2024) highlights the critical importance of culturally sensitive support during these transitions, particularly for patients from refugee or migrant backgrounds who may face compounded experiences of loss and disruption as therapy concludes. This exposes systemic failure to provide continuous culturally attuned care.

To promote continued growth beyond therapy, some therapists recommend selected readings or reflective writing exercises. Encouraging ongoing self-reflection helps to maintain emotional resilience developed during therapy and supports sustained personal development. Holmes (1996) emphasises the need to foster ongoing integration of therapeutic insights, especially in intercultural contexts, where the ending of therapy may awaken complex feelings around identity and belonging. However, these efforts often fall to individual therapists, masking systemic weaknesses and leaving vulnerable patients exposed to premature or insufficient care.

Defining the Group's Focus and Structure

Clear communication about a group's purpose is essential to establish shared expectations and to create a secure therapeutic framework. Groups often centre on shared life challenges or emotional themes – such as adapting to a new culture, coping with loss, or supporting emotional wellbeing. While many groups focus on specific challenges or experiences, I avoid rigid labels such as 'survivors of trauma' or 'grief group', as these can narrowly define or inadvertently expose participants. Instead, I prefer to describe groups simply as 'intercultural group therapy for women' or 'mixed-gender intercultural group therapy'. The focus of the group – its themes, challenges, and emotional work – is addressed within the sessions themselves, rather than through predefined categories. This approach maintains inclusivity and allows participants' experiences to shape the group dynamically, providing patients with the freedom to discuss and explore whatever they wish, a process further shaped by the careful use of language during sessions.

Some participants seek psychoeducation or short-term support, while others embark on longer therapeutic journeys; regardless of focus, providing practical details such as format, seating arrangement (e.g. circle), session frequency (e.g. 12, 24, or 40 sessions), and group size fosters emotional safety and helps participants to feel prepared.

The Role of Language in Group Therapy

Language shapes the therapeutic process, influencing dialogue and emotional expression. For more reserved members, open-ended prompts such as 'How are you feeling today?' or 'What's on your mind?' offer gentle invitations to participate without pressure, thereby allowing emotions to unfold gradually.

With more dominant members, the therapist maintains balance by encouraging active listening and mindful sharing. Phrases such as 'Let's hear from others as well' promote inclusion and help to regulate group dynamics, ensuring that every voice is heard and valued. Thoughtful use of language ensures that all participants, regardless of cultural or personal background, can engage safely and meaningfully in the group process, thereby fostering connection and strengthening cohesion.

Active Participation and Group Principles

Active participation is fundamental. This includes regular attendance, attentive listening, empathetic engagement, and informing the group in advance of absences. Participation does not mean speaking frequently but being emotionally present and responsive.

From the outset, therapists establish key principles – confidentiality, a secure base (Bowlby, 1988), respectful communication, and emotional safety. While some members may initially struggle to engage due to distress or unfamiliarity, these principles are gradually internalised, providing a structured yet flexible framework for meaningful therapeutic work.

In intercultural settings, it is essential that patients understand and agree to group principles before joining, ensuring that they are emotionally prepared for the journey. Occasionally, a patient may unexpectedly encounter someone they know – such as a family member – during the first session. When this happens, the therapist must thoughtfully remove one or both individuals to protect the group's safety and integrity.

Establishing Clear Group Guidelines

Clear guidelines ensure emotional safety. Participants are expected to follow key principles such as punctuality and confidentiality, and to avoid behaviours harmful to themselves or others. A critical part involves learning to express emotions – anger or sorrow – within respectful relational boundaries. The aim is not to suppress emotion but to cultivate recognition, articulation, and constructive regulation.

For example, individuals are encouraged to verbalise anger without insults or abusive language. Physical aggression is strictly prohibited. Emotions should be communicated in ways the group can collectively process and support. By fostering an environment where emotional communication is both structured and open, participants can engage meaningfully while maintaining psychological safety.

Clinical Experience with Challenging Group Dynamics

Early in my group analysis work in the UK, a male participant persistently directed hostile remarks towards me, including accusations and offensive language that I struggled to fully understand as a newcomer to the country. Despite efforts by the group and the analyst to help him to recognise the inappropriateness of his behaviour – particularly its racist and misogynistic undertones – there was no meaningful change. The analyst ultimately referred him for individual work and gently removed him from the group. This decision reaffirmed my sense of safety, value, and respect within the therapeutic space.

This experience underscored a key principle: group therapy depends on each participant's readiness to engage. If a patient is not emotionally prepared or motivated, the process may feel forced and less effective. A shared understanding of the group's purpose and individual responsibility is essential for fostering trust and strengthening the therapeutic alliance.

Supporting Emotional Changes

Some patients may feel pressured to join a group by external sources such as general practitioners (GPs), nurses, or social workers. It is vital that participation remains their own decision. Group therapy can evoke deep emotional responses affecting not only the individual but also their family and wider social relationships. Supporting patients to prepare their families for potential emotional changes helps to create a more stable and understanding environment beyond the group.

Addressing Early Endings

Sometimes a patient may choose to end therapy early due to its intensity. I respond with empathy, recognising that a patient's desire to leave may reflect internal conflict rather than true readiness to conclude therapy. The patient may need additional time to process emotions before they are genuinely ready to leave the group, rather than using departure as a way to avoid difficult feelings. The group often wishes the participant to stay, so efforts are made to explore their reasons for leaving. If the patient remains determined, I encourage attendance for a few more weeks to allow space for reflection and emotional processing – both for themselves and the group.

For example, one male patient considered leaving the group several times over a period of months. Through ongoing dialogue and gentle encouragement, he stayed engaged. Eventually, he disclosed a deeply personal experience: at the age of two, his mother had given him to his aunt, who could not have children. He had carried lifelong feelings of rejection. This disclosure marked a turning point, enabling him to remain until he was genuinely ready to conclude therapy. The group responded with empathy, deepening its emotional tone and encouraging others to reflect on their own early losses.

In open-ended groups, I manage a waiting list to maintain cohesion. In contrast, short-term, closed groups have fixed membership. As a member approaches the end of their time in the group, I support all participants in recognising this transition, providing space to explore its emotional impact and what it symbolises for the group. This process fosters growth and honours the experiences of both those concluding and those continuing their therapeutic journey.

Exploring Unconscious Behaviours and Group Resistance

Group therapy often reveals unconscious behaviours that shape the group's dynamics. Resistance to change may appear as avoidance, deflection, or controlling actions that disrupt the group's flow. The therapist's role is to help members to recognise these defence mechanisms and explore the fears or anxieties beneath them. For example, some individuals may shift the focus onto others to protect themselves from vulnerability.

Effective therapy relies on active verbal participation – speaking, listening, and engaging meaningfully. As trust within the group grows, it creates a safe space for expressing difficult emotions. Facilitated by the therapist, members develop authenticity, allowing hidden interpersonal dynamics to surface and be explored with empathy and thoughtful curiosity.

Leadership in Group Therapy

Group therapy is a dynamic, reciprocal process in which individuals influence, and are influenced by, the group. The therapist must embody several key leadership qualities, including the following:

- Comprehensive training: A solid foundation in psychotherapy and group dynamics is essential for effective leadership.
- Personal experience: First-hand participation in group therapy deepens the therapist's empathy and insight.
- Wholehearted listening: The therapist must remain attuned to both verbal and non-verbal cues, offering genuine attention to members' emotions and needs. This echoes Karen Horney's emphasis on authentic empathy and understanding the patient's true self beneath defensive behaviours (Horney, 1950).
- Patience and feedback: Balancing patience with clear, direct feedback supports the group's progress.
- Neutrality: While complete neutrality is rarely possible, the therapist must remain aware of their own biases and emotional responses. This self-awareness helps to contain reactions, preventing interference with the group process and maintaining a safe, supportive environment.
- Active facilitation: Encouraging participation and guiding discussion helps to keep the group focused and engaged.

Managing Countertransference

Equally important is the need to manage countertransference, whereby the therapist reflects on their own emotional responses. Self-reflection is essential to understand whether these feelings stem from personal experiences or represent projections of the patient's emotions. A skilled therapist adopts a flexible, intercultural approach, thereby fostering growth both in individuals and within the group as a whole.

Intercultural Therapy for the Dominant Group

Intercultural therapy is relevant not only for people from Black and minority ethnic backgrounds but also for White individuals. Culture shapes everyone's identity, values, and emotional expression, including those of the dominant or majority group. For White individuals, intercultural therapy provides a space in which to explore their cultural assumptions, unconscious biases, and inherited beliefs – often overlooked as the 'norm'. It supports deeper self-awareness, challenges privilege and blind spots, and enhances relational understanding in diverse settings. In an increasingly multicultural world, such awareness is essential for personal development and meaningful connection.

Leaderless Groups as a Therapeutic Experiment

Although I do not generally favour leaderless groups, they can offer valuable insights into group dynamics. In long-term groups, I occasionally introduce such sessions to observe how the group functions without a designated leader. Key areas for evaluation include:

- Attendance and participation: Do members remain engaged in the absence of an identified leader?
- Group dynamics: How do members of the group relate to one another within a less structured setting?
- Sharing and withholding: Do members feel more at ease to speak, or do they tend to withhold contributions without leadership present?

Sustaining and Adapting Group Therapy: Challenges, Structure, and Inclusive Practice

Earl Hopper (2003) emphasises the therapist's role in recognising and addressing challenges as they emerge within the group. Thoughtful and responsive engagement with these difficulties can deepen the therapeutic process and support the group's continued development.

The careful selection and assessment of group members is crucial, as each individual significantly shapes the group's dynamics. Establishing a therapy group requires thorough planning, particularly during the formative phase. The therapist plays a central role in shaping the group culture and must approach this responsibility with skill and care. As Foulkes (1975) observed, the therapist's involvement at this stage has a considerable influence on the group's future success. Key considerations include:

- What type of group is being formed?
- Where will it take place?
- How many members will participate?
- What are their needs, and how will these be addressed?
- Does the therapist possess the necessary training and experience?

Groups may be closed or open-ended. Closed groups require full commitment from the outset and run for a set duration, ranging from several weeks to a number of years. Long-term commitment is essential from both the therapist and the group members. Foulkes himself continued his group work until his death in 1976, illustrating the depth of dedication this work demands.

I facilitated a charity-based therapy group for 14 years, which I discuss further in the clinical section of this book. Although supported by a health authority, the group was eventually closed due to new management's limited understanding of its long-term value. I have also supervised therapy groups for over a decade and currently lead several reflective groups for therapists across various sectors. These groups provide practitioners with a space in which to explore professional challenges and deepen clinical insight – an approach consistent with the reflective supervision practices outlined in *Intercultural Supervision in Therapeutic Practice* (Ababio, 2024).

The Power of Connection and Engagement in Group Therapy

Creating a safe and welcoming space is central to effective group therapy. The transformative potential of therapy lies not solely in technique, but in the human connections it fosters. Shared understanding and support can illuminate experiences that might otherwise remain shrouded in darkness (Yalom, 1995).

Individuals who appear passive may be experiencing disconnection and hopelessness, often thinking, 'Group therapy is pointless'. This sentiment may conceal a deeper fear of exclusion or invisibility. When such feelings are acknowledged and explored, they can lead to meaningful psychological growth.

In some cases, silence may not reflect disengagement but can serve as a protective strategy. Kinouani (2020) argues that silencing can be a response to power dynamics within the group – particularly for those carrying the trauma of marginalisation. For some, speaking up has previously resulted in hostility or erasure. In these moments, the group must learn to recognise that silence itself can carry the weight of past violations, and that bearing witness is as vital as speaking.

Unconscious emotions – such as unresolved grief – may feel familiar but impede progress. Genuine transformation often requires directly confronting trauma (Herman, 1992). Although avoidance may provide a sense of control, it can create distance from the self and others (van der Kolk, 2015).

Group sessions typically last 90 minutes, although this may vary depending on the group's size and focus. Groups working with societal trauma may meet for shorter durations. Weekly or twice-weekly meetings are common, while daily sessions tend to occur in inpatient or hospital-based settings. The emotional resilience required for frequent meetings highlights the importance of consistent structure in building trust, especially among traumatised patients (Folkman and Lazarus, 1985).

The physical environment also plays a significant role in engagement. The group room should offer privacy and calm, with seating arranged in a circle to promote openness. Small touches – such as tissues or flowers – can contribute to a welcoming and supportive atmosphere.

While an individual therapist may lead a group, larger or more complex groups may benefit from the involvement of co-therapists to assist in emotional processing and the monitoring of group dynamics. Ongoing professional reflection following sessions is also essential (Yalom, 1995).

Women's Voices in Group Therapy

Therapists must maintain consistency in their approach while adapting to economic constraints, particularly in systems where therapy is undervalued. They are also called upon to challenge societal assumptions – especially those related to womanhood – by resisting discrimination and amplifying silenced voices within the group. In addition to what happens within the group itself, writing about these experiences extends the group's impact, ensuring that women's voices continue to be heard beyond the therapy room. By writing books, articles, or clinical reflections, therapists can honour these women's experiences and ensure that others can read and hear them, particularly those voices that might otherwise remain unheard. This process also helps reflect on the social and cultural factors shaping their lives.

Feminist therapy initially aimed to challenge traditional gender roles but often focused on the experiences of middle-class, educated women. In the 1980s, therapists such as Susie Orbach (Orbach, 1994) and Luise Eichenbaum (Eichenbaum and Orbach, 1988) helped to broaden the field by including the voices of working-class and marginalised women. Yet much of the feminist therapy literature continues to overlook women from diverse cultural and social backgrounds.

Therapeutic spaces have the potential to challenge societal gender norms underpinning trauma and discrimination. Feminist therapy, which emerged in the 1960s, addresses these concerns by promoting egalitarian relationships and validating patients' lived experiences. It acknowledges the role of societal structures in shaping individual trauma and advocates for both personal empowerment and wider social transformation.

However, early feminist therapy often centred on the experiences of middle-class, educated women. There is now a growing call for greater inclusivity, recognising that race, class, and cultural background intersect with gender. Therapists such as Beverly Greene (1994) have emphasised the need to understand the specific experiences of women of colour. Her work, along with that of Comas-Díaz (1994), highlights the importance of culturally competent care that attends to the complexity of identity and systemic oppression. These contributions extend feminist therapy by acknowledging not only gendered experiences but also the broader sociopolitical forces shaping trauma.

As Kinouani (2020) highlights, exclusion can reproduce silencing even in spaces designed to be inclusive. Without consciously addressing power structures and racialised trauma, the group may replicate the very systems it seeks to challenge. An inclusive lens is essential to reflect the varied experiences of all women.

Group therapy provides a supportive environment where women can connect with others facing similar emotional struggles, despite differing life circumstances. While emotions such as grief, anger, fear, guilt, and shame are universal, their expression and interpretation are shaped by personal, cultural, and social factors. These differences enrich the group, offering multiple perspectives and deepening its emotional fabric (Caruth, 1996). In this setting, women are encouraged to speak openly, witness each other's stories, and offer mutual support. This collective journey transforms isolation into connection and belonging. Over time, the group becomes a source of strength and validation, helping each woman to recognise that, while her experiences are unique, they are part of a broader human narrative. Group therapy thus supports individual growth and fosters a shared sense of empowerment and healing.

Reclaiming Women's Voices Across Borders

These reflections gain particular urgency when viewed through the lens of lived experience – both my own and that of the women I have worked with across diverse cultural contexts.

My journey as a therapist has been profoundly shaped by the resilience and struggles of women I have encountered in Türkiye and across Europe. In eastern Türkiye, during my years as a nurse, I witnessed women seeking refuge in hospitals to escape domestic abuse. Some, tragically, died prematurely, their stories silenced by rigid societal norms. These experiences instilled in me a lasting commitment to advocate for women's voices within therapeutic settings, ensuring that their stories – however painful – are heard and acknowledged.

Domestic violence transcends national borders, affecting women from diverse backgrounds who experience similar forms of trauma. Male patients may also have histories of domestic violence, either as survivors themselves or in relation to their family dynamics. Conversely, some male patients recognise their abusive behaviour and express a desire to change, though many retreat when confronted with the depth and difficulty of the work required. Others engage sincerely, striving for genuine transformation. The journey is rarely straightforward, but shared human experiences of pain and resilience remain constant.

The 1980 military coup in Türkiye was a defining moment in the country's history, leaving deep and enduring scars on its collective memory. Although justified under the pretext of restoring order, the coup entailed widespread suppression of democratic freedoms and individual rights, creating an atmosphere of fear and censorship. As a nurse manager during this period, I witnessed the human cost of such repression. I saw 14-year-old girls subjected to virginity tests – a deeply traumatic and invasive violation of their rights. That these acts occurred within a state-sanctioned framework underscores how political violence infiltrated the most intimate areas of personal and social life.

While I could prevent military personnel from entering examination rooms, I could not stop the procedures themselves. This left me with a profound sense of helplessness and frustration, highlighting the limitations of my role within a system far beyond my individual influence. The violence of that era extended beyond the battlefield into institutions such as healthcare. Detainees faced intense trauma, and healthcare workers carried significant emotional burdens as they navigated systems often at odds with their core values of compassion and care.

Witnessing such injustices – especially when unable to intervene meaningfully – left deep emotional wounds. The contrast between my efforts to shield these young girls and the overwhelming force of systemic violence illustrated the immense challenge of resisting entrenched oppression. It reinforced my belief that regimes governed by fear and control do not merely harm individuals in the present but inflict generational trauma that continues to resonate. Trauma rooted in systemic or state-sanctioned violence leaves enduring wounds. In therapy, addressing such trauma involves recognising its long-term emotional and psychological effects. Healing entails supporting individuals as they confront their deepest fears and vulnerabilities, reclaiming their sense of self-worth and agency.

Although the military claimed that the coup was intended to restore stability, its long-term consequences fostered a culture of silence and fear. The psychological aftermath of that period continues to be felt. These experiences underscored the necessity of advocating for justice, speaking out against oppression, and cultivating spaces where trauma can be processed and healing can begin. They also affirmed my conviction that collective action and solidarity are essential in confronting structural injustice.

These early encounters have profoundly shaped my therapeutic approach. I remain committed to creating spaces where human dignity is upheld and individuals – particularly women – are supported in their healing from historical and personal wounds. These experiences did not merely influence my personal values; they laid the foundation for my professional identity. They taught me that trauma does not occur in isolation; it is deeply interwoven with cultural norms, social structures, and power relations. As I transitioned from nursing to psychotherapy, I carried with me a sustained commitment to amplify women's voices and challenge the inequalities that seek to silence them. Being a woman in this profession has at times presented distinct challenges. For example, in early supervision sessions, some colleagues would unconsciously direct questions or seek approval from male peers, implicitly questioning or overlooking the professional judgement of female colleagues. One male therapist even remarked that female colleagues 'dwell on every case too long' and prefer 'short and sharp discussions', thereby highlighting subtle gendered assumptions about professional style. These experiences underscored how gender can influence perception and authority in clinical settings.

A patient once remarked, 'the first therapist I saw was younger than my daughter. How could she possibly understand me?' Such comments illustrate how age and gender shape the therapeutic relationship. Over time, these dynamics evolve. Young male patients now openly discuss topics once considered taboo. While experience offers depth, younger therapists bring fresh perspectives and may connect more readily with their generation. Ultimately, therapy is a collaborative endeavour in which both therapist and patient learn and grow.

By incorporating these diverse perspectives, we can foster more inclusive and validating therapeutic environments. Honouring the multiplicity of women's experiences ensures that their stories are heard, supporting processes of healing and empowerment across borders (Comas-Díaz, 1994).

Understanding Cultural and Social Factors

Acknowledging similarities and differences is vital to understanding a patient's psychological state. Personal, social, economic, and cultural influences all contribute to distress, and for women these often come with additional societal and familial pressures. Recognising and addressing these imbalances is key to supporting genuine psychological growth.

In Turkish society, certain progress has been made – for example, the removal of the derogatory term *eksik etek* ('incomplete skirt') from the Turkish Language Association's dictionary in 2010 (Türk Dil Kurumu, 2010). This phrase, long used to belittle women, was removed as part of efforts to eradicate sexist and discriminatory language. While symbolic, the change reflects an institutional step towards gender equality. Such shifts take time to influence deeply rooted attitudes and behaviours that continue to normalise violence and inequality.

The undervaluation of female children in Türkiye is often reflected in naming practices. Names such as Yeter ('Enough'), Tamam ('Okay'), Çilem ('Suffering'), Satılmış (a male name meaning 'sold'), and Intizar (a name that reflects anger or resentment towards someone, often wishing them harm) carry negative or limiting connotations that have been historically normalised (Ergün and Tümer, 2016). In group therapy, these naming conventions can serve as starting points for deeper exploration, helping women to understand how cultural narratives have shaped their identities. Therapy provides a space in which to challenge internalised beliefs and reframe identity in more affirming and empowering ways.

Gender Inequality and Cultural Transformation in Therapy

Gender inequality persists across many Asian and South Asian cultures. In some regions, names such as Nakusa and Nakushi, meaning 'unwanted,' reflect underlying gender preferences from birth (Singh, 2015). Female children may be given such names based on cultural beliefs about increasing the likelihood of a male child in subsequent births. These naming practices are embedded within broader cultural systems, including dowry traditions and patriarchal family structures, which can influence women's psychological wellbeing.

A notable example of change occurred in Maharashtra, India, where 285 girls previously named Nakusa or Nakushi ('Unwanted') were given the opportunity to select new names for themselves during a public ceremony. This act allowed the girls to redefine their identities within their cultural contexts. Naming is one of society's earliest ways of conveying values, and changing a name can represent a significant step towards personal agency and self-definition (BBC News, 2011).

Yet deeply rooted cultural inequalities continue to affect women's lives. Some patients report experiences of extreme gender-based violence, reflecting the consequences of entrenched cultural norms (Sen, 1990; Nanda, 2003). Preventive measures exist, such as clinics in London that restrict the disclosure of a baby's sex in order to reduce the incidence of gender-based abortions (NHS England, 2018).

These experiences often emerge during group therapy sessions. Within a safe and supportive environment, trauma rooted in cultural oppression can be processed, allowing meaning and understanding to develop. Therapists must exercise cultural competence and sensitivity, creating spaces that address these experiences while minimising the risk of re-traumatisation.

Therapists also play a vital role in challenging cultural and social norms that perpetuate inequality. Through therapy, women can begin to question inherited expectations and rebuild a sense of self no longer defined by others. Therapy thus becomes a site for both personal growth and potential social transformation.

A key aspect of therapeutic work involves helping women to reflect on how naming practices, family dynamics, and gender roles have shaped their self-perception and sense of self-worth. Addressing these influences supports patients in challenging and reshaping narratives that previously constrained them.

It is essential to recognise that gender inequality is not experienced uniformly. Intersectional factors such as race, class, religion, education, and ethnicity create varied forms of oppression (Crenshaw, 1989; Comas-Díaz, 1994). For example, a working-class woman may face both gender- and class-based discrimination, while a woman from an upper-class background may encounter different challenges. Culturally competent therapy acknowledges and responds to these differences.

Despite progress, gender-based discrimination persists. The shared experiences of women across different contexts highlight the widespread nature of these issues and the need for nuanced, compassionate therapeutic responses. Therapists have a responsibility to amplify women's voices, challenge societal norms, and contribute to meaningful, lasting change. Engaging in this work requires empathy, integrity, and respect for the strength and resilience of women.

References

Ababio, B., 2024. *Intercultural Supervision in Therapeutic Practice: Dialogues, Perspectives, and Reflections*. London: Routledge.

Ababio, E. and Littlewood, R. (eds), 2019. *Intercultural Therapy : Challenges, Insights and Developments*. London: Routledge.

Baskin, M., , 2021. 'Community-Centred Interventions for Improving Public Mental Health and Wellbeing among Adults from Ethnic Minority Groups: A Scoping Review', *International Journal of Environmental Research and Public Health*, 18(3), p. 1040. Available at doi:10.3390/ijerph18031040 (accessed 22 August 2025).

Bateman, A. and Holmes, J., 1995. *Introduction to Psychoanalysis: Contemporary Theory and Practice*. London: Routledge.

Behr, H. and Hearst, L., 2005. *Group-Analytic Psychotherapy; A Meeting of Minds*. London: Whurr.

BBC News, 2011. 'Changing Your Name: The Power of Identity', BBC News, 12 March. Available at https://www.bbc.co.uk/news/magazine-12639423 (accessed 22 August 2025).

Bion, W.R., 1961. *Experiences in Groups*. London: Tavistock Publications.

Bowen, M., 1978. *Family Therapy in Clinical Practice*. New York: Jason Aronson.

Bowlby, J., 1980. *Attachment and Loss*, vol. 3: *Loss, Sadness and Depression*. London: Hogarth Press.

Bowlby, J., 1988. *A Secure Base: Parent-Child Attachment and Healthy Human Development*. London: Routledge.

Caruth, C., 1996. *Unclaimed Experience: Trauma, Narrative, and History*. Baltimore, MD: Johns Hopkins University Press.

Casement, P., 1985. *On Learning from the Patient*. London: Routledge.

Casement, P., 1990. *Further Learning from the Patient: The Analytic Space and Process*. London: Routledge.

Casement, P., 2006. *Learning from Life: Becoming a Psychoanalyst*. London: Routledge.

Comas-Díaz, L., 1994. *Women of Color: Integrating Ethnic and Gender Identities in Psychotherapy*. New York: Guilford Press.

Corey, G., 2016. *Theory and Practice of Counseling and Psychotherapy*. 10th edn. Boston: Cengage.

Crenshaw, K., 1989. 'Demarginalizing the Intersection of Race and Sex: A Black Feminist Critique of Antidiscrimination Doctrine, Feminist Theory and Antiracist Politics', *University of Chicago Legal Forum*, 1, pp. 139–167.

Constantine, M.G. and Sue, D.W., 2006. *Multicultural Competence in Counseling and Psychology*. Thousand Oaks, CA: Sage.

Dalal, F., 2002. *Race, Colour and Processes of Racialisation: New Perspectives from Group Analysis, Psychoanalysis and Sociology*. Hove: Brunner-Routledge.

Day, A. and Schoenrade, P., 1997. *Group Therapy in Clinical Practice*. London: Routledge.

Das, V., 2007. *Life and Words: Violence and the Descent into the Ordinary*. Berkeley: University of California Press.

Eichenbaum, L. and Orbach, I., 1988. *Psychodynamic Group Psychotherapy: A Clinical Manual*. New York: Springer.

Ergün, M. and Tümer, E., 2016. *Intercultural Communication and Therapy Practices in Turkey*. Istanbul: Istanbul University Press.

Falender, C.A. and Shafranske, E.P., 2004. *Clinical Supervision: A Competency-Based Approach*. Washington, DC: American Psychological Association.

Fernando, S., 2010. *Mental Health, Race and Culture*. 3rd edn. Basingstoke: Palgrave Macmillan.

Folkman, S. and Lazarus, R.S., 1985. 'If It Changes It Must Be a Process: Study of Emotion and Coping During Three Stages of a College Examination', *Journal of Personality and Social Psychology*, 48(1), pp. 150–170.

Foulkes, S.H., 1964. *Therapeutic Group Analysis*. London: George Allen & Unwin.

Foulkes, S.H., 1975. *Group Analyses: Foundations of the Psychoanalytic Treatment of Groups*. London: Karnac Books.

Foulkes, S.H., 1984. *Therapeutic Group Analysis*. London: Karnac Books.

Foulkes, S.H., 1991. *Group Analytic Psychotherapy: Method and Principles*. London: Karnac Books.

Gelso, C.J. and Hayes, J.A., 1998. *The Psychotherapy Relationship: Theory, Research, and Practice*. New York: Wiley.

Greene, B., 1994. *Women of Color: Integrating Ethnic and Gender Identities in Psychotherapy*. New York: Guilford Press.

Güngör, D., 2024. 'The Reflective Group Process for Female Workers', in B. Ababio (ed.), *Intercultural Supervision in Therapeutic Practice: Dialogues, Perspectives and Reflections*. London: Routledge, pp. 55–74. Available at doi:10.4324/9781003380214-7.

Herman, J.L., 1992. *Trauma and Recovery: The Aftermath of Violence – from Domestic Abuse to Political Terror*. New York: Basic Books.

Herskovits, M.J., 1955. *Cultural Anthropology*. New York: Alfred A. Knopf.

Holmes, J., 1996. *John Bowlby and Attachment Theory*. London: Routledge.

Hopper, E., 2003. *Therapist Self-Care and Reflective Practice*. London: Routledge.

Horney, K., 1950. *Neurosis and Human Growth: The Struggle Toward Self-Realization*. New York: Norton.

Kareem, J. and Littlewood, R., 1992. *Intercultural Therapy: Themes, Interpretations and Practice*. Oxford: Blackwell Scientific Publications.

Kernberg, O.F., 1984. *Severe Personality Disorders: Psychotherapeutic Strategies*. New Haven, CT: Yale University Press.

Kernberg, O.F., 1998. *Aggression in Personality Disorders and Perversions*. New Haven, CT: Yale University Press.

Kinouani, G., 2020. 'Silencing, Power and Racial Trauma in Groups', *Group Analysis*, 53(2), pp.145–161.

Kinouani, G., 2021. *Living While Black: The Essential Guide to Overcoming Racial Trauma*. London: Ebury Press.

Kirmayer, L.J., 2007. 'Psychotherapy and the Cultural Concept of the Person', *Transcultural Psychiatry*, 44(2), pp. 232–257. Available at doi:10.1177/1363461506070794.

Kirmayer, L.J., 2012. 'Rethinking Cultural Competence', *Transcultural Psychiatry*, 49 (2), pp. 149–164. Available at doi:10.1177/1363461512444673.

Klein, M., 1946. 'Notes on Some Schizoid Mechanisms', *International Journal of Psychoanalysis*, 27, pp. 99–110.

Kleinman, A., 1980. *Patients and Healers in the Context of Culture*. Berkeley: University of California Press.

Lemma, A., 2003. *Introduction to the Practice of Psychoanalytic Psychotherapy*. Chichester: Wiley.

McDermut, W., Miller, I., and Brown, R., 2001. 'The Effectiveness of Group Psychotherapy for Depression', *Journal of Psychotherapy Practice and Research*, 10(1), pp. 56–70.
Miller, L., 2006. *Group Psychotherapy: A Handbook for Practitioners*. 2nd edn. New York: Guilford Press.
Minuchin, S., 1974. *Families and Family Therapy*. Cambridge, MA: Harvard University Press.
Montaigne, M.de [1580] 1993. *The Complete Essays*. Translated by M.A. Screech. London: Penguin Classics.
Moodley, R. and Palmer, S., 2006. *Psychotherapy and Counselling in Practice: A Resource Handbook*. London: Sage.
Murdin, L., 2000. *How Much Is Enough? Endings in Psychotherapy and Counselling*. Hove: Routledge.
Nanda, V., 2003. *Identity and Social Change*. New Delhi: Sage.
NHS England, 2018. *NHS Gender Services*. Available at https://www.england.nhs.uk/ (accessed 13 January 2026).
Nitsun, M., 1996. *The Anti-Group: Destructive Forces in the Group and Their Creative Potential*. London: Routledge.
Orbach, S., 1994. *What's Really Going On Here?*London: Virago Press.
Patel, G., 2024. 'Nafsiyat Refugee Project: An Intercultural Psychotherapy Supervision Model', in B. Ababio (ed.), *Intercultural Supervision in Therapeutic Practice: Dialogues, Perspectives and Reflections*. London: Routledge, pp. 75–87. Available at doi:10.4324/9781003380214-8.
Public Health England, 2015. *The Mental Health of Children and Young People in England*. London: Public Health England.
Public Health England, 2015. *A Guide to Community*. London: Public Health England. Available at https://assets.publishing.service.gov.uk/media/5c2f65d3e5274a6599225de9/A_guide_to_community-centred_approaches_for_health_and_wellbeing__full_report_.pdf (accessed 13 January 2026).
Priebe, S. , 2012. 'Equity of Access to Mental Health Care for Patients from Minority Ethnic Groups: A Systematic Review', *Psychological Medicine*, 42(12), pp. 2393–2407.
Rack, P., 1982. *Race, Culture and Mental Disorder*. London: Tavistock.
Sandler, J., Dare, C., and Holder, A., 1992. *The Patient and the Analyst: The Basis of the Psychoanalytic Process*. London: Karnac Books.
Schiller, D. and Morgan, B., 1996. *Group Psychotherapy: Theory and Practice*. London: Routledge.
Schlapobersky, J., 2016. *From the Couch to the Circle: Group-Analytic Psychotherapy in Practice*. London: Routledge.
Sen, A., 1990. *Development as Freedom*. Oxford: Oxford University Press.
Singh, R., 2015. *Cultural Identity and Social Change*. London: Routledge.
Sommers-Flanagan, J. and Sommers-Flanagan, R., 2018. *Clinical Interviewing*. 6th edn. Hoboken, NJ: Wiley.
Sue, D.W. and Sue, D., 2016. *Counselling the Culturally Diverse: Theory and Practice*. 7th edn. Hoboken, NJ: Wiley.
Thomas, L., 1992. 'Intercultural Therapy', in J. Kareem and R. Littlewood (eds), *Intercultural Therapy: Themes, Interpretations and Practice*. Oxford: Blackwell Scientific Publications, pp. 257–272.
Thomas, L., 1995. 'Psychotherapy in the Context of Race and Culture: An Intercultural Therapeutic Approach', in S. Fernando (ed.), *Mental Health in a Multi-Ethnic Society*. London: Routledge, pp.172–192.

Thomas, A. and Sillen, S., 1972. *Racism and Psychiatry*. New York: Citadel Press.

Tribe, R. and Morrissey, J., 2004. *Working with Vulnerable Children and Families: A Practitioner's Guide*. London: Routledge.

Tseng, W.S. (ed.), 2001. *Handbook of Cultural Psychiatry*. San Diego, CA: Academic Press.

Türk Dil Kurumu, 2010. *Türkçe Sözlük*. Ankara: Türk Dil Kurumu.

Van der Kolk, B.A., 2015. *The Body Keeps the Score: Brain, Mind, and Body in the Healing of Trauma*. New York: Viking.

Winnicott, D.W., 1965. *The Maturational Processes and the Facilitating Environment: Studies in the Theory of Emotional Development*. London: Hogarth Press.

Yalom, I.D., 1995. *The Theory and Practice of Group Psychotherapy*. 4th edn. New York: Basic Books.

Yalom, I.D., 2005. *The Theory and Practice of Group Psychotherapy*. 5th edn. New York: Basic Books.

Yalom, I.D. and Leszcz, M., 2020. *The Theory and Practice of Group Psychotherapy*. 6th edn. New York: Basic Books.

Chapter 3

Personal Experiences and New Approaches in the Therapeutic Process

Psychoanalysis and group therapy aim to uncover unconscious emotions spanning the pre-Oedipal to the post-Oedipal stages. Medium-sized (20–40 participants) and large groups (more than 40 participants) provide a space in which to explore broader social, cultural, and political dimensions (de Maré et al., 1991). These distinctions have informed the way in which I understand and engage with group dynamics in therapy.

My interest in group work began with early life experiences shaped by family life and the sociopolitical environments of Türkiye (formerly Turkey) and Europe. Growing up in a family of eight children and two parents exposed me to a complex web of relationships, although I did not initially realise how these dynamics would later inform my professional journey. Over time, involvement in various social and political movements deepened my awareness of collective processes and their psychological impact.

Family structures provide our earliest models for social interaction. In a large family, relationships often require negotiation, adaptability, and a heightened sensitivity to group undercurrents. Disagreements, shifting roles, and subtle alliances echoed the complex dynamics I would later observe in therapeutic groups. Without knowing it, I had developed an attunement to unspoken group dynamics – an ability that would become invaluable in my work as a group therapist.

As my education progressed, I began to understand how group behaviour is shaped not only by individual unconscious processes but also by broader societal forces. Moving between cultures heightened my awareness of the way in which group identity is influenced by historical, political, and cultural narratives.

During my clinical training, I facilitated a group of six men and four women as part of my internship. My supervisor questioned the group size. On reflection, I realised I had unconsciously recreated my own family structure: a mother, father, five brothers, and two sisters. This moment of recognition was both unsettling and illuminating. It revealed how early familial patterns can resurface in our professional work, often without conscious intent.

Such patterns are not uncommon among therapists. Many are drawn to clinical settings or patient groups that reflect aspects of their own histories. A

DOI: 10.4324/9781003726012-4

therapist who grew up mediating conflicts may later specialise in conflict resolution; another who experienced marginalisation may feel drawn to underserved communities. Personal history often shapes professional choices. However, without self-awareness, these unconscious repetitions can restrict therapeutic flexibility and reinforce unexamined biases (Racker, 1968; McWilliams, 2004).

In my own work, I came to recognise that the structure I had unknowingly recreated was influencing group dynamics in unexpected ways. I found myself assigning roles that mirrored those from my childhood. Authority struggles, sibling rivalries, and subtle alliances emerged – patterns that felt strikingly familiar. This awareness enabled me to step back and reconsider my stance. Rather than being governed by unconscious repetition, I could engage with the group process more deliberately.

This experience marked a turning point in my development. It reinforced the importance of self-reflection in therapeutic work, particularly in group settings where transference and countertransference operate on multiple levels. I became increasingly attentive to how personal history shapes the therapist's role within a group.

Rather than suppressing these influences, I began to explore how they might be integrated into my practice in a constructive way. Awareness of my own unconscious enactments helped me to support patients in recognising and working through their own unconscious processes, particularly as they emerged within the therapeutic relationship. When therapists are attuned to their inner responses, they are better placed to manage the group process with depth and clarity.

Supervision groups provide a vital space in which to safely explore these unconscious patterns. They allow therapists to refine their practice with greater awareness and reduce the risk of becoming unconsciously entangled in group dynamics. This reflective stance is even more crucial in larger groups, where the interplay between individual material and collective dynamics becomes more complex. The therapist's role must shift, not only facilitating individual insight but also tracking the group's evolving processes.

Looking back on my early experiences – in my family, within political and social circles, and throughout my training – I can see how these environments shaped my professional sensibility. They offered an intuitive grasp of group processes while also making me vulnerable to unconsciously repeating familiar dynamics. Recognising this has enabled me to work with greater intention, guided by reflection rather than repetition.

This personal journey of awareness reflects a broader truth in therapeutic work: recognising one's own unconscious patterns is an ongoing process. As therapists, I believe none of us are ever entirely separate from our pasts. Yet, through self-reflection and continuous learning, these histories can shape our practice – informing rather than controlling it. Therapy serves not only the transformation of others but also provides a space for the therapist's own growth.

These reflections take me back to my upbringing. Family gatherings – whether beneath the weeping willow in the garden or in our living room – were central to my early life. Moments of connection, storytelling, and play laid the foundation for my understanding of relationships. I watched my parents offer emotional and practical support to friends in marital distress. Their ability to create space for open dialogue reflected both the strength of their bond and their capacity to support others.

Although my parents sometimes argued, they maintained boundaries that protected us from the intensity of their conflicts. Conversations at home frequently touched on political and economic matters, deepening my awareness of the way in which broader societal forces can shape personal relationships. These early experiences continue to influence my therapeutic approach, reminding me of the vital role that context plays in understanding individual and group dynamics.

Personal History, Sociopolitical Context, and Unconscious Influences in Group Therapy

Drawing on my personal and sociopolitical experiences, I began to explore how unconscious processes – shaped by early relational patterns and family dynamics – influence group behaviour and therapeutic practice.

My childhood was marked by significant sociopolitical events in Türkiye, including the execution of Prime Minister Adnan Menderes, the 1960 military coup, and the Cyprus conflict. Growing up in Adana, I recall frequent power outages during storms and the stifling summer heat, when umbrellas offered shelter from both the rain and the sun. These everyday moments were shaped by an underlying awareness of political unrest and its impact on daily life.

As I grew older, political conversations became increasingly central to our lives. The ideals of the revolutionary figure Deniz Gezmiş left a lasting impression, not only on my family but on the wider community and society at large. Many politicians now acknowledge that his tragic execution was a grave mistake, and it remains a deeply shameful chapter in Türkiye's history.

These early encounters with political discourse deepened my understanding of the inseparability of personal and political realities – a perspective that continues to inform my approach to group therapy. Fanon (1963) also addressed the profound psychological effects of colonisation and social upheaval, illustrating how political conditions penetrate internal experience and identity formation. His work resonates with my reflections on the interplay between collective trauma and individual development.

The experience of being misunderstood often leads to a sense of isolation. Yet those who continue to seek connection often discover an unexpected inner resilience. My own experience as a political refugee in England mirrors this trajectory. Although much of that period was marked by loneliness, forming new relationships provided comfort and significantly shaped my clinical outlook. In group therapy, I strive to create spaces where individuals feel seen, heard, and understood – echoing the nurturing yet complex environments of my early life.

My upbringing has profoundly influenced the way in which I understand human relationships and group dynamics. In therapy, individuals come together with a shared aim: to heal, transform, and grow. This collective endeavour echoes the familial bonds I valued as a child, offering a space to explore emotions, confront fears, and form meaningful connections. Shared experiences foster mutual recognition and group cohesion. My background has shaped my theoretical, clinical, and relational stance, particularly in large-group contexts. I have not avoided difficult emotions such as anger, sorrow, grief, or ideological conflict; instead, I have sought to understand and work with them.

Even in my most challenging moments, I have relied on self-reflection as a tool for growth. This reflective tendency was shaped, in part, by my mother – a resilient woman who, together with my father, raised eight children. In many ways, they managed a group characterised by complex personalities, emotions, and needs. She expressed her emotions openly – grieving in sorrow and rejoicing in happiness. Her simple yet profound principle was: 'When you go to a funeral, you must cry; but when you go to a wedding or a celebration, you should laugh and dance.' I absorbed this approach to life, which acknowledges pain and embraces joy. The ability to feel deeply and reflect is often passed down through example and intergenerational influence. In many respects, my mother embodied the qualities of a psychotherapist despite lacking formal training, while I became one through professional education. Reflecting on her life now, I recognise how much she understood, although as a teenager I rebelled and believed that she knew nothing.

These experiences have shaped the way in which I facilitate group therapy. I aim to create spaces rooted in shared purpose and mutual respect, where individuals can safely reconnect with themselves and their capacity for change. The group becomes a container for rediscovering resilience, processing emotions, and building meaningful connections. This journey has involved personal challenges, and years of reflective practice and analysis have been essential in preparing me to work with patients carrying their own emotional burdens.

The Body and the Mind

This book explores the transformative potential of group therapy, rooted in connection between body, mind, and spirit. My early nursing training affirmed the inseparability of physical and emotional health. Unresolved trauma and chronic stress affect the whole person, as Maté (2003), Levine (1997), and van der Kolk (2015) emphasise. They highlight the profound ways in which trauma and unresolved emotional pain are stored in the body and nervous system, affecting both psychological and physical wellbeing. Maté notes how early life stress can manifest as illness or distress later in life, while Levine focuses on the importance of releasing the physiological energy trapped by traumatic experiences. Van der Kolk examines the way that trauma reshapes brain function and bodily responses, influencing memory, emotion regulation, and overall health. Together, their perspectives highlight the need for therapeutic approaches that combine compassionate awareness with body-based interventions to support holistic healing.

In assessment sessions, I pay close attention to posture, complexion, and energy as indicators of emotional states. The body stores lived experience, and its signals often convey what words cannot. One patient, overwhelmed by trauma, described feeling as though they had a 'wild gorilla' on their back. Over time, sustained group work helped them to release this burden – an example of the group's potential to facilitate deep transformation.

Supporting Recovery and Therapist Development

Each person holds the key to their own recovery, but in group therapy this process is supported and amplified through collective witnessing and shared understanding. Free association and mutual recognition help participants to clarify distorted self-images and move towards greater authenticity. Old wounds can surface and be processed – not in isolation, but within the safety of a connected group.

Difficulties may be personal (intra-psychic), relational (interpersonal), or social (linked to wider conditions). In extreme cases, people may become alienated from themselves and others. Yet the act of seeking support already signals hope. Group therapy enhances emotional awareness and strengthens internal autonomy, positively influencing wider life patterns. As Foulkes and Anthony (1957) observed, the group's central task is recovery.

Therapists, too, require support to manage the emotional demands of their work. Supervision offers a crucial space for reflection and guidance. Many highly skilled individual therapists may lack training in group dynamics, which can inadvertently disrupt group processes. It is essential to recognise that proficiency in one-to-one therapy does not automatically translate into competence in group work. Each modality demands its own theoretical foundation, methodology, and skill set.

To manage the complexities of group therapy with integrity, therapists must commit to ongoing development, self-reflection, and dialogue with peers. This commitment allows them to support their groups with care, competence, and authenticity. Only through sustained reflection can therapists remain attuned to the group's potential for transformation.

Resistance, Transference, and the Therapist's Role in Group Dynamics

Resistance is a natural part of therapy, especially when individuals face the challenge of change. For transformation to occur, therapists must recognise and explore resistance alongside the defence mechanisms that arise within the group. Freud (1926) emphasised that defences may hinder progress but also provide valuable therapeutic insight. In group therapy, resistance is inevitable; however, it can serve as a catalyst for growth, both individually and collectively.

Resistance often intersects with cultural and racial identity. Fanon (1967) highlighted how systemic oppression shapes internalised resistance and psychological defences among Black individuals, thereby complicating therapy. Therapists must approach such resistance with cultural humility and sensitivity.

As patients engage in therapy, they begin to work through resistance, allowing defences to soften and transformation to unfold. The group therapist must remain attentive, actively observing and interpreting emerging behaviours (Foulkes, 1971). Transference plays a central role in this process.

Resistance typically emerges when individuals struggle to release deeply rooted behaviours, projecting emotions onto others and reinforcing their worldview. This negative transference may appear as rebellion, hostility, or fear of surrendering to therapy, thereby blocking growth.

Therapists also face resistance. They may feel tempted to interpret behaviour too quickly, but experience teaches patience and clinical intuition – intervening thoughtfully or sometimes remaining silent. In group therapy, this intuition is grounded in theory, emotional awareness, and clinical experience. Foulkes (1975) described the group analyst as a calm, impartial observer, much like a seasoned chess player anticipating and responding to tensions within the group.

Integrating Personal and Professional Selves

A therapist's identity lies at the heart of their work. While many, myself included, value neutrality and anonymity, a therapist's personal history inevitably shapes their approach.

The integration of personal and professional identities depends largely on the depth of engagement with training and personal analysis. A concerning trend among some trainees and recent graduates is viewing training merely as a route to certification, dismissing personal therapy as unnecessary or unaffordable. This attitude, which prioritises theory over self-exploration, limits genuine professional growth. Without personal therapy, a therapist's capacity to manage complex group dynamics and unconscious processes remains restricted.

The Influence of Training and Cultural Contexts

During my training at Goldsmiths, University of London, much of the curriculum reflected a White, middle-class, Western perspective. Nevertheless, I remained committed to preserving my voice and cultural lens. The group therapy unit at Goldsmiths, once known for its diverse approaches, has since closed due to financial pressures. Recent reports reveal broader university restructuring and significant staff cuts (Hall, 2024).

While I value the democratic spirit underpinning the British education system, I remain sceptical of short-term programmes that claim to address racism or cultural difference. British values such as 'courtesy' and 'nobility' can unintentionally suppress perspectives that challenge the dominant narrative. Sue (2010) warns that superficial diversity initiatives often fail to tackle systemic problems.

Change is inevitable. Meaningful solutions require embracing both innovation and discomfort.

Personal Background and Professional Practice

A therapist's background profoundly shapes their practice. To understand how their personal history influences their work, therapists can reflect on questions such as:

- What kind of family and social environment did they grow up in?
- What are their religious, political, or social beliefs?
- How do their personal values influence their therapeutic approach?

For example, a therapist who wears a headscarf may evoke varied responses from patients, shaped by patients' assumptions and past experiences.

Examples of impact:

- Positive: Patients sharing similar values may feel recognised and understood.
- Negative: Others might question the therapist's neutrality, potentially hindering the alliance between therapist and patient.
- Varied preferences: Some patients prefer therapists who are apparently very different from themselves, believing that difference can offer fresh perspectives or challenge assumptions.

The Group Therapist as a Dynamic Presence

As a group therapist, I draw on clinical research, personal therapy, and group analysis to deepen my professional identity. Group therapy is a living, evolving process, shaped by emotions and interactions. Resistance, transference, counter-transference, projections, idealisations, and reflections reveal human complexity and influence both individual and collective transformation (Foulkes, 1964).

In my experience, the dynamics within groups are also shaped by broader cultural change. Just as the world has evolved over the past 40 years – through technological advances, shifting social norms, and changing cultural contexts – so too does human psychology, affecting how participants relate to one another and how group processes unfold.

The therapist's presence is not passive; it requires ongoing self-reflection, emotional attunement, and flexibility to respond to the group's changing needs with care and integrity. I have found that a mindful, responsive presence supports the group's capacity for understanding, growth, and change.

Maintaining Professionalism and Addressing Personal Biases

Ethical considerations require therapists to manage how personal beliefs and biases may influence therapy. Maintaining professionalism and neutrality ensures that personal views do not interfere with patients' progress. When conflicts arise between a therapist's values and those of their patient, self-reflection, clinical supervision, and ongoing professional development are essential to uphold ethical standards.

Challenges can emerge if a therapist holds unresolved biases – for example, homophobic beliefs – which may create an unsafe environment for LGBTQ+ patients and damage trust and the therapeutic alliance.

Therapists who wear visible religious or cultural symbols must carefully separate personal expression from their professional roles. While such expressions are valid, they must never detract from the patient's needs. Respect for each patient's values remains fundamental.

Therapists must engage in honest self-reflection to identify and challenge biases, particularly those related to culture, disability, sexual orientation, and gender identity. Supervision plays a vital role in uncovering blind spots, promoting inclusive practice, and supporting ongoing professional growth. A culturally competent supervisor can help to manage complex dynamics and ensure that therapy remains centred on the patient's needs. Na'im Akbar (1991) emphasises the importance of addressing cultural trauma in therapeutic settings and urges therapists to stay attentive to the sociocultural contexts that shape their patients' lives.

Ongoing education and reflective practice are essential for reducing unconscious bias, building cultural competence, and enhancing therapeutic presence. Therapists must listen empathetically, avoiding both subtle and overt judgement. Every interaction should foster safety, validation, and trust – conditions fundamental to effective therapy.

Potential Impact on Patients

- Lack of safety: A gay patient may withhold aspects of their identity if they sense judgement, thereby limiting the therapeutic process.
- Internalised shame: When patients perceive bias, however subtle, it can reinforce negative self-beliefs rooted in societal stigma. This internalised

shame can fosters feelings of guilt or unworthiness, weakening trust and openness, and thus the therapeutic alliance.

Therapists must foster a respectful, inclusive environment where personal beliefs never interfere with care.

Clinical Considerations for Therapists Working with Marginalised Sexual Identities

1 Maintain boundaries: Ensure that personal identity does not take precedence over the therapeutic focus or the patient's needs.
2 Respect the patient's journey: Avoid imposing personal experiences; support the patient's exploration at their own pace.
3 Foster inclusivity: Create a safe and affirming space without assuming shared identity or experience.
4 Disclose thoughtfully: Consider self-disclosure carefully. Share aspects such as sexual orientation only when it meaningfully supports the therapeutic process.
5 Practise self-awareness: Stay attuned to how personal beliefs, assumptions, or identity may shape clinical work.
6 Seek supervision: Use regular supervision to reflect on dynamics in the work and maintain clinical objectivity.
7 Recognise LGBTQ+ diversity: Understand that shared identity does not imply shared experience. Patients may navigate complex social, cultural, and institutional dynamics related to gender and sexuality. As Nicolazzo (2017) highlights in her study of transgender students' strategies for managing campus life and institutional inclusion, identity is often lived in negotiation with broader systems. Approach each patient with curiosity, humility, and openness.
8 For instance, a therapist working with a young transgender patient may carefully manage the balance between maintaining professional boundaries and drawing on their own identity to foster empathy and insight. While the therapist's identity might support understanding, they must prioritise the patient's unique journey, allowing space for exploration without assumptions. Similarly, a patient from a conservative cultural background might initially struggle with discussing their sexual identity; here, the therapist's role includes fostering safety and trust without rushing disclosure or projecting personal views.

As Layton (2004) notes, therapists working from within marginalised identities must balance authenticity with clinical discipline. This framework supports all therapists in upholding professionalism, cultivating inclusivity, and providing ethical care.

Referral When Necessary

When a therapist recognises that they cannot manage personal biases or lack the competence required to fully support a patient, referral to a more suitable professional is considered the ethical course of action. This decision, ideally made in consultation with supervision, safeguards the patient's wellbeing and ensures that they receive the appropriate care – particularly in specialised areas such as LGBTQ+ support.

Managing Biases and Maintaining Objectivity

Remaining objective is essential to effective therapy, although this can be particularly challenging for early career therapists. For example, an atheist therapist might overemphasise a religious patient's emotional struggles while overlooking the significance of their faith. Similarly, a therapist with socialist leanings may find it difficult to remain neutral when working with someone fleeing an autocratic or capitalist regime. Unchecked biases such as these can distort therapeutic understanding and undermine the therapeutic relationship.

At times, therapists may experience strong dislike – or even hostility – towards a patient. These feelings should not be ignored; they often point to deeper personal, relational, or cultural triggers. Through supervision and self-reflection, such reactions can be explored and understood, transforming them into opportunities for both professional and personal growth. This process helps to ensure that therapy remains centred on the patient's needs.

Ongoing education and reflective practice are crucial for reducing unconscious bias, building cultural competence, and strengthening therapeutic presence. Therapists should listen with empathy, avoid subtle or overt judgement, and create a sense of safety, validation, and trust – conditions fundamental to effective therapy. Ethical practice also involves working respectfully with patients whose values may differ significantly from the therapist's, requiring humility, empathy, and a consistent prioritisation of the patient's wellbeing over personal convictions.

The Reflective Group Therapist

This book invites readers to become not only skilled facilitators but also reflective professionals – curious explorers of human dynamics. A group therapist cultivates a philosophical mindset that values wisdom, embraces uncertainty, and commits to meaningful change. Therapy is a shared journey of discovery, requiring openness, ongoing self-reflection, and emotional attunement to group complexities.

Group therapists often begin with individual sessions to clarify expectations and identify early relational patterns (Yalom and Leszcz, 2020). As the group forms, the therapist gradually shifts their focus from individuals to group dynamics, encouraging deeper interaction among members (Corey et al., 2018). Far from being detached observers, therapists remain present, maintaining boundaries and offering steady attention – especially to the most vulnerable or envious. Their emotions, insights, and presence continuously influence the group and call for ongoing self-examination.

The Character and Personality of the Therapist

A therapist's character and personality are central to shaping their professional identity. As Sue (2010) emphasises, therapists should cultivate deep self-awareness of their cultural identity, values, and biases to provide culturally responsive care. Character represents the core values and integrity that ground the therapist's work, while personality reflects the adaptable qualities that enable responsiveness to individual patients.

The Therapist's Experiences, Interpretations, and Interventions in the Therapeutic Process

A therapist's character and personality are influenced and expressed through their life experiences, which shape how they manage the present moment in therapy. Personal challenges, such as health issues or family difficulties, can affect their capacity to remain fully present. At such times, seeking supervision or therapy – and, if necessary, taking a temporary break – supports personal wellbeing and professional integrity. Prioritising self-care enables therapists to return with renewed focus and to maintain high professional standards.

The Influence of Training, Supervision, and Personal Therapy

Therapists' growth is shaped by training, supervision, and personal therapy. Supervisors support clinical maturity by offering respectful interventions that deepen understanding without imposing their own views. Theoretical models – from Rogers' focus on the therapeutic relationship to Kareem's emphasis on culture, Klein's psychoanalysis, and Foulkes' group analysis – also shape therapists. Over time, practitioners blend these frameworks with their own personality and experience to develop an authentic style.

In my career, working with various supervisors has broadened my perspective and encouraged me to clarify my views. Each supervision has brought unique insights and helped me to manage complexity. However, not all supervisory advice is applicable to every patient. On one occasion, after I shared a supervisor's comment with a patient, they responded, 'Dilek, this is nonsense. This is not you.' This experience illustrated that supervision should guide, rather than dictate, therapy, and that the therapist's authentic voice must remain central to the work.

A Professional Experience of Strong Countertransference and Its Physical Impact on the Therapist

In one individual session – part of a female patient's preparation for group therapy – I experienced a persistent sense of physical discomfort that I initially could not explain. Sensing emotional tension, I gently remarked, 'Elizabeth, you seem uneasy – almost as if you're carrying something that hasn't yet been spoken aloud. Does this reflect how you've been feeling?' This invitation created space for her to articulate what had remained unspoken. The patient, Elizabeth, revealed that she was three months pregnant but had hesitated to share this due to feelings of shame. She was unmarried and uncertain about the future.

The experience highlighted the physical impact of unacknowledged emotional material in the therapeutic space. As Ogden et al. (2006) emphasise, bodily sensations can signal unprocessed emotions, making the therapist's sensitivity to such cues essential.

The Somatic Dimension in Therapy: Ogden's Perspective

Thomas Ogden (1994) stresses the importance of bodily experience in therapy, noting that emotional trauma and unresolved psychological material are often stored somatically, outside conscious awareness. Both therapist and patient may experience bodily sensations – such as tension or discomfort – that reflect unspoken emotional content.

Ogden regards these somatic experiences as a form of countertransference, providing access to significant unconscious material. Recognising and working with these cues allows therapists to reach deeper emotional layers and facilitate change beyond words. This underscores the body as a vital source of knowledge and insight in psychotherapy.

Preparing for Group Therapy

Effective group therapy requires thoughtful preparation rooted in theory and experience. Key considerations include:

1. Room requirements: A quiet, well-ventilated space that accommodates eight to ten participants comfortably.
2. Scheduling: Session times should consider participants' work and childcare responsibilities.
3. Institutional collaboration: Coordination with relevant organisations ensures appropriate referrals and support.
4. Coordination with individual therapists: Group work should complement, not compete with, individual therapy.
5. Group structure: The format – short-term, long-term, open, or closed – should be clearly defined from the outset.

6 Waiting list: Identifying suitable replacement therapists when needed helps to ensure continuity.
7 Institutional awareness: Staff training or information sessions support a culture of understanding and respect.
8 Documentation: Thorough record-keeping supports clinical, ethical, and legal responsibilities.
9 Confidentiality: Ensuring that all information remains confidential is essential for trust and safety within the group.
10 Co-facilitation: Mutual respect and open communication between co-therapists is essential.

Therapists must also maintain professional insurance, institutional affiliation, and a commitment to continuing development.

Choosing Participants for Group Therapy

S.H. Foulkes stated that 'anyone suitable for individual analytic therapy can participate in group therapy' (Foulkes, 1964). While this holds true in principle, careful assessment is necessary. The therapist must safeguard both individual and group wellbeing. Some individuals may need further preparation or may not be suitable at a particular time.

Evaluating the Rationale for Group Therapy

When considering a referral, the therapist should ask:

- Why is this patient being referred to group therapy?
- Is this the right time for them to join?
- Who made the referral, and what was the rationale for it?

It is important to discern whether the referral reflects a genuine therapeutic need or is simply a practical decision based on available resources. Group therapy should be seen as a valuable modality in its own right – not a secondary option.

Careful Evaluation of Group Therapy Candidates

Some individuals may face challenges in participating effectively in a group, such as:

- Those severely traumatised and unable to express emotions;
- Individuals with highly disruptive behaviours or poor impulse control;
- Those with a history of inconsistent attendance or frequent lateness;
- People seeking quick fixes to deep-rooted issues;

- Participants primarily seeking friendship or romantic connections;
- Individuals with untreated substance misuse;
- Those attending therapy under external pressure;
- People focused on blaming others rather than exploring themselves; and
- Patients who frequently change therapies without commitment.

However, these are not absolute rules. If a person is motivated and determined to change, they may still benefit from group therapy with appropriate support and preparation. Careful selection aims to create a safe and constructive environment, but flexibility and clinical judgement are essential to accommodate individual potential for growth.

Group Therapy: The Workplace and Clinical Reflections

Group therapy, although demanding commitment, can significantly foster emotional growth and offer valuable opportunities for relational development. Participants often begin to recognise that workplace difficulties mirror unresolved personal and familial patterns. Reflecting on family and social dynamics helps them to better understand their current behaviours and attitudes.

In many institutional settings, employees may attribute challenges to colleagues or managers, when these difficulties often stem from unresolved familial conflicts. For instance, a manager might unconsciously project childhood tensions onto their team, perpetuating dysfunctional relational patterns. Even when dissatisfied, individuals may struggle to leave such environments. Without self-awareness, they risk repeating these patterns in future settings.

Drawing on supervision and reflective practice, I often explore these dynamics and recommend group therapy as a constructive intervention. When thoughtfully facilitated, a group of eight or nine participants can offer sufficient containment and support – even for those with limited psychological insight or emotional expression – provided they show a willingness to engage.

Group therapy offers a structured space where individuals experiencing paranoid-schizoid anxieties – a concept originally developed by Melanie Klein – can begin to integrate healthier parts of themselves. Patients with narcissistic or borderline traits frequently start to recognise their emotional dependencies and relational patterns through group interactions (Foulkes, 1964; Hawkins and Shohet, 1989). Over time, the group becomes a vital context for self-reflection, interpersonal learning, and gradual emotional growth.

Within the group, participants learn that they do not need to mask anger with smiles or hide tears when sad. It provides a meaningful setting to explore and work through conflicts rooted in family and social life. It also equips participants with tools to manage workplace tensions, including ongoing difficulties with colleagues or management (Foulkes, 1964; Corey, 2016).

Some individuals initially join group therapy hoping to change others rather than themselves. However, the group process encourages self-reflection, often leading to profound personal transformation (Yalom and Leszcz, 2020).

Frequency of Group Therapy

For some patients, weekly group therapy may be more effective than twice-weekly individual sessions. When patients have reached a sufficient level of emotional stability, attending group therapy twice a week can deepen the process and enhance outcomes, as supported by studies on increased session frequency (Cuijpers et al., 2013; Burlingame et al., 2018). However, this is not an absolute rule, and each patient's needs and circumstances are unique (Foulkes, 1964).

Addressing Initial Discomfort in Group Therapy

Patients with narcissistic or borderline traits may initially struggle with feedback from the therapist or group members, leading them to consider leaving. In such cases, starting with individual therapy may be more suitable. However, each patient is unique, and assessments should focus on the individual, not merely the diagnosis (Bateman and Fonagy, 2004; Skodol et al., 2002). Even patients perceived as difficult can achieve meaningful change with the right support.

The Therapist's Role outside the Group Therapy Setting

Referring someone to group therapy demands clinical skill, experience, and genuine interest. Although personal experience of group therapy is not required, therapists should reflect on their attitudes towards it (Hawkins and Shohet, 1989; Corey, 2016). Patients can sense the clinician's confidence – or lack thereof – which may influence their engagement. A collaborative, transparent approach encourages autonomy.

In some of the organisations in which I have worked, I was the sole group therapist, and at times this left me feeling professionally isolated. There was occasionally a subtle sense of rivalry between individual and group analysts. I often needed to remain consistently diplomatic in order to secure referrals for my groups, while continuing to focus on fostering their development. Furthermore, I observed that when service chief executive officers or senior managers lack clinical knowledge, this can create additional challenges. Instead of supporting clinical work, there may be unintended competition or misunderstanding about the value of therapeutic services. This experience highlighted the importance of organisational support and collaboration across therapeutic disciplines to ensure that group therapy is valued and integrated effectively. Throughout my institutional career, I have often found that managing relationships with managers is as important as managing clinical work itself.

Helpful Assessment Questions for Therapists

These are especially relevant if the patient works in a team setting:

- How does the patient function in group or team environments?
- How do they relate to others at work or in social contexts?
- Are they emotionally expressive or withdrawn?
- Do they have a pattern of leaving groups or relationships?

(Yalom and Leszcz, 2020; Hawkins and Shohet, 1989)

Changing Attitudes Towards Group Therapy

In recent decades, attitudes towards group therapy have shifted, particularly within immigrant communities. Based on my clinical experience, Turkish-speaking therapists contributed to this change by providing psychoeducation. Some 30 years ago, few Turkish or Kurdish patients attended group therapy. Today, demand has increased so significantly that public waiting lists can extend up to a year.

While working in patients' mother tongue is naturally more beneficial, effective communication through interpreters can still support meaningful group therapy experiences. For example, when I facilitated groups with Somali and Chinese women via interpreters – such as during my time with the Family Action organisation – these projects proved successful for the patients.

The Value of Group Therapy

Group therapy offers a space for connection and mutual understanding. It reduces isolation and promotes growth through shared experience. Members practise interpersonal skills and receive feedback in a safe environment. Therapists also observe how individual behaviours unfold socially.

Group therapy reflects real-life relationships. Within this space, patients explore behavioural patterns, reshape self-perceptions, and build awareness through honest feedback. Although sometimes uncomfortable, this deepens reflection and emotional resilience. The group serves as a social microcosm, guided by a steady therapist presence.

Emotional development unfolds gradually. Realisations deepen over time, often long after the session. In my own journey, I gradually came to understand what my own analyst meant by this ongoing unfolding.

Preparing Patients for Group Therapy

Group therapy should be presented as one option among many – not as a fixed solution. Uncertainty is natural. Inviting patients to reflect without pressure respects their autonomy. Even a simple remark such as 'perhaps it's not the right time' may shift perspective.

Therapists must assess readiness, offer reassurance, and create a space for emotional exploration. Their task is to foster meaningful group bonds, gently challenge assumptions, and provide a safe space where relationships – therapeutic and otherwise – can gradually unfold.

Preparing for Group Therapy: What to Expect

Group therapy can be a transformative experience, yet it may feel unfamiliar or daunting for those new to it. Offering clear, practical information beforehand helps patients to understand what to expect and encourages their engagement.

Before the first session, participants should be given essential details, including:

- Meeting logistics (location, schedule, fees – if applicable – and contact information);
- Initial arrangements, such as support for attending the first session;
- Educational materials or orientation sessions for those unfamiliar with group therapy;
- A welcoming message providing details about attendance expectations, confidentiality, fees, and instructions on how to accept a place in the group.

Criteria for Participation

Therapists may apply various criteria to determine group suitability. I value participants who are willing to engage openly, challenge the therapist constructively, and respect group boundaries. Key factors include:

- Genuine motivation and readiness to participate;
- Clear expectations and responsibility for attendance; and
- Willingness to engage with feedback, even if there is initial resistance.

Resistance is common and not necessarily a barrier to progress. However, unexplained absences disrupt the therapeutic process.

Key questions during assessment for suitability for group work include:

- Is the patient seeking to address emotional issues related to relationships?
- Are they open to influencing and being influenced by others in the group?
- Can they tolerate listening to difficult feedback?
- Do they wish to share experiences they find hard to express elsewhere?

A high risk of harm to self or others requires caution but is not necessarily an absolute contraindication, provided that there is appropriate professional collaboration.

Expectations and the Preparatory Phase

Clear expectations include:

- Regular attendance;
- Respect for group boundaries;
- Ongoing self-reflection.

For patients expressing anxiety or hesitation, individual therapy may be recommended initially. The preparatory phase is tailored to ensure readiness and alignment with group therapy goals.

I often ask, 'How do you think group therapy will help you?' Responses vary from clear intentions to uncertainty or deference to medical advice. These answers guide a nuanced exploration of motivation and readiness while respecting the patient's perspective.

Assessment balances listening to both content and delivery, aiming to develop a personal therapeutic style that integrates scientific knowledge with creativity and empathy.

Addressing Absences

If a participant stops attending sessions, a structured follow-up is important:

- Wait two to three sessions before reaching out.
- Contact the patient via email, phone, or letter to understand their situation.
- If there is no response, send a final supportive letter explaining file closure while leaving the door open for future re-engagement.

After a member leaves, the group should be given time to process feelings such as disappointment or sadness. Communication with referring clinicians should be maintained when appropriate.

Professional Strengths and Adaptability

My background in nursing, teaching, and community development has provided a solid foundation for my work in group therapy. This diverse experience helps me to maintain calmness and adaptability in a wide range of situations, ensuring a safe and supportive space for participants. For example, I have managed medical incidents during sessions, such as minor injuries and fainting, responding effectively without disrupting the group process. These skills contribute to creating an environment where patients feel contained and cared for, which supports therapeutic progress.

Crossing Thresholds: Reflections from My Own Group Analysis and the Birth of Mixed-Gender Groups

During my studies at Goldsmiths, my tutor Kevin Power referred me to the late Tom Hamrogue, an approved group analyst, encouraging me to contact him for an initial meeting. I am grateful to Kevin for choosing the right analyst for me – Tom proved to be a pivotal figure in my therapeutic journey.

At the time, email was not yet in common use, so I wrote a letter to Tom, introducing myself as a student and expressing my interest in joining his group. A few days later, he telephoned me. Although I was excited to hear from him, I initially struggled to understand his strong Irish accent. Having only recently arrived in England, I was still adjusting to the variety of accents I encountered. I had to ask him several times to repeat the meeting address, and he kindly obliged. Our exchange – between my Turkish accent and his Irish one – was a challenge. These days, however, I am far more at ease with diverse accents.

On the day of our meeting, I arrived early at the Institute of Group Analysis. Tom welcomed me warmly and, after a brief wait, invited me into the consultation room. Before he could begin, however, I launched into sharing my story. Despite his youthful appearance, Tom's grey hair and calm, reassuring presence immediately put me at ease and helped me to feel ready to embrace the therapeutic process. He listened with genuine interest and patience, thereby deepening my sense of comfort.

At the end of our meeting, Tom mentioned that he would show me the group room, but inadvertently forgot to do so. We agreed that I would begin group therapy in September.

On the day of my first session, I arrived an hour early, confident that I knew the address, and passed the time exploring nearby shops. However, I ended up getting lost and arrived 15 minutes late. Once there, I didn't know which room to go to and, in desperation, I opened several doors, interrupting other groups. The puzzled looks from the therapists remain vivid in my memory.

Feeling overwhelmed, I waited in the main hall, hoping to spot Tom as the groups ended. Anxiety and guilt churned within me. After 15 minutes, a grey-haired man approached. 'Excuse me, do you know where Tom Hamrogue's office is?' I asked. With a kind smile, he replied, 'You must be the new member. Come with me – I'm one of his patients too, and I'm late just like you.'

The world seemed to open up. Together, we found Tom's office tucked away in a cosy little library. Tom greeted me warmly and asked about my late arrival. I expressed my frustration with childlike sincerity: 'Why did you forget to show me the room during our first meeting?' John, the man who had helped me, admitted that he hadn't wanted to come that day but had finally stopped resisting. His jealousy of the 'new member' had triggered his own lateness – an event that ultimately benefited both of us and the group.

John later shared that he had long been jealous of his younger sister. Over the years, he often told me that I reminded him of her – the sister he loved but also envied. At times, these transference feelings left me frustrated and uncertain how to respond. My own experience of siblings was quite different. In a family of eight children, I was the eldest daughter. I had five brothers and two younger sisters. Throughout my childhood, I was cherished and never the target of envy. If envy existed, it was between my brothers and was not directed at me.

Despite our cultural, emotional, and intellectual differences, John and I shared many moments of solidarity – and occasional conflict. Even in anger, he seemed like an older brother who both envied and loved me deeply.

A flawed or incomplete situation can still lead to something meaningful when reflected upon thoughtfully. This was how my personal journey into group analysis began. My unexpected entrance and innocent questioning of Tom helped me to find my place in the group and sparked a wave of emotional reactions, including some jealousy among the members. Tom came to represent a nurturing and supportive father figure. I remained in the group for many years, long after fulfilling the requirements of my training.

Curiously, Tom's forgetfulness created a unique emotional atmosphere for both me and the group – one that contributed significantly to the shaping of my therapeutic identity. It also reminded the group that authority can, in fact, be challenged – and that it's okay to do so. Many members of the group were passive and fearful of questioning authority. My directness came as a shock; as someone from a minority background and with an accent, openly voicing such thoughts disrupted the usual group dynamic. By simply speaking up and asking questions, I offered an alternative way of being within the group.

Creating Mixed-Gender Groups

Early in my practice, I facilitated both English-speaking mixed-gender groups and women-only groups for Turkish and Turkish Cypriot individuals. During a Turkish-language individual session, a Kurdish male patient I was working with made a striking observation:

> 'Ms Dilek, your Turkish groups are always for women, but your English groups are mixed gender. Why aren't there mixed groups for us? My problem is with my wife; I want to understand myself in relation to women. Besides, I don't speak English. If only there were mixed groups in Turkish.'

His words stayed with me. Around the same time, I was deeply affected by the tragic death of a female former patient, who had been killed by her husband after seeking a divorce.

These two events prompted serious reflection on my practice. The patient's insight became a guiding principle and led me to stop running women-only groups outside of women's therapy centres. He was absolutely right: men also need opportunities to grow, learn, and change. Such growth can only occur through meaningful, structured dialogue with women in safe, contained spaces. Determined to challenge entrenched prejudices, I began creating environments where Turkish-speaking Kurdish, Turkish Cypriot, and Turkish men and women could come together for open and transformative conversations.

Early in my career, I felt a lot of anger towards male patients. This was because of my own personal experiences with male dominance, which had affected me deeply both in my life and at work. When I told my supervisor, Dr Harold Behr, about this, he said something simple but important: 'They are your patients, here to ask for help – not your partner or your friends.'

That sentence made me stop and think. It helped me to start to understand male patients better and to respond with kindness and professionalism.

Addressing Prejudices and Stereotypes

The decision to start mixed-gender Turkish-speaking therapy groups required confronting both personal and societal biases. When I shared my plans, I faced resistance – even from colleagues. A British colleague asked, 'How can Turkish women sit alongside men in therapy?' Her comment revealed the persistence of cultural stereotypes across communities. Similarly, some British colleagues held assumptions or prejudices about men, particularly Turkish men. These views were also echoed by Turkish-speaking community workers, including ethnic minority therapists. These concerns were not unfounded, given that many Turkish and Kurdish women in London have experienced injury or abuse from men of all nationalities. However, when a Turkish or Kurdish man seeks help, I tend to view the situation differently.

I recognised that these prejudices were deeply rooted – not only in societal norms but sometimes even within the individuals who might benefit from therapy. I understood that challenging these stereotypes required not only intention but also action: a practical demonstration of the benefits of mixed-gender interaction and a commitment to creating an environment where every voice could be heard.

Despite initial resistance, I persevered and established mixed-gender Turkish speaking groups. Over time, these groups became powerful spaces for transformative dialogue. Participants – both male and female – were often surprised to hear honest feedback from each other. This exchange challenged their assumptions about gender roles and interpersonal dynamics. The safe, structured environment enabled individuals to confront their biases and learn from one another, leading to a richer and more inclusive therapeutic experience.

The Emotional Landscape of Men and Women

Societal norms often discourage men – particularly those from Turkish, Kurdish, or Asian backgrounds – from seeking help or expressing vulnerability. While epidemiological data suggest that women report higher rates of depression, many men's psychological struggles remain hidden. Internalised beliefs – such as 'men must be strong' – lead many to pretend they are coping, even when they are not. This facade prevents them from accessing the support they need and creates a dangerous silence that deepens emotional distress. In my experience, this contributes to the perception that women are more depressed than men, when in reality many men remain outside the therapeutic system, their suffering overlooked or unspoken. I recall reading research suggesting that natural miscarriages tend to affect male foetuses more than female foetuses, perhaps because male foetuses are neurologically and physiologically more vulnerable to stress in the womb (Di Renzo et al., 2007; Sandman et al., 2013). This vulnerability may partly explain why females often demonstrate greater emotional and physical resilience. Clinically, I have also observed that many mothers seem particularly protective of their sons, raising the question of whether, on some unconscious level, they sense this underlying fragility.

Between 2004 and 2010, a significant number of Turkish and Kurdish men living in London died by suicide. In contrast, women are more likely to seek help and openly share their struggles. Although women attempt suicide more frequently, the male suicide rate is significantly higher. This stark disparity highlights the lack of accessible resources and support systems for men – a problem not limited to Turkish-speaking communities, but one that affects men across Europe and beyond. These trends underscore the urgent need for mental health services that are sensitive to gender-specific challenges and societal expectations (Derman, 2017).

Many men, shaped by cultural norms, struggle to express emotions such as anger, sadness, or vulnerability. Feelings like envy and competition are frequently suppressed, influenced by longstanding expectations that prize stoicism and self-reliance. Without safe spaces in which to explore these emotions authentically, they may manifest as violence, aggression, or, in extreme cases, tragic outcomes such as murder. It is not uncommon to hear individuals insist, 'I'm definitely not envious or jealous', even while battling hidden inner turmoil.

Freud's early work on repressed emotions, including *Studies on Hysteria* (Freud and Breuer, 1895), *The Interpretation of Dreams* (Freud, 1900), and *Inhibitions, Symptoms and Anxiety* (Freud, 1926), laid the foundations for understanding how suppressed feelings may produce psychological and physical symptoms. This insight echoes my own observations in group therapy, where patients often reveal that behind a composed facade lie powerful, unresolved emotions.

Similarly, in Türkiye, the widespread use of evil eye beads, protective prayers, and rituals to ward off the 'evil eye' may reflect an underlying concern with envy and emotional vulnerability. While these practices are rooted in cultural tradition, they can also be seen as an indirect acknowledgement of internal emotional struggles. Though not always consciously linked to psychological distress, such expressions suggest a collective awareness of the impact of unspoken feelings – an awareness that may benefit from further exploration within therapeutic settings.

References

Akbar, N., 1991. 'Mental Disorder Among African Americans', in R.L. Jones (ed.), *Black Psychology*. Berkeley, CA: Cobb & Henry, pp. 339–351.

Bateman, A.W. and Fonagy, P., 2004. *Psychotherapy for Borderline Personality Disorder: Mentalization-Based Treatment*. Oxford: Oxford University Press.

Burlingame, G.M., Strauss, B. and Joyce, A.S., 2018. 'Change Mechanisms and Effectiveness of Small Group Treatments', in M.J. Lambert (ed.), *Bergin and Garfield's Handbook of Psychotherapy and Behavior Change*. 7th edn. New York: Wiley, pp. 717–757.

Corey, G., 2016. *Theory and Practice of Counseling and Psychotherapy*. 10th edn. Boston: Cengage.

Corey, G., Corey, M.S., and Corey, C., 2018. *Theory and Practice of Counseling and Psychotherapy*. 10th edn. Boston: Cengage.

Cuijpers, P., van Straten, A., Andersson, G., and van Oppen, P., 2013. 'Psychotherapy for Depression in Adults: A Meta-Analysis of Comparative Outcome Studies', *Journal of Consulting and Clinical Psychology*, 81(5), pp. 747–758.

De Maré, P., 1975. 'The Politics of Large Groups', in L. Kreeger (ed.), *The Large Group: Dynamics and Therapy*. Chichester: Wiley, pp. 145–158.

De Maré, P., Piper, D., and Thomson, M., 1990. *The Large Group: Dynamics and Therapy*. London: Routledge.

De Maré, P., Piper, R., and Thompson, S., 1991. *Koinonia: From Hate Through Dialogue to Culture in the Large Group*. London: Karnac Books.

Di Renzo, G.C., Rosati, A., Sarti, R.D., Cruciani, L., and Cutuli, A.M., 2007. 'Does Fetal Sex Affect Pregnancy Outcome?', *Gender Medicine*, 4(1), pp. 19–30. Available at doi:10.1016/j.genm.2007.01.001 (accessed 18 September 2025).

Derman, S., 2017. *A Report on Suicides in Turkish and Kurdish Communities*, KIPDF. Available at: https://kipdf.com/a-report-on-suicides-in-turkish-and-kurdish-communities_5aad3a1f1723dd8318360954.html (accessed 1 June 2025).

Fanon, F., 1963. *The Wretched of the Earth*. Translated by C. Farrington. New York: Grove Press.

Fanon, F. (1967) *Black Skin, White Masks*. New York: Grove Press

Foulkes, S.H., 1964. *Therapeutic Group Analysis*. London: Allen & Unwin.

Foulkes, S.H. (1971) *Introduction to Group-Analytic Psychotherapy*. London: Hogarth Press

Foulkes, S.H., 1975. *Group Analyses: Foundations of the Psychoanalytic Treatment of Groups*. London: Karnac Books.

Foulkes, S.H. and Anthony, E.J., 1957. *Group Psychotherapy: The Psychoanalytic Approach*. London: Karnac Books.

Freud, S., 1900. *The Interpretation of Dreams*. London: Hogarth Press.

Freud, S., 1926. *Inhibitions, Symptoms and Anxiety*. London: Hogarth Press.

Freud, S. and Breuer, J., 1895. *Studies on Hysteria*. Standard Edition, vol. 2. London: Hogarth Press.

Hall, Rachel, 2024. 'Goldsmiths Academics Strike Over 'Incomprehensible' Redundancies', *The Guardian*, 28 March. Available at https://www. https://www.theguardian.com/education/2024/mar/28/goldsmiths-academics-to-strike-over-incomprehensible-redundancies (accessed 9 June 2025).

Hawkins, P. and Shohet, R., 1989. *Supervision in the Helping Professions*. Milton Keynes: Open University Press.

Layton, L., 2004. *Who's That Girl? Who's That Boy? Clinical Practice Meets Postmodern Gender Theory*. London: Routledge.

Levine, P.A., 1997. *Waking the Tiger: Healing Trauma*. Berkeley, CA: North Atlantic Books.

Maté, G., 2003. *When the Body Says No: Understanding the Stress-Disease Connection*. Toronto, ON: Knopf Canada.

McWilliams, N., 2004. *Psychoanalytic Psychotherapy: A Practitioner's Guide*. New York: Guilford Press.

Nicolazzo, Z., 2017. 'Exploring the Ways Trans Collegians Navigate Academic, Romantic, and Social Relationships', *Journal of College Student Development*, 58(4), pp. 526–544. Available at doi:10.1353/csd.2017.0041 (accessed 23 August 2025).

Ogden, T.H., 1994. 'The Analytic Third: Working with Intersubjective Clinical Facts', *International Journal of Psycho-Analysis*, 75, pp. 3–19.

Ogden, P., Minton, K., and Pain, C., 2006. *Trauma and the Body: A Sensorimotor Approach to Psychotherapy*. New York: W.W. Norton & Company.

Racker, H., 1968. *Transference and Countertransference*. London: International Universities Press.

Sandman, C.A., Glynn, L.M., and Davis, E.P., 2013. 'Is There a Viability-Vulnerability Tradeoff? Sex Differences in Fetal Programming', *Journal of Psychosomatic Research*, 75(4), pp. 327–335. Available at doi:10.1016/j.jpsychores.2013.07.009 (accessed 18 September 2025).

Skodol, A.E., Gunderson, J.G., McGlashan, T.H., Dyck, I.R., Stout, R.L., Bender, D.S., and Oldham, J.M., 2002. 'Functional Impairment in Patients with Schizotypal, Borderline, Avoidant, or Obsessive-Compulsive Personality Disorder', *American Journal of Psychiatry*, 159(2), pp. 276–283.

Sue, D.W., 2010. *Microaggressions in Everyday Life: Race, Gender, and Sexual Orientation*. Hoboken, NJ: Wiley.

Sue, D.W. and Sue, D., 2016. *Counseling the Culturally Diverse: Theory and Practice*. 7th edn. Hoboken, NJ: Wiley.

Van der Kolk, B.A., 2015. *The Body Keeps the Score: Brain, Mind, and Body in the Healing of Trauma*. London: Penguin.

Yalom, I.D., 1995. *The Theory and Practice of Group Psychotherapy*. 4th edn. New York: Basic Books.

Yalom, I.D., 2005. *The Theory and Practice of Group Psychotherapy*. 5th edn. New York: Basic Books.

Yalom, I.D. and Leszcz, M., 2020. *The Theory and Practice of Group Psychotherapy*. 6th edn. New York: Basic Books.

Chapter 4

Effective Supervision in Intercultural Group Therapy

The Therapeutic Parallel and Winnicott's Concept of the 'Good Enough Mother'

To appreciate the importance of supervision in therapy, it is helpful to consider Donald Winnicott's concept of the 'good enough mother' (Winnicott, 1953). Just as a mother's patience and emotional containment allow her child to grow and adapt to a complex world, supervision offers therapists the emotional support and containment essential for effective practice (Behr, 1995; Hawkins and Shohet, 1989). Winnicott's metaphor highlights the value of holding space for difficult emotions – without overreacting or taking control.

Much like the 'good enough mother', a therapist must manage overwhelming emotions in the therapeutic space – providing support while ensuring that they are not overwhelmed (Bion, 1961; Foulkes, 1975). Supervision enables therapists to reflect, maintain boundaries, and preserve their emotional wellbeing (Behr, 1995; Hawkins and Shohet, 1989).

Although Winnicott did not directly address race or culture, his concept of emotional containment is essential across diverse contexts (Kareem and Littlewood, 1992). His emphasis on unconditional care and the creation of 'holding environments' offers a powerful model for intercultural work (B. Brown, 2012; C. Brown, 2024).

The Importance of Supervision

Race significantly shapes clinical development, professional positioning, and accountability (C. Brown, 2024; Sue and Sue, 2016). Supervisors from dominant cultures – even those with diverse experience – may struggle to engage meaningfully with race unless they critically examine their own identity and positionality (Ababio, 2024; Dalal, 2006). The lack of diversity within psychoanalytic and therapeutic professions compounds this, making it harder for White supervisors to recognise and respond to cultural realities (Fernando, 2010; Kinouani, 2021).

Many institutions fail to prioritise high-quality supervision, citing financial constraints. Yet inadequate support contributes to burnout, emotional fatigue,

DOI: 10.4324/9781003726012-5

and reduced patient care capacity (McDermut et al., 2001; Sommers-Flanagan and Sommers-Flanagan, 2018). Supervisors must provide a reflective, culturally aware approach (Ababio, 2024; Kareem and Littlewood, 1992), offering a space in which to examine clinical relationships, identify patterns, and explore unconscious processes (Ogden, 1994; Bion, 1961).

Key Considerations in Supervision

Effective supervision demands critical awareness. Supervisors must reflect on questions such as:

- Should the emphasis be on the patient's needs or on the patient-therapist dynamics?
- How does the supervisor's presence shape the therapeutic process?
- To what extent should external factors, such as institutional or political pressures, be taken into consideration?
- How do Oedipal dynamics emerge, and how might they be addressed?

Supervision helps therapists to recognise early family patterns and their emotional responses (Foulkes, 1975; Racker, 1968; Behr, 1995).

Supervision for Experienced Therapists

Supervision is essential for reflection and professional growth throughout a therapist's career (Behr, 1995; B. Brown, 2012). Emotional demands can be significant, regardless of experience (Sommers-Flanagan and Sommers-Flanagan, 2018), and creating a safe space for therapists to explore doubts fosters resilience and professional development (Hawkins and Shohet, 1989; B. Brown, 2012). Without supervision, even experienced therapists risk burnout and may struggle to practise effectively. As an experienced therapist, I continue to engage in supervision and receive regular professional support because I believe that this constitutes an ethical responsibility for all therapists. This practice allows me to sustain my work as a psychotherapist, while also finding personal fulfilment and enjoyment in it.

Addressing Suicidal Tendencies in Patients

Working with patients experiencing suicidal tendencies is demanding (McDermut et al., 2001). Supervisors provide emotional support, self-reflection, and guidance in clinical strategies (Hawkins and Shohet, 1989; Behr, 1995). Supervision must offer a safe environment where difficult cases are examined without fear of criticism (Ogden, 1994; C. Brown, 2024).

Developing Observational Skills in Group Therapy

Supervisors encourage structured reflection on sessions, including participation levels, seating arrangements, and group responses (Foulkes, 1975; de Maré et al., 1990). This improves therapists' observational skills and strengthens professional grounding (Behr, 1995; Hawkins and Shohet, 1989).

Systemic Awareness in Therapy and Supervision

Understanding systemic factors within therapeutic and organisational contexts is essential. In NHS settings, limited resources, high demand, and bureaucratic pressures affect care quality (Priebe et al., 2012; van der Kolk, 2015; Hall, 2024). Awareness of these pressures enables supervisors and supervisees to engage constructively, developing strategies for resilience and clinical integrity (Fernando, 2010; Kinouani, 2021).

Conclusion

Therapy and supervision must extend beyond the clinical encounter to include systemic and interdisciplinary perspectives (Sommers-Flanagan and Sommers-Flanagan, 2018; Priebe et al., 2012). Professional responsibility requires therapists to critically reflect on clinical skills and systemic influences (Sue and Sue, 2016; Ababio, 2024). Supervision should support reflection, critical resistance, and professional integrity amid structural pressures (Behr, 1995; Hawkins and Shohet, 1989; Hall, 2024).

References

Ababio, B., 2024. *Intercultural Supervision in Therapeutic Practice: Dialogues, Perspectives and Reflections*. London: Routledge.

Behr, H., 1995. *Personal Analysis and Supervision*. London: Routledge.

Bion, W.R., 1961. *Experiences in Groups and Other Papers*. London: Tavistock Publications.

Brown, B., 2012. *Daring Greatly: How the Courage to be Vulnerable Transforms the Way We Live, Love, Parent, and Lead*. New York: Gotham Books.

Brown, C., 2024. 'Beyond Recognition', in B. Ababio (ed.), *Intercultural Supervision in Therapeutic Practice: Dialogues, Perspectives and Reflections*. London: Routledge, pp. 21–36.

Dalal, F., 2002. 'Culturalism inmulticultural psychotherapy', in R. Moodley and S. Palmer (eds.) *Race, culture and psychotherapy: Critical Perspectives in Multicultural perspectives*. London: Brunner-Routledge.

De Maré, P., Piper, D., and Thomson, M., 1990. *The Large Group: Dynamics and Therapy*. London: Routledge.

Fernando, S., 2010. *Mental Health, Race and Culture*. 3rd edn. London: Palgrave Macmillan.

Foulkes, S.H., 1975. *Group Analyses: Foundations of the Psychoanalytic Treatment of Groups*. London: Karnac Books.

Hall, Rachel, 2024. 'Goldsmiths Academics Strike Over 'Incomprehensible' Redundancies', *The Guardian*, 28 March. Available at https://www.theguardian.com/education/2024/mar/28/goldsmiths-academics-to-strike-over-incomprehensible-redundancies (accessed 23 August 2025).

Hawkins, P. and Shohet, R., 1989. *Supervision in the Helping Professions*. Milton Keynes: Open University Press.

Kareem, J. and Littlewood, R., 1992. *Intercultural Therapy: Themes, Interpretations and Practice*. Oxford: Blackwell Scientific Publications.

Kinouani, G., 2021. *Living While Black: The Essential Guide to Overcoming Racial Trauma*. London: Ebury Press.

McDermut, W., Miller, I., and Brown, R.A., 2001. 'The Role of Supervision in Managing the Emotional Impact of Patient Care', *Journal of Clinical Psychology*, 57(2), pp. 225–234.

Ogden, T.H., 1994. 'The Analytic Third: Working with Intersubjective Clinical Facts', *International Journal of Psycho-Analysis*, 75, pp. 3–19.

Orbach, S., 1994. *Interventions in Supervision: Enhancing Professional Development*. London: Routledge.

Priebe, S., Burns, T., Cavallaro, R., Catty, J., Fioritti, A., Knapp, M., Lauber, C., Ruggeri, M., Salize, H.J., Schene, A., and Tomov, T., 2012. 'Equity of Access to Mental Health Care for Patients from Minority Ethnic Groups: A Systematic Review', *Psychological Medicine*, 42(12), pp. 2393–2407.

Racker, H., 1968. *Transference and Countertransference*. New York: International Universities Press.

Sommers-Flanagan, J. and Sommers-Flanagan, R., 2018. *Clinical Supervision: A Competency-Based Approach*. 2nd edn. Hoboken, NJ: Wiley.

Sue, D.W. and Sue, D., 2016. *Counseling the Culturally Diverse: Theory and Practice*. 7th edn. Hoboken, NJ: Wiley.

Van der Kolk, B.A., 2015. *The Body Keeps the Score: Brain, Mind, and Body in the Healing of Trauma*. London: Penguin.

Winnicott, D.W., 1953. 'Transitional Objects and Transitional Phenomena', *International Journal of Psycho-Analysis*, 34, pp. 89–97.

Chapter 5

Theoretical and Practical Insights into Understanding Large Groups

Building on the earlier exploration of group dynamics and systemic pressures within therapeutic and organisational settings, this chapter turns to the broader psychological processes at work in large groups, particularly during times of social crisis. Work by de Maré et al. (1991) has been central in defining and examining the unique dynamics of large groups, which differ fundamentally from smaller, more intimate therapeutic settings. Their insights provide a foundation for understanding how group size shapes psychodynamic processes, collective behaviour, and the potential for transformation.

While my early work focused on small groups, the social unrest that erupted in London, United Kingdom, on 6 August 2011 significantly widened my perspective on the psychological dimensions of large group behaviour, especially in moments of collective crisis. The unrest began as a protest against the police killing of Mark Duggan, a 29-year-old Black man, but quickly escalated into widespread riots and looting, causing severe economic, social, and psychological harm. The destruction of homes, historic buildings, and local businesses displaced many and deepened feelings of insecurity and disillusionment within affected communities. Over the course of a week, nearly 2,000 children and young people were arrested, lives were lost, and many others injured. The scale and intensity of the riots exposed longstanding tensions in British society, particularly concerning policing, racial injustice, and economic inequality (Riots Communities and Victims Panel, 2012; Ministry of Housing, Communities and Local Government, 2013).

In the aftermath of the disturbances in London, politicians and the public sought explanations, yet the discourse was often clouded by racist ideologies that oversimplified events, disproportionately blaming Black and immigrant communities while ignoring deeper structural issues. Media narratives reinforced stereotypes, reducing the riots to criminality and moral decline rather than addressing systemic inequalities and historical grievances.

One case that challenged this dominant narrative was that of Laura Johnson, the daughter of a millionaire, who was arrested for looting. Reported by the BBC on 5 April 2012, her involvement complicated the racial and class-based framing of the riots. It highlighted the socio-economic diversity of those

DOI: 10.4324/9781003726012-6

involved and pointed to broader motivations than those suggested by prevailing discourses. Nevertheless, much media coverage remained focused on individual blame, avoiding engagement with the structural and psychological conditions underlying the unrest.

Notably, insights from crowd psychology were largely absent from public and political discussions. Theories of deindividuation, collective identity, and group contagion could have illuminated why individuals behaved as they did within the crowd. Instead, responses centred on punitive measures, sidestepping deeper reflection on social alienation and economic hardship that fuelled collective behaviour. Stott and Drury (2016) provide a critical analysis of policing strategies during crowd events, arguing that heavy-handed or confrontational approaches often escalate tensions rather than contain them. Their work suggests that understanding the crowd's social identity and motivations is crucial for managing unrest constructively.

This highlights the need for a more nuanced and systemic approach – one that integrates psychological insight with an understanding of structural conditions. Interdisciplinary inquiry, drawing on psychotherapy, social psychology, and systemic inequality studies, can offer a fuller picture of how large groups respond to collective distress, particularly in societies marked by deep divisions and historical wounds.

Psychoanalytic and social theory emphasise that unconscious processes are shaped by social and cultural contexts. Factors such as race, class, and culture are not only external realities but also internalised, influencing identity and group dynamics. This perspective helps to explain the complex emotional and psychological responses seen in large groups during moments of social crisis, when issues such as racial injustice and economic hardship converge.

In line with the social identity approach (Reicher et al., 2010), individuals in large groups often behave according to their shared social identities and group norms. This framework helps to explain how collective emotions such as anger and defensiveness emerge in response to perceived social threats and injustices.

Insights and Experiences from 1977

In 1977, after graduating from Florence Nightingale Nursing College in İstanbul, Türkiye (formerly Turkey), I was appointed to the State Hospital in central Konya, under the aegis of the Turkish Ministry of Health and Social Services. The hospital's size and heterogeneous workforce provided a clear illustration of large group dynamics within an institutional context (Kreeger and de Maré, 1975).

Although I was the only nurse at the hospital with the formal qualifications required for the role, the chief physician was initially reluctant to appoint me to a senior position. However, after a period of overseeing the operating theatre, I was appointed head nurse. My responsibilities included oversight of staff working conditions, coordination with medical colleagues, and the introduction of an in-service training programme informed by contemporary nursing education. More than 100 nurses, administrative staff, and support personnel participated in the programme, marking an early engagement with large group processes within a professional organisational setting. Retrospectively, these challenges can be understood in the context of the broader political climate in Türkiye during the 1970s, a period characterised by significant social and ideological tension (Zürcher, 2004).

Curiosity, Suspicion, and Organisational Anxiety

Regular meetings among nursing staff attracted increasing attention from hospital administrators and senior medical personnel. Initial curiosity frequently evolved into suspicion, with questions raised regarding the purpose and content of these gatherings. In an environment shaped by political polarisation, such collective activity was readily interpreted as potentially subversive.

Large group meetings brought together individuals from diverse professional, social, political, and religious backgrounds, including clinical, administrative, and support staff. Despite these differences, initial collaboration was achieved, demonstrating the integrative potential of large group work (Kreeger and de Maré, 1975).

As group cohesion developed, resistance emerged both within the organisation and from external sources. Local media framed the educational activities as politically motivated, reflecting broader societal anxieties. Such responses illustrate how large groups promoting dialogue and cohesion may be perceived as threatening within hierarchical or authoritarian systems. Internal opposition also arose, consistent with what Nitsun (1996) describes as anti-group phenomena, whereby destructive dynamics emerge in response to anxiety generated by change and collective engagement.

Escalating tensions culminated in incidents involving intimidation and physical threat, which were inadequately addressed by institutional authorities. These responses reflected prevailing social norms and power structures, particularly in relation to gender, political affiliation, and professional autonomy.

From a group analytic perspective, this example illustrates how large group settings can activate unconscious social, political, and cultural conflicts. Large groups may intensify collective anxieties, particularly during periods of societal instability (Kreeger, 1975). This case demonstrates how organisational and societal forces can converge to undermine group processes that challenge established structures.

A Journey through Roles and Locations

My career took me through a variety of roles and locations: working in Dersim (Tunceli), at an orthopaedic hospital in Urla, at İzmir Karşıyaka State Hospital, and later at Istanbul Zeytinburnu Chest Diseases Hospital and Şişli

Nursing College. Each post brought its own mix of social, political, and personal challenges. In time, circumstances required me to leave Türkiye and continue my work in London, which provided opportunities to work in public health institutions, while also allowing space for reflection on psychotherapeutic practice and professional development.

In 1990, participation in an international meeting of Turkish-speaking migrant women in the Netherlands offered further insights into large group dynamics. The participants represented a range of ethnic backgrounds, including Kurdish, Armenian, Turkish, and Laz, and engaged with diverse perspectives encompassing socialist, Marxist, feminist, and homemaker viewpoints. Structured across large, medium-sized, and small group formats, and interspersed with informal exchanges, the event provided opportunities for both collective discussion and individual reflection, consistent with the dynamics described by Anthias (2002) and Brah (1996).

The gathering illustrated several phenomena commonly observed in large group contexts. Emotional intensity frequently emerged, reflecting the interaction of personal, social, and political factors. Participant behaviour varied across different group formats, revealing the influence of unconscious processes on interaction (Bion, 1961). Conflicting positions within the group occasionally dominated proceedings, contributing to tension and undercurrents of anxiety, consistent with Volkan's (2004) observations regarding the imprint of historical and social experience on large group behaviour.

Observations during the event highlighted the limitations of theoretical knowledge in managing emotional complexity (Bion, 1962). Creative expression, such as drawing or other symbolic activity, can function as a mediating tool for processing emotion, serving both reflective and communicative purposes (Winnicott, 1971). Such mechanisms may support participants in managing affective experiences within large groups, particularly when verbal communication is constrained.

My subsequent engagement with other large groups reinforced the need for both practical and theoretical training to develop the capacity to manage complex emotional and social dynamics. Guided participation in groups that integrate experiential learning with theoretical frameworks facilitated the development of resilience, reflective capacity, and awareness of both individual and collective processes (Foulkes, 1964; Benjamin, 1995). Postgraduate and master's studies in group analytic therapy provide both academic and practical grounding for understanding large group dynamics. Historical knowledge of the field, including the development of group analysis and its theoretical foundations (Foulkes, 1975; Rosenbaum, 1974, 1996; Pines, 1983), facilitated the integration of theory with practical experience, supporting a coherent understanding of how group processes shape both individual and collective experience.

Participation in multicultural and multilingual groups in various countries – including England, Türkiye, Greece, the Netherlands, France, Italy, Spain,

Hungary, Morocco, Germany, and Switzerland – consistently demonstrated that large groups are arenas in which unconscious anxieties, biases, and tensions often surface (Dalal, 2002; Hopper, 2003; Weinberg, 2007). Effective facilitation requires intentional structuring and careful guidance to support healthy communication, promote self-reflection, and enable constructive engagement with emotional and relational processes (Bion, 1961; Obholzer and Roberts, 1994).

Overall, these experiences underscore that the development of professional competence in working with large groups depends on the integration of theoretical knowledge, experiential learning, and reflective practice. Awareness of unconscious dynamics, cultural and social context, and group processes enables facilitators to support constructive engagement and foster meaningful learning and transformation within large group settings.

Large Group Dynamics in Türkiye

In Türkiye, large group dynamics are shaped by a complex interplay of historical trauma, cultural identity, and sociopolitical change. Situated at the crossroads of Eastern and Western influences, the country experiences persistent tensions that affect cohesion and belonging. Rapid political and social transformation, often accompanied by instability, have contributed to diminished trust within communities, fostering uncertainty and disconnection.

During periods of organisational or social turbulence, authoritarian or punitive leadership approaches can exacerbate alienation within groups. Individuals often respond to anxiety with defence mechanisms such as projection, denial, and intellectualisation, as documented in psychodynamic and organisational studies (Hinshelwood, 1991; Obholzer and Roberts, 1994). While these mechanisms can help to manage immediate anxiety, they may distort perception, constrain reflection, and limit a group's capacity for collaborative functioning. When explored within a supportive environment, however, they offer opportunities to address unspoken fears and facilitate authentic interpersonal engagement.

Observations across healthcare and institutional settings indicate that instability and shifting allegiances influence group interactions. Individuals may project confidence to mask anxiety or withdraw emotionally to avoid difficult conversations. Although these strategies can reduce immediate tension, they limit deeper engagement. Regional differences, for example between Eastern provinces with strong local heritage and Western hospitals shaped by distinct social values, further illustrate how personal and collective histories, as well as local social norms, subtly shape group behaviour and relational patterns (Hinshelwood, 1991; Obholzer and Roberts, 1994).

These dynamics provide a foundational context for understanding how group behaviour unfolds in both professional and communal settings, and they set the stage for exploring practical experiences and insights gained through direct engagement with large groups.

Insights from Large Group Experiences

Large groups offer unique opportunities for insight that may not arise in individual or small group therapy. In these settings, social, political, and cultural influences often unspoken elsewhere surface openly. Personal histories and collective narratives intertwine, revealing assumptions, biases, and emotional dynamics that shape interactions (Foulkes, 1964; de Maré et al., 1991).

Participants encounter parts of themselves – fragile, defensive, or judgemental – that can be difficult to recognise in other contexts. Unlike the contained space of individual therapy, large groups reflect both personal and shared challenges, highlighting the ongoing negotiation between individuality and belonging (de Maré et al., 1991).

Dialogue is central to this process. More than exchanging words, dialogue is a gradual unfolding through which differing views are expressed, reflected upon, and understood. It creates a space in which diverse perspectives coexist without the need for agreement or dominance (Isaacs, 1999). Genuine dialogue involves presence, engagement, and tolerance of ambiguity, fostering shifts in perspective and emotional responses over time (de Maré et al., 1991).

In an increasingly divided world, sustaining dialogue across differences is essential for social cohesion. Understanding individual experience within groups requires attention to both communication and the unconscious processes that shape group behaviour.

Le Bon's Mass Psychology and Freud's Psychoanalytic Expansion

The insights gained from direct engagement with large groups can be further understood through classical and psychoanalytic theories of group behaviour. Foundational work by Le Bon, Freud, and later Foulkes provides a framework for interpreting the unconscious and social dynamics observed in these settings.

Gustave Le Bon (1895) argued that individuals in crowds lose personal responsibility and rational control, becoming highly suggestible and emotionally driven. Anonymity, contagion, and suggestibility create a collective mindset whereby people often act in ways they would not alone. While influential, Le Bon's theories have been criticised for generalising and portraying crowds mainly as irrational and destructive.

Building on Le Bon, Freud (1921) explored the unconscious dynamics of groups. He highlighted how identification with a leader and internalised ideals can bind members together, sometimes reducing personal autonomy. Freud also described how individuals can temporarily lose their sense of personal identity under group influence, with the group overriding self-control. These insights revealed the tension between individual desires and group demands, and they laid the groundwork for understanding group cohesion, leadership, and collective belonging in therapy and social psychology.

Freud's work, although foundational, has limitations. Critics, such as Dalal (2001), argue that his distinction between the individual and the group is too simplistic and that broader social and cultural contexts – the social unconscious – also shape group behaviour. Considering these factors helps us to understand groups more fully, combining psychoanalytic insight with social context.

Foulkes (1964) extended Freud's ideas by introducing the concept of the 'matrix' – a shared web of relationships and communication connecting group members. This matrix influences both conscious and unconscious interactions, encompassing not only individuals but also cultural and societal forces. Foulkes observed that group members often project their feelings onto this collective field, stirring powerful shared responses. Skilled facilitators, attuned to the matrix, can guide these currents towards deeper understanding and connection.

The matrix reveals how group members are interwoven, like threads in a tapestry, each influencing the whole. Foulkes' work remains central to large group therapy and continues to guide modern approaches to group analysis (Foulkes and Anthony, 1957). Building on these insights, it becomes clear how healthy group connections and authentic dialogue can serve as agents of societal and emotional transformation.

These theoretical insights provide a foundation for examining contemporary large group settings, in which diverse cultural, linguistic, and social factors interact with unconscious group dynamics to shape both individual and collective experience.

Transforming Connections through Healthy Relationships

Managing social, familial, and community relationships requires honest dialogue that recognises social, political, and cultural realities. Group therapy can support this process of transformation by fostering awareness of unconscious and relational dynamics (Foulkes, 1975; Hopper, 2003).

Foulkes' work highlights that emotional, social, and cultural effort is essential for meaningful dialogue to thrive in large groups (Foulkes, 1975). Yet for dialogue to flourish, societies burdened by trauma must confront and reshape harmful norms, including racism, homophobia, misogyny, and violence (hooks, 2001; Fanon, 1967). Challenging these entrenched patterns is vital for cultivating integrity, authenticity, and healthier interpersonal connections.

This process involves critical examination of cultural values – releasing those that cause harm and embracing those that foster genuine dialogue and meaningful attachment. Through such reflection, societies can nurture authentic connections and enable lasting transformation (Buber, 1958; Isaacs, 1999). It is important to recognise that individual experiences form part of personal history but do not define the entirety of identity.

Distinct Characteristics of Large Groups

Large groups frequently evoke strong emotions such as anger, fear, and disappointment. For instance, the killing of a 29-year-old Black citizen by police in London provoked widespread unrest, illustrating how collective anger can escalate into panic or violence (Mohdin and Murray, 2011). Similarly, disappointment or frustration within groups may result in silence, withdrawal, or avoidance, reflecting underlying emotional and relational tensions.

Such emotional responses are shaped by individual histories, including early family security, supportive relationships, and personal resilience or vulnerability (Bowlby, 1988). In contexts of crowd behaviour, these dynamics can manifest as chaotic or irrational actions, with individuals experiencing the sensation of being swept along, akin to waves in a storm (Le Bon, 1895; Freud, 1921).

Therapy groups, however, operate differently. Participants enter these spaces intentionally, seeking engagement, reflection, and mutual support. Within a structured and facilitated environment, large groups provide opportunities to process emotions collectively, explore interpersonal dynamics, and foster a shared culture of growth and understanding (Yalom, 1995).

The Role of the Group Therapist

A group therapist does not act as a strict moral authority, nor do they pursue perfection. Rather, they function as a gardener, tending to a diverse and sometimes unruly ecosystem, creating conditions conducive to growth without imposing it (Foulkes, 1984).

Large groups provide fertile ground for insights that may not arise in smaller, more structured settings. Within this environment, participants gradually reveal hidden emotions and reactions, such as arrogance, vulnerability, destructiveness, and harsh self-judgement (Hopper, 2003). The group acts as a reflective surface, exposing unconscious biases and defensive patterns. Although resistance and discomfort often occur, these tensions can clear the air, creating space for new understanding (Bion, 1961).

As awareness increases, members transform not only their self-perception but also their relationships with others (Hopper, 2003). Following intense large group encounters, participants often engage in smaller groups to process the emotional impact and gain clearer insight into emerging dynamics. This reflective practice provides a foundation for discussions on migration and related themes.

Reflections on Large Group Dynamics

As the process unfolds, emotional resilience and self-awareness develop. Participants begin to communicate more meaningfully, learning to listen deeply, reflect thoughtfully, and accept diverse viewpoints. The group often mirrors broader societal dynamics, becoming a space for both personal and collective development (Foulkes, 1975; Pines, 1983). Through increasing awareness, members transform not only their self-perception but also their relationships with others (Hopper, 2003).

Large groups – typically exceeding 30 members (de Maré et al., 1991) – offer unique opportunities to explore social, cultural, and political dynamics. Unlike smaller therapeutic groups, they can surface generational memories, collective anxieties, and repressed emotions that shape participants' experiences. As Pomerance Steiner (cited in de Maré et al., 1991) suggests, large groups serve to investigate and question social and cultural conditions, extending the focus beyond the individual and family to broader collective dynamics.

Hopper (2003) identified the social unconscious as a powerful undercurrent in large groups, where collective anxieties and unprocessed social histories silently influence behaviour. Volkan (2001) emphasised that large group dynamics often mirror societal trauma and unresolved historical grievances, particularly in culturally diverse or politically divided contexts. Managing these complex dynamics requires careful facilitation. Skilled co-facilitators provide emotional containment, multiple perspectives, and guidance through turbulent currents of group emotion, enabling participants to navigate waves of fear, exclusion, and confusion effectively.

Experiential Contexts in Large Group Work

Turkish-Speaking Group

In a Turkish-speaking women's group in the Netherlands, participants operated within strong defensive structures shaped by political history and social pressure. Emotional expression was often constrained, contributing to experiences of isolation among both participants and facilitators. These dynamics reflected broader patterns observed among women who had lived under conditions of oppression in Türkiye. From a professional perspective, this setting provided an opportunity to observe how political and emotional dimensions intersect within group processes, and how such intersections may be recognised and integrated within therapeutic work.

European Intercultural Workshop: Exposure to Large Group Processes

From 25 to 28 May 1995, I attended the 4ème Séminaire Interculturel Européen (Fourth European Intercultural Workshop) in Paris, representing the Nafsiyat Intercultural Therapy Centre. This was my first significant encounter with large group work in an intercultural therapeutic context.

The four-day workshop brought together more than 300 participants from diverse professional, linguistic, and cultural backgrounds. It was structured to provide intensive experiential learning through engagement in both large and small group settings. The atmosphere was deliberately immersive, allowing emotional, relational, and cultural dynamics to emerge with minimal external structuring.

Dialogue within the large groups developed organically through shared words, phrases, and emotional expressions, creating moments of connection as well as misunderstanding. Contributions ranged from the seemingly incidental to the deeply affect-laden, with some statements carrying significant emotional impact. For certain participants, the intensity of the experience proved overwhelming, leading to withdrawal or unreflected flight from emotionally charged states such as anxiety, anger, or hostility. These responses illustrated the emergence of primitive emotional states that are frequently mobilised in large groups, including hate, fear, and disappointment. Engagement with such dynamics requires both emotional capacity and reflective containment. Participants who remained engaged were able to observe how individual responses were shaped by collective processes, offering opportunities for both personal insight and professional development.

Workshop Structure

The workshop was organised around three distinct but inter-related group formats:

- Large group sessions: All participants and supervising analysts met together in a single hall for 75 minutes. No common language was imposed, and participants were free to speak in their preferred language. While this openness facilitated intercultural expression, at times it generated experiences of exclusion and misunderstanding.
- Small group sessions: These groups were organised by language, each lasting 90 minutes and facilitated by two analysts. The smaller setting allowed for deeper exploration of emotional responses, relational patterns, and emerging themes from the large group.
- Cultural and educational reflection groups: These independent spaces were available to participants who wished to explore shared cultural backgrounds, including experiences of religious education or its absence. These groups operated without designated leaders, enabling open exchange around personal and collective values.

More than ten therapists and analysts from a variety of cultural and professional backgrounds facilitated the workshop. I participated in an English-speaking small group co-facilitated by Marleno Spero and Malcolm Pines, both senior figures in group analytic practice. The majority of participants were psychology trainees or practising mental health professionals.

This experience contributed to a growing understanding of how large groups function as sites where individual histories, cultural narratives, and collective emotions converge. It also provided an experiential foundation for later reflections on migration, belonging, and intercultural group dynamics (a topic developed in Chapter 6 in this volume).

Large Group Dynamics and Emotional Challenges

Large groups often become a crucible for pressing social concerns – issues of sociology, politics, culture, tradition, and economics. These discussions challenge both the conscious and unconscious mind, evoking discomfort and prompting deep self-reflection. Effective leadership is essential, requiring skill, patience, creativity, and psychological containment. Without such guidance, personal traumas can erupt like 'emotional bombs', leading individuals to respond with aggression or withdrawal.

Managing such complexity typically involves multiple therapists who facilitate sensitive assessment and constructive dialogue. These facilitators act as skilled captains, guiding the group through shifting emotional tides and providing containment and varied perspectives to help participants to remain afloat during intense waves of group dynamics. Large groups can feel overwhelming – immense and turbulent. Within this ocean of human experience, unresolved traumas, collective anxieties, and deep-seated conflicts may surface unexpectedly, provoking fear or aggression. Participants can feel emotionally adrift, caught in currents of exclusion, frustration, or confusion. Unlike smaller groups, the vastness exposes generational memories and repressed emotions beneath the surface, enabling recognition and processing.

De Maré et al. (1991) described large groups as unique spaces in which to address social, cultural, and political traumas. The challenge lies not in the presence of emotion but in maintaining clear thinking amid turbulence. Without careful guidance, chaotic behaviours may emerge, resembling violent currents pulling participants off course. Volkan (2001) observed how large group dynamics mirror societal trauma and unresolved historical grievances, especially in culturally diverse or politically divided contexts. Hopper (2003) introduced the social unconscious as a powerful undercurrent where collective anxieties and unprocessed social histories silently shape group behaviour beyond individual awareness. The first therapeutic large groups emerged in England in the early 1970s, aiming not only to recognise and process unconscious material but also to promote social understanding, dialogue across differences, and collective healing.

Cultural Encounters and Experiences of Exclusion: Linguistic and Cultural Dynamics at the European Intercultural Workshop

The 1995 workshop comprised highly educated participants from White European and Asian backgrounds, representing France, Italy, Israel, Germany, Iran, India, Yugoslavia (now Serbia and Montenegro), Sweden, Ireland, Egypt,

Norway, the People's Republic of China, Japan, Denmark, Switzerland, and several Eastern European countries. In these large group dialogues, participants explored social, communal, economic, and familial issues, providing a therapeutic space in which to process emotions, share perspectives, and reflect on cultural experiences.

Several weeks before the event in Paris, participants were sent written guidelines outlining expectations for the group process, including free expression, regular attendance, active participation, and confidentiality. Despite the intention to create an inclusive multilingual environment, the practical realities of language created uneven access to meaning. Discussions conducted in English, German, French, and Italian limited the full participation of some attendees, with nuances inevitably lost in translation. This linguistic gap intensified a sense of otherness and evoked feelings commonly associated with exclusion, including frustration and alienation.

These responses were acknowledged and explored within smaller group settings, where participants had greater opportunity to articulate the emotional impact of partial inclusion.

One day, in the large group, I stood up and spoke in Turkish: 'I don't understand what you're talking about, and now you won't understand me either.' Within the multiplicity of voices, this use of the Turkish language functioned as a symbolic act, momentarily equalising the imbalance created by language and restoring a sense of agency.

The intervention initially generated confusion and surprise; however, several participants responded in Turkish, disclosing their own personal or familial connections to Türkiye. For a brief period, a shared linguistic and cultural space emerged within the larger group. Subsequent discussions in the small groups reflected curiosity about this exchange and opened wider conversations about exclusion, understanding, and the emotional consequences of linguistic dominance.

This episode highlighted the way in which language operates not only as a medium of communication but also as a marker of power, inclusion, and belonging within large groups. It reinforced the importance of recognising and addressing structural and cultural asymmetries in group settings, particularly where dialogue is intended to support reflection, equality, and mutual understanding.

Reflections on Large Group Dynamics

Large groups can be conceptualised as vast, complex systems – immense, deep, and sometimes turbulent. Participants navigate waves of emotion, currents of unconscious processes, and occasional conflicts. Within this dynamic environment, moments of connection and understanding emerge, but unpredictable dynamics can also challenge engagement. Effective facilitation requires attention to underlying emotions, careful dialogue, and cultural sensitivity, ultimately fostering a climate of shared trust and equality. This aligns with the ancient Greek concept of *koinonia*, which symbolises a shared dialect that unites participants and opens communication channels amid complexity (de Maré et al., 1991). Hopper further identified the social unconscious as a powerful undercurrent, where collective anxieties and unprocessed social histories silently shape group dynamics and responses.

Large group work allows participants to explore the interplay between personal, familial, and societal dynamics. The structured therapeutic environment provides opportunities to notice subtleties in emotional responses and relational patterns, supporting the integration of cognitive, emotional, and social awareness. This facilitates recognition of defensive strategies, emotional regulation, and the negotiation between individual expression and collective belonging.

Contextual factors, such as cultural and political backgrounds, influence engagement in large groups. For example, in Turkish-speaking women's groups, participants' engagement may be shaped by social and political pressures. Defence mechanisms, including reliance on intellectual or theoretical frameworks, can be employed to manage anxiety or difficult emotions, which may contribute to emotional withdrawal or perceived isolation within the group. These dynamics often reflect broader social patterns, including histories of living under oppression, where emotional expression may be constrained and roles rigidly defined.

By contrast, participation in structured large group workshops with therapeutic guidance can enhance awareness of emotional subtleties and relational responses. Structured settings support reflection on both personal and social aspects of experience, enabling participants to explore complex emotional and political dimensions and to integrate multiple aspects of self within a safe and contained environment.

Key Themes and Observations from the Paris Large Group

Several key themes emerged from the Paris large group, highlighting both emotional processes and structural dynamics:

- Emotional awareness: Participants gained insight into their own feelings and recognised that the group climate supported reflection, even amid turbulent dynamics.
- Suppression of emotions: Some participants initially held back feelings due to the size, diversity, and unfamiliarity of the group, illustrating how defensive responses can emerge.
- Challenges of connection: Differences in cultural, linguistic, and personal backgrounds occasionally created distance, emphasising the delicate balance required to maintain relational stability.
- Defence mechanisms: Psychological barriers arose in response to group tensions. The structured environment provided a safe space to explore these defences, fostering connection and potential transformation.

- Emotional understanding and transformation: Participants described clarity emerging from shared expression, likened metaphorically to moving from turbulent waters to calm seas (de Maré et al., 1991; Bion, 1961; Pines and Spero, 2015; Klein, 1946). Long-held emotional burdens were released, allowing renewed strength and ease to emerge.

Additional observations on large group dynamics included:

- Social conditions for peace: Individual and collective wellbeing are foundational for fostering sustainable social understanding (de Maré et al., 1991).
- Cultural context: Groups composed of participants from diverse backgrounds require careful facilitation to navigate differences and support deeper emotional insight. Structured settings enable exploration of cultural and emotional diversity while providing containment and guidance.

Intellectualisation can be a common response in large groups, potentially limiting emotional engagement; thus, effective facilitation, mutual dialogue, and cultural awareness are essential to support participants in navigating these complex dynamics (Bion, 1961; Harwood and Pines, 2006).

Emotional Awareness and Creative Expression in Large Groups

Large groups, with their inherent emotional complexities, often elicit engagement with internal resources. Emotional tension that may be difficult to articulate can emerge, and participants sometimes use creative forms of expression to process these feelings. Artistic activities such as ceramics, embroidery, and painting have been observed to provide structured outlets for intense emotions, supporting emotional regulation and insight. In this context, creative expression functions as a method for surfacing, exploring, and reflecting on affective experiences in a contained and constructive manner (Klein, 1946).

Large Group Experiences and Healing

Large group experiences can serve as powerful vehicles for collective healing, particularly through shared social rituals. In Türkiye, events such as football matches, political demonstrations, funerals, weddings, and henna nights play a central role in shaping emotional and social bonds. These communal spaces foster a sense of belonging. Yet, when poorly structured, they may give way to destructive outcomes, highlighting the fragility of large group dynamics.

For example, celebratory gunfire at weddings – intended as a gesture of joy – has sometimes resulted in fatal consequences. Such tragedies reflect the dangers of surrendering to heightened mass emotion, where individual control is lost in the swell of collective psychology. Similarly, political rallies may become arenas of hostility, especially when unresolved grievances are amplified. These examples illustrate how unexamined emotional undercurrents can drive destructive behaviours in large groups (Volkan, 2001).

Large group dynamics can be likened to a river that nourishes the communities along its banks but, if unchecked, can flood and devastate the land it touches. This dual potential – both reparative and harmful – underscores the need for sensitive facilitation and awareness of emotional undercurrents within the Group (de Maré et al., 1991).

When group dynamics are thoughtfully facilitated, with space for honest and respectful dialogue, large group settings can provide opportunities for societal healing. Communal rituals offer a space for processing grief, loss, and transition. Without structure or meaningful conversation, however, these gatherings risk reinforcing divisions or escalating tensions.

While large groups reveal complex emotional currents, social tensions, and cultural differences, often in intense and unpredictable ways, small groups, by contrast, provide a safer and more contained space where these insights can be explored, processed, and integrated. Issues such as racism, migration, and exclusion – amplified in large settings – can be addressed thoughtfully, allowing participants to deepen their understanding of both personal and collective experiences. The transition from large to small groups thus offers a continuum of therapeutic engagement, supporting more nuanced and meaningful personal and collective healing (Klein, 1946; Pines, 2015).

Large group work is inherently complex, requiring a careful balance of individual emotion, cultural sensitivity, and group psychology. Facilitators must manage diverse emotional currents and cultural sensitivities, requiring specialised skills and ongoing awareness to harness the healing potential of large groups effectively. Thoughtful facilitation can transform potential chaos into opportunities for collective resilience and healing, laying important groundwork that is later developed in smaller, more intimate therapeutic settings.

References

Ababio, B., 2024. *Intercultural Supervision in Therapeutic Practice: Dialogues, Perspectives and Reflections*. London: Routledge.

Anthias, F., 2002. 'Where Do I Belong? Narratives of Place, Social Division and Cultural Hybridity', *Sociology*, 36(3), pp. 437–455.

Anthias, F. and Yuval-Davis, N., 1992. *Racialized Boundaries: Race, Nation, Gender, Colour and Class and the Anti-Racist Struggle*. London: Routledge.

Behr, H., 1995. *Personal Analysis and Supervision*. London: Routledge.

Benjamin, J., 1995. *Like Subjects, Love Objects: Essays on Recognition and Sexual Difference*. New Haven, CT: Yale University Press.

Bion, W.R., 1961. *Experiences in Groups*. London: Tavistock.

Bion, W.R., 1962. *Learning from Experience*. London: Heinemann.

Bober, B., 2000. *Feminist Theory: From Margin to Center*. 2nd edn. Cambridge, MA: South End Press.

Bowlby, J., 1988. *A Secure Base: Clinical Applications of Attachment Theory*. London: Routledge.
Brah, A., 1996. *Cartographies of Diaspora: Contesting Identities*. London: Routledge.
Brown, B., 2012. *Daring Greatly: How the Courage to Be Vulnerable Transforms the Way We Live, Love, Parent, and Lead*. New York: Gotham Books.
Buber, M., 1958. *I and Thou*. New York: Scribner.
Dalal, F., 2001. *Group Therapy: A Critical Overview*. London: Routledge.
Dalal, F., 2002. *Race, Colour and the Processes of Racialization: New Perspectives from Group Analysis, Psychoanalysis and Sociology*. Hove: Brunner-Routledge.
De Maré, P., Piper, D. and Thompson, B., 1991. *Koinonia: From Hate, through Dialogue, to Culture in the Large Group*. London: Karnac Books.
Foulkes, S.H. and Anthony, E.J., 1957. *Group Psychotherapy: The Psychoanalytic Approach*. Harmondsworth: Pelican Books/Penguin Books.
Kreeger, L., 1975. *The Large Group: Dynamics and Analysis*. London: Routledge and Kegan Paul.
Kreeger, L. and de Maré, P., 1975. *The Functioning of Social Systems in Groups: Group-Analytic Studies*. London: Routledge and Kegan Paul.
Fanon, F., 1967. *Black Skin, White Masks*. Translated by C.L. Markmann. New York: Grove Press.
Foulkes, S.H., 1957. *Group Psychotherapy: The Psychoanalytic Approach*. London: Karnac Books.
Foulkes, S.H., 1961. *Introduction to Group-Analytic Psychotherapy: Studies in the Social Integration of Individuals and Groups*. London: Heinemann.
Foulkes, S.H., 1964. *Therapeutic Group Analysis*. London: Allen & Unwin.
Foulkes, S.H., 1975. *Group Analyses: Foundations of the Psychoanalytic Treatment of Groups*. London: Karnac Books.
Foulkes, S.H., 1984. *Therapeutic Group Analysis*. London: Karnac Books.
Freud, S., 1921. *Group Psychology and the Analysis of the Ego*. London: The International Psycho-Analytical Press.
Grinberg, L. and Grinberg, R., 1989. *Psychoanalytic Perspectives on Migration and Exile*. London: Routledge.
Harwood, I.N.H.and Pines, M., 1998. *Self Experiences in Group: Intersubjective and Self Psychological Pathways to Human Understanding*. London: Jessica Kingsley Publishers.
Hinshelwood, R.D., 1991. *Clinical Klein*. London: Free Association Books.
Hopper, E., 2003. *Therapist Self-Care and Reflective Practice*. London: Routledge.
hooks, B., 2001. *All About Love: New Visions*. New York: Harper Perennial.
Isaacs, H., 1999. *Group Dynamics: A Practical Guide*. London: Kogan Page.
Isaacs, W., 1999. *Dialogue and the Art of Thinking Together*. New York: Doubleday.
Klein, M., 1946. 'Notes on Some Schizoid Mechanisms', in *Envy and Gratitude and Other Works 1946–1963*. London: Hogarth Press, pp. 1–24.
Le Bon, G., 1895. *The Crowd: A Study of the Popular Mind*. London: T. Fisher Unwin.
Ministry of Housing, Communities and Local Government, 2013. *Government Response to the Riots, Communities and Victims Panel's Final Report*. London: Department for Communities and Local Government. Available at https://www.gov.uk/government/publications/government-response-to-the-riots-communities-and-victims-panels-final-report (accessed 13 January 2026).
Mohdin , A. andMurray , J., 2011. '"The Mark Duggan Case was a Catalyst": The 2011 England Riots 10 Years On', *The Guardian*, 30 July. Available at https://www.theguardian.com/uk-news/2021/jul/30/2011-uk-riots-mark-duggan (accessed 22 August 2025).

Nitsun, M., 1996. *The Anti-Group: Destructive Forces in the Group and their Creative Potential*. London: Routledge.
Obholzer, A. and Roberts, V., 1994. *The Unconscious at Work: Individual and Organizational Stress in the Human Services*. London: Routledge.
Pines, M., 1983. *The Large Group*. London: Routledge and Kegan Paul.
Pines, M., 2015. 'Reminiscences and Reflections on My Life in Psychiatry and Psychotherapy', *Contexts*, C68, June.
Reicher, S., Spears, R., and Haslam, S.A., 2010. 'The Social Identity Approach in Social Psychology', in M.S. Wetherell and C.T. Mohanty (eds), *The SAGE Handbook of Identities*. Sage, London, pp. 45–62.
Riots Communities and Victims Panel, 2012. *After the Riots: The Final Report of the Riots Communities and Victims Panel*. London: Riots Communities and Victims Panel.
Rosenbaum, M. (ed.), 1974. *Group Psychotherapy from the Southwest*. London: Gordon and Breach Science Publishers. (Reprinted by Routledge, 2014).
Rosenbaum, M. (ed.), 1996. *Handbook of Short-Term Therapy Groups: Resource for Mental Health Professionals*. Lanham, MD: Rowman & Littlefield.
Stott, C. and Drury, J., 2016. 'Contemporary Understanding of Riots: Classical Crowd Psychology, Ideology and the Social Identity Approach', *Public Understanding of Science*, 26(1), pp. 2–14. doi:doi:10.1177/0963662516639872.
Tuckett, D., 2005. 'Does Anything Go? Towards a Framework for the More Transparent Assessment of Psychoanalytic Competence', *The International Journal of Psychoanalysis*, 86(1), pp. 19–49.
Volkan, V.D., 2001. *Bloodlines: From Ethnic Pride to Ethnic Terrorism*. London: Farrar, Straus & Giroux.
Volkan, V.D., 2004. *Blind Trust: Large Groups and Their Leaders in Times of Crisis and Terror*. Charlottesville, VA: Pitchstone Publishing.
Weingarten, K., 2007. 'The Connectedness of Supervision and Social Justice', *Journal of Systemic Therapies*, 26(2), pp. 1–15.
Weinberg, H., 2007. *Short-Term Group Psychotherapy: An Introduction*. London: Routledge.
Winnicott, D.W., 1960. 'The Theory of the Parent-Infant Relationship', *International Journal of Psycho-Analysis*, 41, pp. 585–595.
Winnicott, D.W., 1971. *Playing and Reality*. London: Tavistock.
Yalom, I.D., 1995. *The Theory and Practice of Group Psychotherapy*. 4th edn. New York: Basic Books.
Zürcher, C., 2004. *The Post-Soviet Wars: Rebellion, Ethnic Conflict, and Nationhood in the Former Soviet Union*. London: Palgrave Macmillan.

Chapter 6

Immigration and its Impact on Group Therapy

Migration as an Emotional Experience

Migration is more than a physical relocation; it represents a profound emotional and psychological journey. As León and Rebeca Grinberg (1989) describe in their psychoanalytic work on exile and migration, the process involves migratory mourning – a layered grief that encompasses the loss of homeland, identity, language, social status, and familiar cultural frameworks. These losses create deep internal disruptions that challenge a person's sense of self and continuity.

Refugees and migrants often confront the difficulties of adapting to a new environment, including cultural differences, language barriers, and social integration, while reflecting on contrasts between their homeland and the host country, such as climate, lifestyle, and social norms.

Family Dynamics and the Emotional Weight of Migration

Raising children in a new country presents unique difficulties. Refugees must navigate unfamiliar healthcare systems, adapt to new educational frameworks, and overcome cultural and linguistic barriers. Balancing two cultures while raising children can be emotionally demanding, requiring continuous negotiation between past and present. Many also explore their sense of belonging within family life, confronting tensions around gender roles, cultural expectations, and emotional support. These experiences reveal the emotional weight of migration and its impact on family dynamics, a crucial aspect in understanding the social and psychological complexities of displacement (Grinberg and Grinberg, 1989).

Taking leave of people, places, and a once-familiar way of life can evoke emotions ranging from sorrow to relief. Grief is deeply intertwined with migration, shaped by the loss of loved ones, homeland, and identity. These emotional experiences influence how individuals navigate the journey of relocation (Grinberg and Grinberg, 1989).

DOI: 10.4324/9781003726012-7

Managing Past and Present

Migration involves reconciling past and present, loss and renewal. Migrants must integrate new cultural values while preserving essential aspects of their identity. This process can be likened to a tree whose roots remain firmly embedded in the soil of the homeland, while its branches reach outward into new environments (Grinberg and Grinberg, 1989).

The circumstances surrounding migration – its timing, destination, and conditions – profoundly shape individual experiences. Inadequate support structures may contribute to emotional distress and depression. Although countries such as the United Kingdom are frequently portrayed as democratic havens, refugees may nonetheless encounter racist attitudes and forms of social exclusion. Comparisons between migrants' countries of origin and their host societies can lead to disillusionment, as hopes for a 'lesser of two evils' do not always result in the safety and stability anticipated.

Even those seeking safety may face prejudice and hostility, at times from actors or institutions intended to provide support. Racism, destructive emotions, and violence remain global concerns. Bonilla-Silva (2003) highlights how racism frequently operates through subtle, systemic mechanisms rather than overt acts. This form of 'colour-blind racism' obscures persistent inequalities and unconscious biases embedded within societies. Those who seek to challenge these injustices, including immigrant professionals, must also reflect on their own implicit attitudes. Racism thus emerges as a deeply entrenched social phenomenon, the persistence of which necessitates sustained critical attention.

Reflections on Envy and Misjudgement

While working with refugees, I witnessed a revealing moment during a team meeting. A colleague expressed her frustration: 'You know that Chilean refugee? I can't believe she bought a music system I wouldn't even consider for my own home. It's unbelievable. She's a poor refugee, yet she has a mobile phone! She's wearing beautiful, expensive clothes I could never afford.'

At the time, mobile phones were not yet in common use. The team listened sympathetically, asking questions to help the colleague to reflect on her feelings. I felt the urge to respond bluntly, thinking that she might be envious of the Chilean refugee. Instead, I paused and chose a more measured approach. I suggested: 'I wonder if some feelings of envy might be coming up in relation to this refugee.'

My comment surprised the team, but it expressed a truth often left unacknowledged. Even professionals can experience envy – yet recognising such emotions within ourselves without judgement is essential. I am grateful to psychoanalytic theory and to authors such as Melanie Klein, whose work has informed my understanding of both myself and others, and has supported a calm and reflective stance in challenging situations. This particular moment also reminded me why choosing the right words and speaking thoughtfully is important in both therapy and everyday life.

Melanie Klein (1957), who developed the psychoanalytic concept of envy, suggested that envy can obstruct personal growth. The envious part of the self resists insights that foster development, choosing instead to attack or devalue them.

Although Klein did not address cultural or migration issues specifically, her theory helps to illuminate emotional reactions – such as unconscious hostility or devaluation – that can arise in any therapeutic context, including intercultural work.

The Chilean refugee's reality was more complex than my colleague had imagined. Her clothes were gifts from the family whose house she cleaned. The music system – her only indulgence – was bought on a limited budget and paid for in instalments. Music was not a luxury but her way of staying connected to life. Before enduring a year in prison during Pinochet's regime, she had been an opera singer. The mobile phone served as a practical means of communication with social workers and loved ones, rather than as a status symbol. It was provided by social services.

Refugees are often misjudged. While some migrate for economic reasons, many seek asylum to escape war or persecution. The woman in this story had previously lived in relative comfort but was forced to flee her country as a result of political activism. Her story reflects resilience and the human need for connection and dignity, rather than materialism.

Another illustrative incident concerns a middle-class colleague who sometimes came to work wearing worn-out clothes, including a torn jumper. Given that she typically dressed elegantly, this choice of attire prompted inquiry. She explained, 'I work with refugees. It is better to appear this way around them. I do not want to trigger their envy.' However, the refugees themselves reportedly criticised this deliberate presentation, interpreting it as inauthentic or patronising. This episode highlights how well-intentioned attempts at empathy may be misaligned with patients' perceptions. In this context, respect was articulated through standards of cleanliness and neatness consistent with professional care.

Shared Human Needs and Desires

Human desires transcend race, gender, background, or ethnicity. Most people seek:

- Happiness and peace;
- Respect, belonging, and stability in a new society;
- A balance between preserving their culture and embracing new influences.

Is True Integration Possible?

Integration becomes difficult when the dominant culture holds negative expectations. Refugees may face racism, discrimination, and economic hardship (UNHCR, 2023). Yet despite these obstacles, many refugees demonstrate remarkable resilience and find ways to rebuild their lives (Papadopoulos, 2007).

Refugees' Realities in Their New Countries

Refugees often arrive in their host countries full of hope, only to confront harsh realities. Many lose significant sums to smugglers and are detained in reception centres (Refugee Council, 2023). Even those granted entry frequently endure long periods of uncertainty while awaiting residency decisions and fearing deportation.

When residency is granted, initial relief often gives way to new challenges. Prolonged waiting periods – sometimes lasting decades – prevent refugees from attending funerals, weddings, or reuniting with family (Amnesty International, 2022). This leads to deep emotional isolation and a sense of invisibility.

Language barriers further marginalise refugees, branding them with simplistic labels that erase their individuality and complexity:

- The silent Kurdish woman.
- The confused Somali man.
- The angry child.

Meanwhile, evaluative statements similarly reduce individuality:

- 'She doesn't understand what I'm saying.'
- 'I don't think we can get anywhere with this woman.'

Such labels and descriptors fragment identities and erase individuality. Struggling to plan for the future, some refugees idealise their homeland, saying: 'If only I had stayed in prison and breathed my own country's air.'

The Role of Kindness and Therapy

Support from local communities – especially landlords or neighbours – can be life-changing. In safe, welcoming environments, refugees begin to care for themselves, process their emotions, and reconnect with life. Group therapy also provides a vital space for healing, sharing, and learning (Tribe and Thompson, 2009a).

The Process of Adaptation for Immigrants

Several factors affect adaptation:

- The circumstances of arrival;
- Whether the person came alone or with family;
- The emotional impact of leaving loved ones behind.

When an artist is forced to work as a cleaner, or a doctor to wash dishes, they often undergo a profound identity crisis. Like a tree transplanted into new soil, immigrants must root themselves anew while adapting to unfamiliar conditions. Those with strong inner resources and a supportive environment adapt more effectively, finding new ways to reconstruct their lives (Bhugra, 2004). Some professionals may undertake temporary work in roles outside their main field, providing firsthand insight into the challenges of identity shifts during career transitions.

Supporting Asylum Seekers and Survivors of Torture

Asylum seekers and survivors of torture require comprehensive social, medical, and psychological support to facilitate their recovery and integration. Under the European Convention on Human Rights, countries are legally obliged to provide such support; however, in practice these obligations are frequently inadequately fulfilled (Council of Europe, 1950). This gap between legal obligations and actual provision of care highlights systemic challenges within host countries.

Systemic discrimination compounds the difficulties faced by asylum seekers. Recent inquiries into institutional racism, such as those concerning policing practices in the UK, suggest that some progress has been made (Independent Office for Police Conduct, 2024). Nonetheless, inequalities persist in various sectors, including healthcare and therapeutic services, which can hinder access to appropriate support for survivors of trauma.

Survivors of torture require patient, respectful, and trauma-informed care. Many survivors suppress distressing memories as a protective mechanism, often to shield their families from further pain. Dismissive attitudes or remarks such as 'It's all in the past' or 'Move on' risk invalidating survivors' experiences and deepening their silence. Professionals working with this population should prioritise the following principles:

- Attentive listening with patience and genuine interest.
- Avoidance of judgement and intrusive questioning.
- Respect for privacy and emotional boundaries.

Creating a safe and empathetic environment is fundamental to enabling survivors to share their narratives and begin the process of healing and rebuilding their lives.

It is important to recognise that refugees do not require pity but rather appropriate, professional support grounded in respect for their autonomy and resilience. The fact that a refugee has navigated significant obstacles to reach a destination such as London – and has engaged in therapy – demonstrates their resourcefulness and agency. Unfortunately, many Western therapists approach refugees primarily through a lens of vulnerability or neediness, at times overlooking their roles as individuals and family members with their own capacities and cultural identities.

Therapeutic approaches should focus on recognising and amplifying refugees' strengths rather than their vulnerabilities. In clinical settings, I have encountered remarks during team discussions such as 'How will they manage this week? They cried a lot in the session', implying that emotional expression equates to instability. This overlooks the fact that refugees maintain active lives, relationships, and often participate in communities where their native language is spoken.

Maintaining awareness of these contextual factors is crucial. Understanding a refugee's existing resources and support networks allows for the development of personalised, culturally sensitive care plans that support recovery and empowerment.

Emotional Challenges and the Need for Support

Working with refugees requires deep empathy and strong support systems. Survivors of torture often find it easier to share their experiences with strangers they are unlikely to see again. This is known as emotional displacement (Herman, 1997). In contrast, opening up to friends can make them feel more vulnerable. If friends, overwhelmed by the emotional weight of these experiences, inadvertently breach confidentiality, it can increase the survivor's sense of isolation and shift the focus from healing to disappointment.

Therapists and professionals who support refugees may experience emotional strain arising from the challenges of their roles. Many hesitate to seek help themselves, fearing that it might be seen as a sign of weakness. In reality, recognising the need for support shows strength. Carrying the burden of past trauma is like walking with a hidden load – only in safe company can this burden be set down. Sharing emotional burdens helps professionals to remain resilient and effective in their work.

Immigration and Contributions

Immigration has long shaped the UK's cultural and economic landscape. In the 17th century, Huguenots fleeing religious persecution transformed southern England with large-scale construction and marshland reclamation projects (Gwynn, 2001). Since then, migrants have made notable contributions across multiple sectors of society – from Nobel laureates such as Albert Einstein and Sigmund Freud to artists, musicians, and writers such as S.H. Foulkes and Lucian Freud (Kushner, 2003). Their legacies highlight the transformative power of migration. Throughout history, many refugees and migrants have enriched their new societies in remarkable ways. For example, V.S. Naipaul, born in Trinidad to Indian parents, introduced diverse narratives to English literature. These individuals embody resilience and the powerful impact that migrants can have across fields such as literature.

Immigrants have also revitalised industries such as food and the arts. London's culinary scene reflects the flavours of countless homelands – from

Turkish, Kurdish, Ethiopian, African and Indian to Colombian and Iranian. For migrants, food is not merely sustenance; it is like a warm embrace from the past, nourishing both body and soul and offering comfort far from home. Each traditional meal becomes a vessel carrying stories, flavours, and the history of a homeland, shared lovingly across generations and borders. Together, these meals bridge the emotional distance between past and present.

Food as a Cultural and Emotional Connection

Food carries memory. For immigrants, it becomes more than nourishment – it is a lifeline to lost landscapes, a gentle echo of voices left behind. In London, communal spaces such as Cem Evi and Bozca-Der (Kurdish and Turkish organisations) offer more than shelter; they are sanctuaries where stories are shared over meals, and where celebration and mourning are wrapped in the aromas of home. In these spaces, rituals such as Ashura transform humble dishes into sacred offerings – symbols of resilience, healing, and continuity. They anchor people in the past while helping them to manage the present.

When friends and family members visit from Türkiye, they often bring lemons, oranges, and other treasures from their gardens. These gifts are cherished, carrying the memory of the sun, the scent of home, and the warmth of loved ones. In the past, foodstuffs such as simit, a circular Turkish bread, were rarely available in the UK; today, however, many Turkish shops, restaurants, and cafés provide them.

Immigrants have not only carried their food across continents; they have revitalised entire industries. London's culinary landscape is a mosaic of spices and stories – from the bold richness of Turkish dishes to the delicate balance of Iranian stews. For many, food is a bridge between the life they left behind and the one they are building. It is a warm embrace across borders, a way to say 'I am still here', even when everything has changed. These meals nourish the soul as much as the body, carrying memories folded into every recipe, every shared table, every bite.

Food is more than sustenance for immigrants – it is identity made tangible. Each recipe, each spice, each act of preparation carries a piece of a homeland, a language spoken not with words but with flavours. In new lands, the act of cooking becomes a quiet declaration: 'I belong, and I remember.' It is a way to maintain cultural continuity, to teach children the tastes and textures of their heritage, and to resist the erasure of memory that distance can bring.

Shared meals become ritualistic anchors in an unfamiliar world. Community kitchens, family gatherings, and informal celebrations are spaces where stories are passed down alongside recipes. A simmering pot of mercimek çorbası (lentil soup) or a tray of baklava (a sweet pastry made of layers of filo pastry filled with nuts and sweetened with syrup or honey) is not merely food – it embodies history, comfort, and resilience. In these moments, immigrants transform ordinary ingredients into acts of preservation, care, and connection.

The importance of food also extends to adaptation. Ingredients are sometimes replaced, recipes modified, and traditions blended with local customs. Yet even when they have been changed, the essence remains: a bridge linking the past with the present, linking those who have left with those who have arrived. The kitchen becomes both laboratory and sanctuary, a space where memory and innovation coexist.

Food also serves as a medium for dialogue between cultures. Immigrant dishes offered in markets, cafés, and festivals invite curiosity and appreciation from others, turning what was once private sustenance into shared cultural knowledge. In this way, food not only preserves identity – it cultivates understanding, empathy, and belonging.

Ultimately, the immigrant's relationship with food is a testament to endurance. Each bite carries stories of departure and arrival, of loss and adaptation, of longing and joy. It is a subtle, daily assertion that no matter how far one has travelled, home is never truly lost – it is always carried, lovingly, on the tongue and in the heart.

Migration Across Time and Space: Dreams of Return and the Meaning of Home

Migration is a timeless thread woven through human history. From Mary and Joseph's flight to Egypt in the Christian tradition to the Prophet Muhammad's migration to Medina in Islam, the search for safety and belonging has endured across centuries. In contemporary times, crises such as the Syrian conflict have forced thousands to flee, with Turkish cities such as Mersin and Adana serving as waystations for refugees. This influx has been accompanied by increased reports of racism in Türkiye, reflecting a broader challenge faced by many host nations (Human Rights Watch, 2023).

Migrants endure a constant journey – driven by the quest for safety, connection, and hope. Although overshadowed by loss and sorrow, migrants bring with them the essence of their homelands like seeds, ready to take root in foreign soil. Refugees often harbour a persistent dream: the hope of one day returning to the country they were forced to leave. This yearning, deeply rooted in memory and identity, sustains them through hardship and displacement

Many long-term migrants experience a complex relationship with their country of origin. Even after extended periods abroad, visits can reveal profound cultural shifts, with familiar landscapes and social rhythms appearing to have altered during their absence. In such cases, the life established in the host country often becomes the primary reference point, creating a sense of belonging abroad while simultaneously highlighting estrangement from home.

In cities such as London, migrants often develop deep connections to the cultural vibrancy and creative opportunities found there, which can foster both engagement and inspiration. Over time, the host city becomes a central point of identity, while visits to the country of origin are experienced more as moments of connection than attempts to reclaim a past life.

This process can be further complicated by political and social pressures in the host country. Recent proposals by nationalist politicians in the UK to deport migrants, for example, create additional psychological burdens, intensifying the sense of displacement and the challenge of reconciling memory with adaptation. Such dynamics illustrate the ongoing negotiation of identity, belonging, and home that many migrants face over time.

This tension mirrors the delicate balance that many refugees must navigate: between memory and adaptation, between the heart's longing and the mind's quiet acceptance of change. Home is no longer simply a place of origin; it is where life unfolds, where passions are nurtured, and where a meaningful existence can be built – even far from the landscapes of childhood.

Challenging Inequality in Psychotherapy

In therapy and clinical training, it is essential to recognise and challenge embedded racial and cultural biases. Discrimination continues to persist within psychotherapy training and professional institutions in the UK. High tuition fees and limited opportunities for international students often deepen exclusion (Tribe and Morrissey, 2004). While White British students may also encounter challenges during their studies, students born abroad – regardless of whether they were raised in Europe – often face additional obstacles related to accent, religion, or cultural background, which may require greater effort to succeed academically. These added challenges may contribute to higher withdrawal rates among some international students. At the same time, it is important to recognise that all students, regardless of colour or background, can experience difficulties during their education (Tribe and Morrissey, 2004).

Encouragingly, the past decade has seen growing momentum for change, largely thanks to the perseverance of practitioners from diverse backgrounds. This progress requires both emotional and intellectual stamina. Yet research still shows that the majority of students in psychology and psychotherapy programmes in the UK are White Europeans, highlighting the urgent need to dismantle barriers rooted in race and class (British Psychological Society, 2014).

Addressing these disparities demands more than systemic reform; it calls for deep personal reflection. Therapists must examine not only the structures in which they operate but also their own assumptions and practices. While overt racism may be more easily recognised, unconscious bias often remains unnoticed. Cultivating self-awareness enables therapists to model meaningful change and to build trust with patients who have experienced exclusion. Although uncomfortable, this process is central to ethical practice. All therapists – regardless of background – share this responsibility (Fernando, 2010).

Training, Resentment, and Resilience

Psychotherapy training is both emotionally and academically demanding. Students from diverse backgrounds may encounter challenges shaped by cultural expectations, prior experience, or individual circumstances. These challenges can include factors such as accent, appearance, or differing cultural norms, while others may experience distinct pressures within the training environment. Developing strategies to manage these challenges fosters resilience, diligence, and professional competence. Supportive supervision and recognition of effort enable students to reach their potential, while moments of tension or envy – common in any competitive setting – can provide opportunities for reflection and professional growth.

Facing Racism and Belonging

My understanding of racism arises from both lived experience and academic study. I have encountered subtle and overt forms of discrimination in my professional and personal life. Within the institutions where I work, unconscious bias persists among White British colleagues and patients alike (Patel et al., 2000). I view racial prejudice as a psychological wound that demands careful attention. Clinically, I meet all my patients with compassion, while addressing discriminatory attitudes among colleagues firmly yet tactfully. Psychotherapists must examine and question their own assumptions. This is a challenging but necessary task.

In recent years, more international students have pursued psychology training; however, high costs remain a significant barrier. Many choose shorter, more affordable routes; Tribe and Thompson (2009b) highlight the financial and systemic challenges faced by international psychology trainees. Despite the UK's rich history of psychotherapy, institutional support remains limited. Some students confronted by persistent obstacles respond with frustration or attempt to fully assimilate into White European norms – often at the expense of their cultural identity. I have encountered therapists who are uncomfortable with their heritage, even when working in their native languages, such as Turkish or French.

Institutions must move beyond tokenism and embed diversity at the core of teaching and practice. This includes reviewing admissions procedures, providing financial aid, diversifying curricula, and ensuring that supervision actively addresses issues of race, culture, and identity. Change cannot rely on goodwill alone; institutional frameworks must evolve to reflect the lived realities of those entering the profession. Otherwise, diversity risks becoming a hollow ideal – celebrated in theory but neglected in practice (Williams and Rasool, 2000).

Confronting Racial Bias in Therapeutic Practice

Raising awareness about discrimination is neither simple nor quick. It is a gradual and demanding process shaped by lifelong social conditioning. To work effectively with people from diverse backgrounds, therapists must continually reflect on their own assumptions, prejudices, and unconscious projections that may influence their clinical work. This internal work requires emotional honesty and consistency. Just as patients bring inherited fears into therapy, therapists also carry their own histories and biases (Thomas, 1992). While these points may appear repetitive, such reiteration is necessary. Regularly revisiting them helps to ensure that they are systematically integrated into professional practice and mindset.

Scholars such as Littlewood, Lipsedge, and Fernando have made important contributions to our understanding of race and mental health (Littlewood and Lipsedge, 1997; Fernando, 2010). Their research reveals stark inequalities in access to therapy: those with greater economic resources are more likely to receive care, while people from Black and other ethnic minority backgrounds face multiple systemic obstacles (Bhui et al., 2007). These barriers are not only institutional but are also perpetuated by clinicians.

Some European therapists interpret the behaviours and expressions of minority patients through the lens of White, Western norms. What is unfamiliar is too often labelled pathological, reinforcing bias and deepening mistrust in mental health services. Patel et al., (2000) and Williams and Mohammed (2009) highlight how discrimination acts as a chronic stressor, shaping both health outcomes and clinical interpretations – a pattern supported by research on diagnostic bias in cross-cultural contexts. This can lead to unnecessary diagnoses and further marginalisation. Consequently, patients from Black, Asian, Turkish, Kurdish, Iranian, Latin American, and other minority groups often mistrust mental health services, fearing stigma and institutionalisation.

Patel et al. (2000) examine how unconscious bias persists among White British practitioners and patients, influencing interactions and care within mental health settings. Their findings indicate that systemic and interpersonal prejudices contribute to unequal treatment and erode trust in healthcare. Such persistent bias creates significant barriers for minority patients, limiting both access to mental health support and the quality of support received.

Hospital admission rates in the UK remain disproportionately high for Black and minority ethnic patients, highlighting ongoing disparities in mental health care. Research indicates that many of these individuals could benefit from psychotherapy, yet they are often directed towards medication and hospitalisation (Fernando, 2010). Addressing these disparities requires therapists to engage directly with marginalised communities and consider the perspectives and experiences of those they serve.

Internalised racism affects both patients and clinicians. In my work, I have encountered both openness and scepticism. While some patients immediately recognise me as a professional, others struggle to trust me. Such resistance – a common defence – often reflects deeper psychological and cultural tensions. Patients must feel safe to voice their doubts. Therapists, in turn, must respond with patience and insight, fully attuned to the emotional dynamics within the therapeutic space.

The real challenge – and opportunity – lies in embracing what feels unfamiliar and building relational bridges across difference. Working with defensive patterns, both in patients and ourselves, requires resilience and the courage to remain independent in our thinking. Confronting internalised bias is essential to fostering a truly inclusive therapeutic culture (Patel et al., 2000).

Cultural Sensitivity and Trust in Therapy: Managing Identity and Internalised Racism

Therapists must enter the therapeutic relationship with cultural awareness, genuine curiosity, and an openness to learning. It is not enough to empathise solely with the patient's internal world – we must also acknowledge their external, social realities. Racism, embedded in societal structures, often leads individuals to internalise negative perceptions, at times identifying with the very systems that marginalise them (Littlewood and Lipsedge, 1997).

Consider some everyday examples. Some immigrants feel compelled to adapt their names to conform to English norms:

- 'Who has the time to explain how their name is pronounced all the time?'
- 'I don't want anyone to know my child is Muslim.'
- 'I don't want it to be obvious that my child is Turkish.'

At first glance, such decisions may seem practical and intended to ease social interactions. Yet the pressure to conform often fosters self-alienation and emotional detachment. Over time, the cumulative impact of assimilation – combined with unacknowledged experiences of exclusion – can manifest as psychological distress or even physical symptoms (Williams and Mohammed, 2009).

The Turkish diacritics ü and ö, as in the author's name Dilek Güngör, retain distinctive sounds that do not exist in English. The frequent pressure to alter such characters highlights broader issues of linguistic erasure and cultural misrecognition in institutional settings.

Immigrants sometimes choose names for their children that are more accessible to English speakers – often at the expense of the rich sounds, cultural significance, and cherished traditions of their heritage languages. While such choices are understandable, they may contribute to a gradual erosion of cultural identity. What may seem like minor inconveniences can, over time, evolve into profound suffering. However, with appropriate therapeutic support, healing becomes possible.

Whatever challenges a patient may bring, they will always recognise whether their therapist is truly listening. A therapeutic approach grounded in respect, empathy, and cultural sensitivity enables patients to feel seen and heard. This foundation of trust is essential for meaningful therapeutic work – particularly when addressing the complex interplay between culture, identity, and internalised racism (Fernando, 2010).

A Path Towards Healing

There are, of course, exceptions. Some individuals change their names for reasons of safety. The group analyst Siegmund Heinrich Fuchs, for instance, adopted an Anglicized surname while fleeing Nazi Germany. He is now known as S.H. Foulkes, and although his original name later became known, the change served as a vital protective measure at the time.

Many refugees and asylum seekers change their names – not always officially, but socially – when they first arrive in a new country. Introducing themselves under a different name can serve as a form of self-protection in response to real or perceived threats. As they settle and feel safer, some gradually reclaim their original names, both socially and professionally. This process illustrates that recovery is not only about addressing past trauma but also about restoring one's identity, voice, and sense of self.

Addressing Bias and Shared Backgrounds in Therapy

A recent interaction with a Turkish colleague highlighted the nuanced complexities of bias within therapeutic practice. She expressed admiration for my work with certain patient groups but framed this in a manner that suggested that these patients were particularly challenging or less capable of engaging in therapy: 'I admire you; how do you work so effectively with such ignorant groups? I can't manage that.'

This exchange reflected a common misconception about who therapy is for and revealed an internalised form of bias. The language used implied that individuals from certain backgrounds are less capable of engaging meaningfully in therapeutic work. Underlying her words was an unacknowledged sense of superiority – perhaps grounded in her education or life experiences – that positioned her above the very people she claimed to support.

This encounter serves as a reminder that biases can remain deeply embedded, even among practitioners. It underscores the need to confront such assumptions while also appreciating the unique perspectives that patients from diverse backgrounds bring to therapy. For therapists, ongoing self-reflection and honest examination of one's assumptions are crucial for creating a genuinely inclusive and respectful therapeutic space (Thomas, 1992).

Ironically, this same colleague – herself from a rural, economically disadvantaged, and educationally limited background – often asked, 'Why can't I communicate?' Her struggle illustrates that sharing a similar class or cultural background with patients does not automatically lead to connection. On the contrary, it can introduce blind spots.

I explained to her that effective therapeutic work does not depend on shared identity, but rather on the therapist's internal work and willingness to engage with people from all walks of life. Without such self-awareness, the therapeutic relationship risks being clouded by unexamined prejudices and internalised narratives (Littlewood and Lipsedge, 1997).

Recognising these dynamics is essential if we are to develop an empathetic and effective practice – one that integrates both the therapist's and the patient's cultural and social realities.

Intercultural Group Therapy: A Lived Perspective

My identity as a group therapist and my commitment to an intercultural analytic approach are deeply rooted in my lived experience, clinical work, and journey as a refugee therapist in Europe. We no longer live in a world shaped solely by singular perspectives – those tied to one culture, one colour, or one worldview. Today, technology intersects with sociological, anthropological, psychological, economic, and political realities, all of which influence our inner lives in ways we may not immediately recognise (Fernando, 2010).

My therapeutic approach considers individuals and communities within their broader social and historical contexts, addressing internal conflicts, spiritual struggles, and the external conditions shaping people's lives (Kareem and Littlewood, 1992). Racism is not confined to any one group; in clinical work, it is essential to explore these dynamics with White British, Irish, or other European patients. At the same time, working with minority patients – whether Turkish, Kurdish, or others – does not automatically lead to easier communication or deeper empathy. Relationships with patients from similar cultural backgrounds can present particular challenges that require careful attention and reflection (Lago, 2011).

Some Black and ethnic minority therapists, in seeking legitimacy within the dominant clinical culture, may unconsciously imitate Western therapeutic models to the point of losing essential aspects of their cultural identity. While learning from Western traditions is valuable, authentic therapeutic work requires a balance – honouring one's heritage while engaging critically and creatively with dominant models. Embracing, rather than suppressing, our full identity brings depth, richness, and integrity to clinical practice (Fernando, 2010).

Growing up with a Kurdish and Turkish background in Türkiye, I had to overcome complex social tensions and prejudice. Although my heritage was rarely openly discussed, discrimination was ever-present. These early experiences shaped my sense of self – caught between pride in my roots and societal shame. Recognising this internal conflict has been essential to my therapeutic work, heightening my awareness of how cultural narratives influence identity and mental health, particularly for those managing marginalisation or dual cultural belonging. This insight reinforces my commitment to cultural sensitivity and empathy, guiding my work with patients from diverse backgrounds.

Trauma, Identity, and Cultural Dynamics in Contemporary Therapeutic Practice

Trauma has evolved significantly in today's rapidly changing world. We are no longer in Freud's Vienna, shaped by a White, middle-class bourgeois society, nor in mid-20th-century Türkiye. Globalisation has led to an unprecedented level of migration, linking lives across continents. Mass communication and online therapy now allow people to connect across borders in ways once unimaginable.

As cultures intertwine, the nature of trauma and its treatment must also transform. Therapy must reflect the complexities of our interconnected world, taking into account the social, cultural, and historical dynamics that shape individual experiences and responses (Bhugra and Becker, 2005).

In clinical practice, these global changes intersect with class, culture, and personal histories. Despite assumptions that psychotherapy primarily suits educated, middle- or upper-class individuals, minority therapists like myself have challenged this view. My clinical work spans a wide range of patients – from workers and people from rural backgrounds to highly educated professionals.

I have observed that the emotional defences of highly educated individuals can sometimes be more rigid, whereas for working-class people and those from rural, agrarian backgrounds the main challenge often lies in confronting the self. For middle-class patients, additional pressures – social expectations, status concerns, and financial stress – can make self-exploration more difficult (Hollway and Jefferson, 2013).

Some patients may initially hesitate to engage in therapy with a Turkish therapist. This reluctance often stems from unresolved personal experiences or lack of trust. Moreover, therapists may feel uneasy when working with patients from similar cultural backgrounds. Over-identification can blur boundaries, making it harder to maintain emotional distance or offer fresh perspectives (Lago, 2011).

For example, a patient requested a Kurdish-speaking therapist. They were aware that I am Turkish but did not know that I am of Kurdish origin. When informed that no Kurdish-speaking therapist was available, they initially refused. Later, upon learning of my Kurdish background – although I speak only Turkish – they agreed to attend therapy sessions. This case highlights that the concern was not language alone, but trust linked to ethnic identity. Political tensions in Türkiye made the patient feel cautious, illustrating the importance of cultural sensitivity beyond language.

Creating a therapeutic space that is both safe and effective requires clear boundaries and an emotionally differentiated presence grounded in genuine empathy. This demands ongoing self-reflection and personal work – essential professional responsibilities. Without them, therapy risks being compromised by unconscious bias or unresolved personal material (Kareem and Littlewood, 1992). Unlike many other professions, therapists cannot rely solely on technical skill while privately managing emotional turmoil. A fragmented or unsettled self may inadvertently cause harm. It is the therapist's self-awareness, emotional clarity, and honesty that give therapy its transformative power.

Conclusion

Authenticity and responsibility in therapy require therapists to acknowledge mistakes honestly and reflect on how their own and their patients' cultural backgrounds shape the therapeutic relationship. As globalisation reshapes societies and trauma crosses borders, therapy must adapt to the complexities of identity, culture, and social context. Therapists need to remain aware of how class, ethnicity, and political tensions influence patients' experiences and their trust in the therapeutic space.

Effective therapy calls for therapists to embrace vulnerability and cultural humility, creating a space where trust can flourish despite differences. In doing so, they support individual healing and foster inclusive, respectful therapeutic environments. This commitment to openness and cultural responsibility is essential for cultivating genuine connection and lasting change in an interconnected world.

References

Amnesty International, 2008a. *The Punishment of 'Honour' Killings: A Global Human Rights Crisis*. London: Amnesty International.

Amnesty International, 2008b. *'Honor' Crimes: A Global Perspective*. London: Amnesty International Publications.

Amnesty International, 2022. *Trapped in Limbo: Refugees and Family Reunification*. London: Amnesty International.

Amnesty International, 2023. *Ending Honour-Based Violence*. Available at https://www.amnesty.org/en/what-we-do/violence-against-women/honour-based-violence/ (accessed 3 August 2025).

Bhugra, D., 2004. *Cultural Psychiatry*. London: Routledge.

Bhugra, D. and Becker, M.A., 2005. 'Migration, Cultural Bereavement and Cultural Identity', *World Psychiatry*, 4(1), pp. 18–24.

Bonilla-Silva, E., 2003. *Racism without Racists: Color-Blind Racism and the Persistence of Racial Inequality in the United States*. Lanham, MD: Rowman & Littlefield.

British Psychological Society, 2014. *Diversity and Inclusion at the Heart of the BPS*. Leicester: British Psychological Society. Available at https://www.bps.org.uk/ (accessed 1 June 2025).

Bhui, K., Warfa, N., Edonya, P., McKenzie, K., and Bhugra, D., 2007. 'Cultural Competence in Mental Health Care: A Review of Model Evaluations', *BMC Health Services Research*, 7, p. 15. doi:doi:10.1186/1472-6963-7-1.

Council of Europe, 1950. *European Convention on Human Rights*. Strasbourg: Council of Europe.

Fernando, S., 2010. *Mental Health, Race and Culture*. 3rd edn. Basingstoke: Palgrave Macmillan. Available at https://www.bloomsbury.com/uk/mental-health-race-and-culture-9780230212718/ (accessed 22 August 2025).

Grinberg, L. and Grinberg, R., 1989. *Psychoanalytic Perspectives on Migration and Exile*. New Haven, CT: Yale University Press.

Gwynn, R.D., 2001. *Huguenot Heritage: The History and Contribution of the Huguenots in Britain*. London: Sussex Academic Press.

Herman, J.L., 1997. *Trauma and Recovery: The Aftermath of Violence – From Domestic Abuse to Political Terror*. New York: Basic Books.

Hollway, W. and Jefferson, T., 2013. *Doing Qualitative Research Differently: A Psychosocial Approach*. London: SAGE.

Human Rights Watch, 2023. *World Report 2023: Events of 2022*. Available at https://www.hrw.org/world-report/2023 (accessed 22 August 2025).

Independent Office for Police Conduct, 2024. *Race Discrimination Report*. Available at https://www.policeconduct.gov.uk/sites/default/files/documents/iopc-race-discrimination-report-Nov24.pdf (accessed 12 August 2025).

Kareem, J. and Littlewood, R. (eds), 1992. *Intercultural Therapy*. Oxford: Blackwell Scientific Publications.

Klein, M., 1946. 'Notes on Some Schizoid Mechanisms', *International Journal of Psycho-Analysis*, 27, pp. 99–110.

Klein, M., 1957. *Envy and Gratitude and Other Works 1946–1963*. London: Hogarth Press.

Kushner, T., 2003. *Remembering Refugees: Then and Now*. Manchester: Manchester University Press.

Lago, C., 2011. *The Handbook of Transcultural Counselling*. Maidenhead: McGraw-Hill Education.

Littlewood, R. and Lipsedge, M., 1997. *Aliens and Alienists: Ethnic Minorities and Psychiatry*. 3rd edn. London: Routledge.

Papadopoulos, R.K., 2002a. *Therapeutic Care for Refugees: No Place Like Home*. London: Karnac Books.

Papadopoulos, R.K., 2002b. 'Refugees, Home and Trauma', in R.K. Papadopoulos (ed.), *Therapeutic Care for Refugees: No Place Like Home*. London: Karnac Books, pp. 9–39.

Papadopoulos, R.K., 2007. 'Refugees, Trauma and Adversity-Activated Development', *European Journal of Psychotherapy & Counselling*, 9(3), pp. 301–312.

Patel, K. and Lord, A., 2000. 'Using Action Research to Study Ethnic Minority Sex Offenders', *Prison Service Journal*. Available at https://www.researchgate.net/publication/301636845_Lord_A_Patel_K_2000_Using_Action_Research_to_Study_Ethnic_Minority_Sex_Offenders_Prison_Service_Journal (accessed 22 August 2025).

Patel, N., Bennett, E., Dennis, M., Dosanjh, N., Mahtani, A., Miller, A., and Nadirshaw, Z., 2000. *Clinical Psychology, 'Race' and Culture: A Resource Pack for Trainers*. Leicester: British Psychological Society.

Refugee Council, 2023. *Annual Report and Accounts 2023/24*. Available at https://www.refugeecouncil.org.uk/documents/364/Annual_Report_Financial_Statements_2023-24.pdf (accessed 22 August 2025).

Thomas, L., 1992. 'Intercultural Therapy: Themes, Interpretations, and Practice', in J. Kareem and R. Littlewood (eds), *Intercultural Therapy*. Oxford: Blackwell Scientific Publications, pp. 133–145.

Tribe, R. and Morrissey, J. (eds), 2004. *Handbook of Professional and Ethical Practice for Psychologists, Counsellors and Psychotherapists*. Hove: Brunner-Routledge.

Tribe, R. and Thompson, K., 2008. *Working with Intercultural and Refugee Trauma: An Overview of Therapeutic Approaches*. London: Routledge.

Tribe, R. and Thompson, K. (eds), 2009a. *Working with Intercultural and Refugee Trauma: Theoretical and Practical Perspectives*. London: Routledge

Tribe, R. and Thompson, K., 2009b. *Working with Interpreters in Mental Health*. Hove: Routledge.

United Nations High Commissioner for Refugees (UNHCR), 2023. *Global Trends: Forced Displacement in 2023*. Geneva: UNHCR. Available at https://www.unhcr.org/globaltrends (accessed 22 August 2025).

Williams, D.R. and Mohammed, S.A., 2009. 'Discrimination and Racial Disparities in Health: Evidence and Needed Research', *Journal of Behavioral Medicine*, 32(1), pp. 20–47.

Williams, R. and Rasool, H., 2000. 'Mental Health Services for Black and Minority Ethnic Communities', in S. Fernando (ed.), *Mental Health in a Multi-Ethnic Society: A Multidisciplinary Handbook*. London: Routledge, pp. 157–176.

Chapter 7

Clinical Practice in Group Therapy

Turkish-Speaking Group Psychotherapy: A Three-Year Journey

The Turkish-speaking population in the United Kingdom is diverse, encompassing a broad spectrum of ethnic, religious, and regional identities. These include not only ethnic Turks but also Kurds, Turkish Cypriots, Armenians, Bulgarians, Arabs, and Roma – each shaped by their distinct cultural, linguistic, and historical experiences. While sharing a common language, these groups are often affected by deeply rooted tensions resulting from political conflict, social division, and collective trauma, both within Türkiye (formerly Turkey) and in the diaspora.

Religious diversity added further complexity, with participants identifying as Sunni Muslims, Jews, Alevis, or Christians, while some had no religious affiliation. Although these varied identities often remained unspoken, they strongly influenced group dynamics. Participants' migration histories differed as well: some arrived as refugees or asylum seekers, while others migrated for education, marriage, or economic reasons. Jewish participants shared distinct migration experiences shaped by historical and political contexts.

Initially, the idea of therapy was met with scepticism by the Turkish and Kurdish communities in London, largely because of longstanding mistrust of formal institutions – particularly among older generations and those who had experienced systemic marginalisation.

Culture plays a central role in shaping mental health, and therapeutic relationships in such diverse settings cannot be separated from the broader sociopolitical context. The beliefs, values, and lived experiences of each group member must be understood in relation to the historical and contemporary forces that have shaped them. Over time, therapeutic support gained recognition as a valuable resource for coping with the psychological impact of migration, displacement, family breakdown, and intergenerational conflict.

Çiğdem Kağıtçıbaşı's (2017) cultural psychological approach, which emphasises the self within its cultural and social framework, has deeply informed my work. Her research on individualism versus collectivism in Turkish culture provided insight into how differing orientations towards personal autonomy

DOI: 10.4324/9781003726012-8

and family-centred values influenced participants' engagement in therapy. Within the group I facilitated, cultural elements such as family dynamics – often rooted in collectivist traditions – and the significance of hierarchy were clearly reflected in the way in which participants related to one another and to the group process.

Group Composition and Structure

This therapy group ran for three years, beginning with an eight-month preparatory phase. During this period, I prioritised continuity of sessions while navigating the challenges and opportunities presented by collaboration with various institutions.

The group comprised women aged 21 to 68, each of whom had lived in the UK for three to 18 years. Although they shared a common language – Turkish – their cultural identities and migration histories were quite diverse. Participants included Turkish Cypriots, Kurds, women from Türkiye, an Armenian woman, and a Bulgarian immigrant fluent in Turkish.

These varied backgrounds encompassed a wide range of experiences, including trauma, displacement, intergenerational conflict, and social isolation. Such differences significantly influenced the group's dynamics. Attending to the intersections of culture, migration, and identity was vital in fostering a therapeutic space where participants felt seen, heard, and understood.

The First Meeting

In our initial session, Yasemin, the Armenian participant, hesitated before saying 'Dilek Hanım' (a respectful Turkish form of address similar to 'Ms Dilek'), 'please don't mention that I'm Armenian to the rest of the group.'

I explained the importance of sharing personal information – not only for her own therapeutic journey but also to support the group process. While I could not promise confidentiality, I offered a supportive stance, acknowledging that her eventual openness might benefit both herself and the group.

Initial Themes

During initial assessments, most women presented with physical symptoms – many of which were psychosomatic – including:

- Chest, head, and back pain;
- Stomach ulcers;
- Insomnia;
- Sexual dysfunction affecting relationships.

Other significant concerns emerged:

- Feelings of loss and grief;
- Insecurity and dependency (linked to dependent personality traits);
- Inability to leave abusive marriages, despite emotional, financial, and physical violence;
- Alcohol dependency, self-harm, and suicidal thoughts.

Breaking the Silence

At the first group session, the women gathered quietly, united by cautious curiosity. I welcomed them, and a prolonged silence followed – common in newly formed groups. They looked around uncertainly; I was the only familiar face from prior individual meetings.

Eventually, Kaderim, a survivor of domestic violence, broke the silence: 'What does this silence mean? Why aren't we talking? I feel awful.' Her courage shifted the dynamic. Smiling, 68-year-old Sacide remarked: 'I think a baby girl has just been born.'

In some parts of Türkiye – particularly where these women come from – the birth of a baby girl is traditionally not celebrated. In Turkish culture, the phrase 'a baby girl has been born' during a moment of silence serves as a ritual acknowledgement of the delicate, unspoken tension in the room – the quiet birth of new emotions or truths. Such silence often carries an undercurrent of sadness and unease.

The group appeared puzzled until Tülay responded, her voice tinged with both curiosity and frustration: 'When a baby girl is born, there's sadness in the room. People hold their breath … but why? Boys only stay with their mothers until they marry. Girls, though, remain loyal for life – yet no one seems to value that.'

Tülay's tears prompted deep reflection among the group on the roles of women within their families and the expectations rooted in feudal cultural traditions. 'I hope this group will be a place where we can grow new feelings and share fresh perspectives', another woman said.

Shared Struggles

This exchange opened the space for deeper stories to emerge. Accounts of familial neglect, societal pressure, and long-held grief over their perceived insignificance as daughters began to surface. Laughter, tears, and sorrow filled the room, fostering a raw and honest connection.

Kaderim shared her dislike of her name: 'Well, my parents almost named me Kadersiz [which means without destiny]. The registry clerk intervened and suggested something "better". I've never liked my name – maybe that's why I feel so unlucky!' Her self-deprecating humour struck a chord, encouraging others in the group to reflect on the meaning of their own names and the weight of familial expectations.

Unlike my English-speaking groups, in which trust often took weeks to build, this group shared deeply personal experiences almost immediately. Their shared cultural and linguistic background created an immediate sense of familiarity. It was not language alone that brought them together; rather, they were connected by collective experiences of displacement, loss, and survival.

Many had fled violence, endured economic hardship, or faced discrimination – both in their countries of origin and in the UK. Some had been forced into marriage; others had left families behind in search of safety. The burden of being both immigrants and women – often feeling metaphorically and literally homeless – profoundly shaped their identities. These shared histories enabled a deep emotional resonance that facilitated early disclosure.

However, the initial sharing often took the form of venting rather than reflection. Much of the anger was directed outward, with limited self-awareness. As their therapist, I adopted a patient stance, allowing the process to unfold. Gradually, they shifted from addressing me to engaging with one another, thereby fostering mutual understanding and solidarity.

Shared histories and collective experiences often nurture a sense of community and recognition among individuals facing similar adversity.

The Role of Names

By the third session, names had become powerful metaphors for the women's experiences. One participant remarked: 'My name is Gurbet [absent from home]. It's as if my mother knew – my whole life has been lived in exile.' Another said: 'Dilek hanım, did you plan this group on purpose? Look at us – each of us has a peculiar name. And then there's you, Dilek [wish or desire]. It's clear your mother wished for you!'

This observation marked a turning point. The group began not only to reflect on their shared experiences but also to consider my presence in their journey – deepening the therapeutic relationship further.

Early Challenges and Growth

At first, the women expressed frustration with my therapeutic stance, hoping for immediate answers. Gradually, they came to realise that no external force could resolve their pain. As they began to take ownership of their healing, they spoke more openly about feelings of rejection and womanhood – often competing to be heard.

Despite their cultural differences and individual traumas, common themes emerged: rejection, femininity, family violence, and belittlement. These shared experiences gradually fostered a sense of safety and unity within the group.

Some participants began to recognise the defensive behaviours of others, while still resisting awareness of their own. This interplay of vulnerability, resistance, and connection laid the foundation for the group's ongoing therapeutic journey.

Ayşe's Story within the Group

Ayşe, a 28-year-old mother of five children and four months pregnant, joined the group in a whirlwind of emotion – oscillating between joy and overwhelming anxiety. With another child on the way, she was under immense societal and familial pressure. 'Please pray for me. If I don't have a son, my marriage will surely end!' Her words revealed a deep fear shaped by cultural expectations. Having a son was seen as essential to securing her place within the family and tribe. This pressure was articulated in terms of thoughts of self-harm, underscoring the extent of her distress.

Her desperation exposed the emotional toll of these demands, intensified by her mother-in-law's threats and her husband's indifference. 'My mother-in-law told my husband she's looking for another wife who can give him a son. It's so unfair. I really don't want a girl. Her fate would be the same as mine.' Ayşe's words reflected not only her despair but also a resistance to passing on the oppression she had endured.

Sacide responded: 'You must listen to your inner world. What it's telling you matters – not what your mother-in-law or your husband says.' She recalled a well-known Turkish saying:

'Those who cannot hear their inner voice become deaf to the world.'

Ayşe's fear also echoed a saying often heard in traditional households: 'He who doesn't beat his daughter will later beat his knees in regret.' This deeply troubling proverb embodies the belief held by some Turkish families that daughters must be strictly controlled to prevent future shame. Ayşe, visibly distressed, shared: 'I already have too many daughters to control. I don't want another.'

Her words carried both exhaustion and sorrow – an internalised fear of perpetuating the same constraints placed upon her. Such messages weighed heavily not only on Ayşe, but on many women in the group, shaping their sense of self, motherhood, and the futures they imagined for their children.

Sacide, one of the older members of the group, responded calmly but firmly: 'Those sayings were made by men. Don't listen to them. We need to challenge these wrong ideas, not carry them forward.' Her voice brought a steady presence to the room – a reminder that cultural beliefs can be questioned, and that change often begins with such moments of courage and clarity.

A Space for Reflection

When Gülser asked, 'Why does your husband listen to his mother?' her question carried both frustration and disbelief, highlighting the complex power dynamics in Ayşe's marriage.

I reflected on Ayşe's emotions: 'It sounds like you're carrying a great deal of frustration and hurt about the dynamics in your relationship, particularly around family expectations and support. How are you feeling about everything right now?' Although I aimed to create space for Ayşe's feelings, the group rushed to offer advice – unintentionally overshadowing the emotional weight of her experience.

I offered another reflection: 'You deserve to feel important and valued in your relationship. Have you had a chance to talk to your husband about how this makes you feel?' Ayşe's voice trembled with emotion as she replied:

> If I have a son, I would worship him forever … But I'm afraid to find out the baby's gender. When I told the medical team that my other children were girls, the nurse didn't say anything. It's forbidden to reveal the gender. They say women tend to abort if it's a girl … I can't do that. It feels wrong. But I really want a boy.

Her words struck a deep chord. As tears streamed down her face, the room grew still. A shared sorrow began to emerge. What had initially been her pain soon became a moment of collective mourning.

Shared Stories and Emerging Bonds

As one woman shared her story, others nodded in quiet recognition. There is truth in the

Turkish saying: *Kadın kadının yurdudur* ('a woman is a home to another woman'). Within the group, this sense of shared refuge became tangible.

In the early sessions, the women spoke of being born as girls and of giving birth to daughters. Familiar remarks were exchanged:

- 'But girls are the best.'
- 'What's so great about boys?'
- 'My mum loved my brother more.'

These light-hearted observations gradually gave way to deeper reflections – on marriage, family roles, immigration, homelessness, financial hardship, and infidelity. Regret often surfaced alongside tears: 'I honestly don't want to have sex with him; I get no pleasure from it. I'm only doing it so he doesn't go to that Polish woman. I pretend to enjoy it. What else can I do? But I don't know how much longer I can stand this.'

Sacide cut through the emotion with a sharp remark: 'So, you're two-faced, are you?' To everyone's surprise, her bluntness sparked honesty rather than defensiveness: 'You're right, honestly.' Something shifted. The group drew closer, and a unique rhythm began to emerge. The women started comparing their struggles – who was on the highest dose of antidepressants, who had a GP, who listened best, and who had suffered the most.

Although these women were illiterate and from rural backgrounds, they were incredibly rich in folk wisdom. They often shared proverbs – some nurturing, others troubling – that I had never heard before. One woman reminded the group: *Birlikten kuvvet doğar* ('strength comes from unity'). Another added with a smile: *Kız evlat cennettir* ('a daughter is paradise'). And someone else whispered: *Kadın isterse dağları deler* ('if a woman wills it, she can pierce mountains').

Through their sayings, I gained a deeper understanding of how profoundly these internalised beliefs had shaped these women's lives, revealing both the strength and the burdens they carried. They were able not only to recall existing sayings but also to create new, positive ones – like artists shaping hope and resilience through words.

Challenges and Tensions

At times, their frustration was directed at me:

- 'Can you truly help us to overcome our depression?'
- 'Talking to the neighbours would be better! Nothing seems to change anyway!'

Some questioned whether group therapy was enough and suggested that one-to-one sessions might be better. I occasionally responded with provocative comments to help them to express anger – emotions many had silenced for most of their lives. Painful memories emerged:

- 'My mother tongue is Kurdish, so I only learned Turkish when I started school. The teacher used to hit us if we didn't speak Turkish.'
- 'My father never hugged me. Now my husband is the same. He doesn't love me. He's worse than my father – he hits me.'
- 'My mother used to call me a "stupid girl." And here I am, still stupid. Why am I even alive? Why am I still with this violent husband?' The woman's voice broke, and tears began to flow down her cheeks.

The women tried hard to understand why they continued to live in chaos and with men who did not value them. Many had internalised blame, carrying deep shame rooted in early neglect and violence. Their self-worth had been eroded over time, making it difficult to imagine that they might deserve better. I hoped that, through the group, they would begin to feel this pain rather than just speak it – to become emotionally aware of how these patterns had shaped their lives. Only then could they begin to break the cycle. Some tried to please me, while others expressed their pain more directly. At times, they appeared as passive children seeking approval; at others, as rebellious teenagers defying authority.

Progress through Connection

Gradually, the group began to feel safer with one another. My consistent approach – listening with patience and genuine interest – helped to build trust. Although the sessions often circled back to familiar themes, something began to shift:

- 'I don't know why, but I feel bad when I come to the group.'
- 'I get annoyed with all of you, but when I go home, I miss you.'
- 'I regret what I've said.'
- 'Do you see us as your family?'

The women started to reflect on the group itself, recognising family patterns, feelings of jealousy, longing, and connection. Some felt excluded from their families; others wrestled with what belonging truly meant.

That uneasy feeling some described – feeling bad upon arriving – was not resistance to the group, but a quiet realisation that the group was about *remembering*, not forgetting. While their friends and family members might have encouraged them to move on quickly, the group invited them to confront and process their past. They began to understand that true progress could not occur without first sorting through the pain and unresolved experiences they had long suppressed.

I was no longer merely the facilitator. They began to trust me – and each other. Rather than reacting, they tried to understand. My presence began to hold meaning, helping the group to manage its emotional life and make sense of their stories. Yet competition remained. Rivalries surfaced, echoing sibling dynamics. The women competed for attention and care, even as a sense of closeness grew.

Then came a moment of rupture and depth. Gülsüm spoke: 'My father was violent towards my mother. In turn, my mother would beat us out of anger towards him. I prayed for their deaths!' Her voice trembled: 'But when my mother died of cancer, I was devastated … I felt as if I had killed her.' Tears streamed down her face. 'My father is still alive, and he treats his current wife with the utmost care. My mother was the one who endured all the suffering.' Her words struck the group deeply. A heavy silence followed. Then Yasemin remarked: 'We've all suffered, haven't we? Maybe in different ways, but we have all carried the same weight.'

A Turning Point

Yasemin's comment lingered, drawing the group into a moment of shared recognition. It prompted reflection on the women's common experiences, shifting the focus from difference to shared struggle. This marked a turning point. Together, they began to confront internalised biases, prejudices, and identity tensions within the safe space they had co-created.

The cultural and religious tensions that had surfaced earlier gave way to more reflective dialogue. Yasemin's insight helped the group to recognise that, despite their different backgrounds, it was their shared pain and resilience that bound them. This understanding deepened their connection and mutual respect.

As I observed this shift, I sensed a defining moment in their therapeutic journey. The group was no longer merely a space in which to express pain or compete for attention – it was becoming a place where stories were challenged and supported. This change reflected the essence of group therapy: a movement from wanting to be heard towards learning to listen, empathise, and respond with care.

Their emotional oscillation – between idealisation and criticism – mirrored deep-rooted longings for validation and safety. It was as though the women were constantly testing the group, their reactions shaped by earlier experiences of abandonment and disappointment. In this dynamic, I became both a source of comfort and a potential threat – someone who might, like others before me, withdraw or disappoint.

This interplay of comfort and fear marked a significant phase in their therapeutic process. The aim was not to erase difference but to meet it with empathy. Each narrative added a thread to a shared tapestry of repair.

Sabiha's description of the group as a 'powerful organic medicine' aptly captured what was taking place. The group had become a living, breathing presence, shaped by each woman's contribution. Its rhythm was not imposed but emerged naturally, as they explored trust, connection, and vulnerability. Within this space, they encountered forms of care and validation long absent from their lives – yet a lingering fear remained: that it could all vanish.

This recurring anxiety around abandonment formed a major emotional barrier. Immersed in the group process, they vacillated between hope and fear. The guilt stirred by their doubts revealed the depth of their vulnerability. Even within the safety of the circle we had built, they remained alert to the risk of rejection.

This tension revealed a fundamental truth about therapy: healing requires the courage to be vulnerable and the resilience to endure discomfort. The women's struggle between closeness and distance reflected longstanding wounds. The task was to create a space in which they could stay with these tensions long enough to discover that what they feared most could also become a path to connection and healing.

Gradually, the intense projections, both idealising and critical, that were directed at me began to soften. This marked an important development in the group's therapeutic process. As trust deepened, the women began to explore the more layered aspects of their identities:

- Why had they come to the UK?
- Where were they from?
- What did it mean to be Alevi or Sunni?

Lale, who was Cypriot, stated in a tone that conveyed superiority: 'We Cypriot people are more civilised.' Tülay, a Kurdish Alevi, swiftly responded: 'No way! We Kurdish-Alevi people are much more progressive. You've become slaves to the English!'

Suddenly, the group's energy shifted. What had once been a contest over suffering became a form of rivalry over region, religion, and modernity. I listened closely, choosing not to intervene.

Then Yasemin, who had remained silent until that point, spoke up. Her voice broke the tension and spared me from stepping in: 'What is this discrimination? Isn't that why we came here in the first place?' She paused, then added: 'So what? I'm Armenian. Does that change anything? Are you going to kick me out of the group because of who I really am? What matters is being a good human being.'

Yasemin was attempting to bridge the gap. She wanted to name her Armenian identity and its impact, yet she was afraid. Her outburst, especially given her usual composure, surprised the group – and opened a new direction. They began to encourage her. 'It's great that you're expressing yourself just as you are,' I said.

Yasemin reflected on the impact of societal discrimination, explaining that she had asked me not to disclose her Armenian identity. Another group member, Sacide, responded with ironic curiosity about the secrets people might keep, despite those that she herself maintained. This exchange illustrates how societal pressures and internalised secrecy can shape group dynamics, highlighting the influence of wider social and cultural contexts on disclosure, identity, and trust within the group.

'I've kept myself hidden', Yasemin admitted, her tone soft with vulnerability. 'But after the dream I had last weekend, I decided to speak openly in the group and stop hiding.' She then shared her dream in vivid detail. The group, once quick to attack, now listened with curiosity and reflection. As they explored ethnicity, culture, language, and accent, they began to see that speaking the same language or coming from the same city did not imply that they were all the same.

They went on to share their reasons for seeking therapy, their struggles with individuality, and their complicated relationships with family and society. Topics such as racism, the roots of depression, and the pain of abuse emerged. In recognising each other's presence in the here and now, they experienced a shared emotional awakening.

By the 18th month of therapy, an unexpected development occurred. The group, once mired in conflict and comparison, began working together with more cohesion than I had anticipated. It was the final week of this phase.

Tülay said: 'Haven't all our problems come from religious issues?' As tears welled up, she described how her brother had been murdered in the Maraş massacre at the age of 11, and how she had hidden behind a herd of goats in a barn while the rest of her family was killed. The atmosphere shifted.

Competition and grievances dissolved. The group turned instead to listening, understanding, and offering thoughtful questions and support.

The women spoke of being belittled by their families and communities and, without realising it, how they had mirrored that pain within the group. A growing awareness, both individual and collective, began to emerge. As their understanding of relationships deepened, they started to question past behaviours. Reflecting on their histories, they looked to the future with greater hope, searching for meaning in the present.

The first session after the summer break began with Fasıla sharing: 'Being the same is easy. What matters is how we exist with our differences. I want to share something else, but I don't know if it's appropriate.' She expressed how much she had missed the group. Encouraged by Tülay, she spoke about a childhood experience of sexual abuse. The revelation shocked and saddened the group, leading to a long silence. Then 68-year-old Sacide also shared her own story: 'I thought I was alone in this. I'm so glad you spoke up, my dear.' That Sacide, a devout and reserved elder respected by the group, had disclosed such a personal memory significantly deepened the level of trust within the group. It felt as though a barrier had been lifted, allowing conversations around sexuality and abuse to begin.

In the weeks that followed, the group explored feelings of shame, guilt, anger, and anxiety – emotions they had long hidden behind the facade of family honour. They began to recognise how these burdens had slowly poisoned them from within. Together, they reflected on difficulties in setting boundaries, generational and cultural tensions in parenting, and the challenges of raising children in London. The group also confronted issues such as sadomasochistic relationship patterns and addiction.

They started identifying how everyday sayings had shaped their insecurities, such as:

- 'Feed the crow and it will peck out your eye.'
- 'Long hair, short mind.'

In response, they began creating their own proverbs – ones that honoured women.

What puzzled them was how much healing happened simply through relationships and conversation – without medication. 'I started therapy without believing in it. I didn't tell anyone. People around me think those who go to therapy are mad. But now I take pride in having the chance to benefit from this treatment – especially with all of you', one woman admitted.

Over a period of 20 months, the group became increasingly comfortable expressing admiration, jealousy, and competition. Initially, some participants had remarked, 'I don't even know what jealousy is.' By the end, they were learning not only to recognise and name their emotions, but to observe how these emotions manifested in their bodies.

The women often assumed that I wouldn't understand their troubles, yet they continued to open up. I only intervened when necessary. The group had begun to function independently, and my silence was sometimes mistaken for distance.

Ironically, the therapist (me) – regarded as someone who 'didn't know' – became a healing presence. The group came to view me as a deep, cool river into which they could pour frustrations they had never expressed to their mothers. This brought both warmth and intense emotional transference that was often negative, but ultimately healing.

Sacide reflected: 'Until this age, I've always been a mother, a mother-in-law, a grandmother. But for the first time, I want to cry like a child, like a teenager. I realise now how much I didn't know.' At the age of 68, Sacide's stories inspired women over 30 years younger than her. A modest woman, she eventually attended sessions without her headscarf and stopped wearing the black gloves she had worn all year. It was as if uncovering her hair and hands mirrored an opening of her heart. Once, she revealed:

> You know, when I was 16, I kissed a handsome boy in the neighbourhood for the first time. There was a nursing home nearby. I could never tell my stepmother about the harassment from an old man who worked there and who was also our neighbour. I wanted so much to share it with my mother … but I couldn't. She wouldn't have believed me.

Some 22 months later, Tülay left the group after deciding to move away from London. Her farewell was filled with sadness. It wasn't just about saying goodbye to her – the room now held memories of people and places they had never properly been able to part from. The emotional bond was strong. All the women brought gifts, such as amulets, scarves, and lacework, as if to say: 'Please don't forget us. Remember us.' These women, who had long felt forgotten and abandoned, were now finding ways to preserve connection.

Yet Kaderim expressed her feelings through anger: 'You're taking all my troubles with you. God knows what you'll do!' Tülay replied: 'But you're staying here carrying my stories. At least this group still exists for you. I have to leave … I wonder if I'll meet any Turkish people where I'm going? I've heard there aren't many Turks there. And racism is another issue.'

Kaderim, who easily showed anger but struggled to express sadness or affection, fell silent. Sacide gently intervened: 'Why don't you just say that you're going to miss her? We will all miss Tülay very much.' Kaderim remained silent for a moment, tears streaming down her face. Bowing her head, she quietly acknowledged Sacide's words.

Group therapy gave the women a deeper awareness of themselves, their families, and the broader society in which they lived. At first, they often spoke over each other, struggling to listen. But, over time, they learned not only to hear one another but also to listen to themselves. They began to take responsibility, to offer support, and to give honest yet respectful feedback.

Revisiting past traumas helped them to understand their present more clearly. They stopped blaming others and embraced their roles as mothers – with less illusion and more acceptance. Through open dialogue, they began to shift deeply ingrained behaviours, becoming more authentic both within and beyond the group. Trust, understanding, love, and respect became the foundation of their connection.

Initially, they had projected jealousy and anger onto those absent, particularly men and distant family members. But with courage and reflection, they reassessed these relationships. Silenced dimensions such as sexuality, femininity, longing, and beauty came into focus. Rather than resisting the group's conclusion, they approached separation as a chance to confront unfinished emotional landscapes in their lives.

This process led to profound internal shifts – not perfect or complete, but real and rooted in awareness.

The Final Session (Three Years Later)

At the final session, each woman arrived elegantly dressed – an unspoken tribute to the depth of their shared journey. The room held a quiet mix of anticipation and reflection. An empty chair was placed among them, symbolising not loss but the invisible bonds they had formed.

Sabire, who once relied on crutches both physically and emotionally, walked in without them.

'I don't need them anymore', she said – a quiet, powerful declaration. The group shared in her silent triumph.

Ayşe followed: 'And my mother-in-law? She hasn't changed – but she no longer controls my emotions. My husband and I had hoped for a boy again, but this time we welcomed another daughter – and we feel nothing but love for her.' Her words carried a calm acceptance and happiness that reflected the change within her.

Sacide, once fearful of loneliness, now embraced solitude:

> I always needed people around me to feel safe. Thoughts of death were never far. I used to think I was old and running out of time. But I see things differently now. I have a rich past and a good life ahead. I've learned to enjoy my own company. Being alone no longer frightens me – it feels peaceful, full of possibility.

Laughter filled the room as the women reflected on shared struggles and moments of growth. Old grief had lifted just enough to make space for something new – vast, grounded, and quietly transformative.

As the session neared its close, someone said, 'It feels like a funeral.' Another added, 'But not a sad one – a funeral for our old selves.' I nodded in agreement.

Freud once wrote that mourning allows emotional transformation – not just for lost loved ones, but for former versions of ourselves (Freud, 1917). A silence followed. Sabire smiled, a quiet, knowing gesture, and then spoke: 'Like ripe fruit falling from a tree – ready for the next stage.'

I recalled a verse from Rumi (2004): 'Don't grieve. Anything you lose comes round in another form.' The group hadn't merely let go. Each woman had gained insight, resilience, and a renewed capacity to move forward. Another line from Rumi resonated: 'Try not to resist the changes that come your way. Instead, embrace them. Let life flow through you' (Rumi, 2004).

Their transformation didn't mean that every wound had healed or that every question had been answered. But they now responded differently – to themselves, to others, and to life. They were no longer the same women who had entered the group three years earlier. They carried more awareness, stronger voices, and deeper bonds – with each other and within themselves.

They left the room lighter, not because everything had been resolved, but because they now held their questions differently. The empty chair no longer marked absence; rather, it represented the space they had made together, a testament to shared growth and resilience. Ayşe's joy in welcoming her daughter symbolised the kind of acceptance and love that the group had nurtured in each woman's life.

Reflective Observations

The group met once a week, yet the work often felt intense and proved meaningful for the women involved. Their journey revealed both pain and resilience, marked by gradual change and enduring strength. What began as a gathering of women carrying grief, trauma, and loneliness gradually developed into a supportive community. Out of isolation, they created a space in which vulnerability could be expressed and shared experience became a source of connection. This transformation, however, was not achieved without difficulty. Facilitating the group required engaging with intense emotions, including anger, experiences of domestic violence, and trauma-related distress, which were often challenging to witness and contain. Sustaining a reflective and supportive stance throughout this process demanded ongoing attention, self-awareness, and emotional effort. Despite these challenges, the steady development of trust and mutual support within the group illustrated the potential for healing and growth within a carefully held therapeutic space.

Their transformation unfolded over a period of three years. Through mutual care and respect, they cultivated a sense of belonging. Each woman reclaimed her agency while discovering strength in openness. This process revealed the resilience that emerges when personal struggles are explored within a group. The collective energy and recognition nurtured individual growth and contributed to a broader cultural shift. The group became more than a therapeutic setting; instead, it functioned as a communal holding environment where grief, longing, and hope could coexist.

This change can be understood through what Winnicott (1971) described as a 'transitional space' – a setting in which play, creativity, and transformation become possible. The group offered such a space, allowing the women to rework long-held narratives and try out new ways of being. In this environment, they softened their defensive edges and allowed something new to emerge between them.

During one session, Ayşe quietly shared the pain of silently suffering the loss of her mother. Her voice trembled, and tears welled up. 'For years, I thought I had to suffer alone', she said, 'but here, I finally felt safe enough to let it out.' Around the room, others offered gentle words or a supportive glance, and the silence turned into a shared moment of understanding. This openness encouraged others to share their experiences and strengthened their connections.

Over time, their interconnected stories wove a narrative of perseverance. Although their pain was deeply personal, it could be held and understood collectively. What had once been too painful to voice became speakable, and what had once isolated them began to bring them together. Ayşe's acceptance of and happiness in welcoming her daughter reflected how personal transformation could ripple outward, influencing family and community.

The group's conclusion was not a final farewell but an acknowledgment that their personal growth extended beyond the therapy room. They became living examples of the strength that emerges from connection and care. Their ritualised conclusion – dressing smartly, naming their grief, referencing metaphors of death and renewal, bringing flowers and fruit, reciting poetry, and creating moments of silence – reflected the importance of mourning not only as an individual process but as a communal one. One member placed an empty chair in the centre of the room, calling it 'the space we made together', while another read a verse by Rumi. Their ability to acknowledge the loss of the group while celebrating its impact showed a form of collective meaning-making, consistent with Freud's idea of mourning as emotional transformation (Freud, 1917).

Although the formal group sessions had come to an end, the seeds of change had been sown, ready to grow in new and unforeseen ways. Each woman carried a part of the collective strength they had built, leaving a lasting legacy of shared resilience, connection, and hope. And I realised, quietly, that they had taken a part of me with them too – their growth and courage had left an imprint on me as well.

Why This Group?

In my practice, I have been mindful of the ethical responsibility to provide culturally appropriate services and to ensure informed consent, particularly within communities facing significant language and trust barriers (UKCP,

2019). While working across different institutions, I became increasingly aware of the unmet need for Turkish-speaking therapy, especially among women. Many faced language-related difficulties that restricted their access to mental health services. This challenge is well documented by Kirmayer et al. (2011), who highlight how linguistic and cultural differences can obstruct effective care for migrant populations. Although community organisations recognised this gap, practical responses were limited.

The majority of these women could not afford private therapy. Often from working-class backgrounds, with little or no formal education, and having migrated from rural parts of Türkiye, their circumstances compounded the difficulty of accessing suitable psychological support (Berry, 1997; Al-Issa and Tousignant, 1997).

In response, I helped to initiate Turkish-speaking therapy groups, beginning with women-only spaces. As interest grew, mixed-gender groups followed, and later men's groups were introduced, facilitated by male therapists. My role was often behind the scenes, ensuring that the process ran smoothly – almost like 'working in the kitchen'. This evolving model continues to provide culturally sensitive spaces where Turkish-speaking individuals can engage in meaningful psychological support (Sue and Sue, 2013; Çakır and Güneri, 2011).

Patient Selection and Early Engagement: Criteria, Strategies, and Initial Steps

New approaches are often met with scepticism. At first, both patients and professionals questioned whether group therapy would be appropriate for Turkish-speaking communities. Nadkarni et al. (2015) note that such hesitation is common, rooted in cultural unfamiliarity and concerns about confidentiality. However, as trust developed, referrals increased – from doctors, psychiatrists, nurses, social workers, and community staff – reflecting a growing recognition of group therapy as a viable and culturally sensitive form of intervention.

Before joining a group, each patient attended at least two individual sessions – sometimes as many as 12. These sessions were used to explore expectations, assess suitability, and reduce reliance on one-to-one therapy, while gently encouraging early group engagement (Corey, 2016).

Many patients carried histories of abuse and deep feelings of shame, guilt, and fear. They struggled with self-blame and societal judgement, often voicing thoughts such as:

- 'It's not my fault.'
- 'I guess I'm the one to blame.'
- 'What's the point of getting better?'
- 'I would be better off dead.'

Some also saw themselves as the most self-sacrificing members of their families and communities. A number of women entered therapy hoping to change others rather than themselves. Despite their suffering, many defended their families – bound by duty, honour, and unspoken codes of loyalty (İnal-İnce and Kaya, 2017). Group therapy created a space in which to explore these conflicts and long-suppressed emotions.

Themes of shame and guilt, deeply shaped by patriarchal and feudal social structures, were particularly pronounced among Kurdish and Turkish patients (Oflaz et al., 2019). Many expressed uncertainties about the therapeutic process, asking questions such as:

- 'If it's going to help me, how will that happen?'
- 'What if someone I know shows up?'
- 'How long will it take for me to feel better?'

These questions reflect a wider hesitation about therapy among Turkish patients. Kağıtçıbaşı (2017) emphasises the cultural importance of interpersonal connection in the healing process, noting that traditional sayings and proverbs convey a collective understanding that recovery is nurtured through human relationships and mutual support. This cultural framework highlights the relevance of relational approaches in therapy, where social bonds are central to psychological wellbeing. Addressing such concerns early was essential. I explained that therapy could be difficult, but always made space for hope, which remained central to the work (Frankl, 1963).

To accommodate childcare needs, sessions were held from 11.00 a.m. to 12.30 p.m., coinciding with school hours. Each group began with clearly defined principles:

- Confidentiality and trust;
- Commitment to regular attendance;
- No contact outside the group.

Every patient received a written letter outlining therapy duration, confidentiality rules, attendance expectations, and the importance of avoiding outside contact with group members. This provided clarity and encouraged commitment, especially for those unfamiliar with therapy.

To bridge waiting periods, I introduced 'holding' sessions – brief calls, letters, or one-off meetings – drawing on Winnicott's concept of the 'holding environment' (Winnicott, 1960). These maintained emotional continuity and safety before the group sessions started. My approach remained exploratory and grounded, using prompts such as:

- 'I wonder if you mean to express that you feel anxious when discussing this topic.'
- 'Perhaps the reason for your behaviour is that you feel unheard in your current situation.'

This structured yet flexible approach supported patients' transition into therapy while fostering trust, engagement, and emotional containment (Yalom, 2005).

Professional and Personal Insights

Working with the Turkish-speaking community presented unique challenges. Being 'too close to home' often meant managing cultural insecurities. Some patients questioned the quality of care provided by a therapist from their own background, expressing personal beliefs such as 'I've heard that people like me get better help from therapists who are more "Western."' This reflected assumptions that Western approaches were superior and their own cultural values less valid (Sue and Sue, 2013).

These perceptions created complex dynamics. Some patients feared that a therapist from their own community might be too emotionally involved, while others questioned the trustworthiness of the process. Confidentiality was a major concern; indeed, patients frequently asked, 'What if people find out?' or 'How can I be sure this stays private?'

To address these worries, I engaged openly with patients' concerns. One Kurdish woman doubted my ability to understand her struggles. I acknowledged the complexity of her experience and affirmed my commitment to appreciating the cultural nuances she brought to the therapy process (Hays, 2008). This helped her to hold both anxiety and mistrust while remaining open to therapy. Together, we explored how her discomfort – particularly regarding my Turkish background – stemmed not only from personal insecurities but also from internalised racism influenced by wider Western narratives (Tummala-Narra, 2007).

I was transparent about ethical responsibilities and professional boundaries, reassuring patients that the therapy space was secure, their stories confidential, and that my role was to support and deepen their self-understanding – not to judge. Ethical practice in psychotherapy requires that therapists adhere to professional standards and codes (UKCP, 2019).

I encouraged reflection on how therapy could be rooted in patients' values. I often said, 'We will explore this together, building on your understanding of what healing means.' This enabled some patients to shift their perspectives, seeing my cultural insight not as a barrier but as a bridge. It created space for gentle questioning of long-held beliefs and the barriers to progress.

Fourteen Years in the Room: A Long-Term Group Therapy Journey with Black and Ethnic Minority Patients

Shared Experiences of Racism and Displacement

This group brought together individuals from diverse parts of the world, each carrying histories marked by displacement, war, and racism. Some had fled active war zones, while others bore intergenerational scars of slavery and colonialism. The group included individuals who were Black, of mixed-heritage, or White-presenting (perceived as White), originating from countries such as Angola, Afghanistan, Uganda, South Africa, Zaire (now the Democratic Republic of the Congo), Eritrea, Ghana, the West Indies, Chile, and Iran. Despite their differences, all members of the group were shaped by the psychological aftermath of racism, marginalisation, and institutional mistrust.

Their belief systems were equally varied, spanning Catholicism, Protestantism, Islam, Buddhism, atheism, and evolving or conflicted faith positions. The group also reflected a broad range of ages, life experiences, and gender identities. English was a second language for all of us – including myself – creating a shared vulnerability and, paradoxically, a sense of equality. Fluency became secondary to our collective commitment to communicate and be understood.

This cultural mosaic did not foster easy trust. What initially united the group was not connection, but caution – a mistrust of systems, professionals, and sometimes each other. We began not with assumptions but with listening. Trust was built slowly through the rhythm of showing up and speaking the truth. Within this fragile space, a transformative process gradually unfolded.

This section offers a glimpse into a long-term group therapy journey that progressed deliberately and patiently, like a slow steam locomotive. Over the years, as members departed and new ones joined, the group maintained continuity while evolving. It began with nine members – five men and four women – each participating for varying durations, from four to nine years. Remarkably, one man and two women remained for the full nine years.

Fourteen years of group therapy cannot be adequately captured in a single chapter, or even a book. Each session held its own story, shaped by the lives, traumas, and interactions of the participants. This section highlights selected moments that illustrate the group's progression and transformative experiences.

During this fourteen-year period, 23 individuals joined at different stages, bringing with them a wide range of cultural and socio-economic backgrounds. This particular cohort included participants from Uganda, Somalia, Eritrea, Sri Lanka, Pakistan, Latin America, Iran, Iraq, Morocco (raised in France), Denmark, and Türkiye, including Kurdish members. These encounters deepened my appreciation for London's vibrant multiculturalism, which continues to draw me in like a magnet.

The group's evolving composition brought both challenge and richness. Each member carried perspectives shaped by their homeland's history, traditions, and struggles. At times, these differences sparked tension but also created space for learning, empathy, and mutual growth. The group became a microcosm of the wider world, where misunderstandings, assumptions, and biases were not avoided but openly explored.

Such diversity highlighted the crucial role of cultural sensitivity in therapy. It became clear that every therapeutic encounter is filtered through a cultural lens. Differences in communication styles, social norms, and emotional expression sometimes caused confusion or frustration. For example, the reserved nature of some participants occasionally clashed with the more expressive styles of others. Yet these contrasts offered valuable opportunities for reflection and connection.

Guiding the group to understand and respect these differences was essential. Over time, members came to see difference not as a barrier but as a window into one another's worlds. Through sustained dialogue, the group gradually dismantled the walls that separated them, recognising the shared humanity that united them despite their diversity.

As the years passed, the group's cohesion deepened. What had once been a source of tension – cultural diversity – became one of its greatest strengths. Members learnt to support one another in increasingly meaningful ways. Through these encounters, the group evolved into a supportive community where trust, empathy, and shared experience transcended cultural boundaries.

The group met at Nafsiyat, a not-for-profit intercultural therapy centre based in London. The sessions brought together patients from Black and ethnically diverse backgrounds and developed into a rich and complex therapeutic space. Over time, themes of cultural identity, belonging, and resistance to change surfaced repeatedly.

Numerous turning points – some subtle, others more pronounced – revealed the deep impact of personal and cultural histories on group dynamics. These varied experiences brought both tension and strength into the room. This section explores the emotional stamina required in long-term group therapy, as well as the shifting patterns of trust, silence, confrontation, and solidarity that emerged.

I also reflect on the role of the group therapist, the evolving nature of leadership, and the personal demands of sustaining such a diverse group over more than a decade. My aim is not to present a fixed model but to offer a lived account of what it means to remain in the room – through conflict and repair, discomfort and growth.

Reasons for Focusing on This Group

As part of my group analytic psychotherapy training, I was required to establish two therapy groups – one lasting at least two years, the other one year – alongside individual therapy and clinical placements. After careful consideration, I chose to collaborate with the Nafsiyat Intercultural Therapy Centre.

The late Lennox Thomas, clinical director at Nafsiyat, supported me throughout this process. His trust and guidance were invaluable. Our professional relationship continued until his death in 2020. The first nine months were spent in consultation, during which I carefully selected patients for group therapy. These evening sessions, held from 6.00 p.m. to 7.30 p.m., proved both challenging and rewarding. Nafsiyat also allowed me to take on additional patients and to facilitate more groups beyond the minimum university requirements, which provided significant learning opportunities.

As a non-profit organisation, the centre faced financial constraints and maintained a long waiting list. I worked on a voluntary basis, receiving supervision in return. My previous roles – as a nurse at St Thomas's Hospital, a health development officer at the former Camden and Islington Health Authority, and a psychotherapist – enabled me to adapt effectively to this new setting.

There was a considerable unmet need for culturally informed group therapy, particularly for patients from Black and ethnic minority backgrounds. Many appeared to have been overlooked within mainstream services, which often lacked the resources or understanding to address their complex needs. Referrers frequently expressed a sense of helplessness in supporting these patients, who came from a wide range of cultural and linguistic backgrounds. Working in this context underscored the importance of developing group therapy models that were both accessible and responsive to cultural diversity.

Overcoming Culture Shock and Challenges at Nafsiyat

At the time, Nafsiyat operated from a modest three-storey house and lacked a spacious group room. I was also the centre's first trained group therapist, as its primary focus had previously been on individual and family therapy.

A Call to Action

My first supervisor outside the university, Lennox Thomas, was both realistic and encouraging. He advised:

> Being a student isn't easy. Nafsiyat isn't wealthy, but we can offer good supervision and a workspace. Be creative – don't expect too much in terms of resources. The room on the top floor is currently being used as storage. Clean it up and use it as your group room!

His pragmatic advice served as a call to action. I set to work and transformed the dusty storage space into a functional group room.

I was determined to create a structured, safe environment for my patients, many of whom had experienced trauma, war, or displacement. Every detail mattered: arranging chairs in a circle, positioning the clock, ensuring that tissues were to hand, and placing a doorbell within reach. With limited resources and minimal administrative support, I often welcomed patients at the door myself. This required not only therapeutic expertise but also cultural awareness. I made a point of researching my patients' countries of origin, learning about their histories, politics, and cultures. Yet it was their personal narratives that offered the deepest insights.

Patient Selection and Group Dynamics

Selecting patients for group therapy was both complex and rewarding. I conducted thorough evaluations to assess suitability. Referrals and self-applications brought in individuals with unique cultural and personal histories, each requiring careful consideration.

A particularly difficult dilemma arose when considering two particular potential members – one from Eritrea, the other from Ethiopia. At the time, the two nations were in active conflict, and both individuals had endured significant losses. Placing them in the same group risked intensifying mutual distrust and unresolved anger. After careful reflection and consultation, I decided to include the Eritrean patient in the group, while seeing the Ethiopian patient individually – prioritising emotional safety and the group's therapeutic potential.

The final group consisted of five men and four women. Through supervision, I learnt to balance patients' individual needs with group dynamics, allowing the therapeutic process to unfold gradually. Over time, I witnessed profound transformations – a testament to the power of connection and understanding in fostering emotional growth.

Starting the Group

The group was scheduled to begin in September, and I felt a surge of anticipation. It would follow an analytic model, meeting once a week for 90 minutes. This moment marked not only the culmination of my training and preparation but also a deep emotional investment. Immersing myself in each patient's story demanded sustained empathy – thinking and feeling alongside them. I often compared therapy groups to a theatre stage, where each member must authentically play their role. Balancing emotional involvement with the necessary therapeutic distance was a delicate and ongoing task.

Understanding the diverse cultural and geographical backgrounds of my patients – and integrating this knowledge into my emotional framework – required both theoretical insight and lived experience. My own twice-weekly group analysis and supervision sessions were invaluable during this period. As someone still relatively new to England, I was also managing my own sense of foreignness and the psychological challenges of being an immigrant. At the same time, I was both a patient in one therapy group and a trainee therapist in another.

Juggling these roles was demanding but deeply enriching. My natural curiosity and love of learning helped me to manage the workload. Despite the challenges, I felt a profound sense of fulfilment – as if this work were my true calling.

Themes and Group Development Process

At the outset, I chose not to disclose that the therapy would be long-term. Instead, I requested a commitment of at least three years, believing that this would allow sufficient time for meaningful therapeutic progress. To ease anxieties, we agreed not to mention that I was a trainee therapist, although I was already a qualified counsellor. Many members came from backgrounds where mental health services were either inaccessible or stigmatised, making trust and safety paramount (Bhugra and Becker, 2005; Tribe, 2002).

The group followed an analytical approach, encouraging members to explore their personalities, emotions, thoughts, and behaviours through their interactions. My role was to facilitate this process – supporting conflict resolution, fostering personal growth, and helping members to reach a point where they felt ready to leave, in line with the principles of analytic group therapy developed by S.H. Foulkes.

Creating a safe, respectful, and confidential environment was my main priority. Within this space, members were encouraged to confront both one another and their internal struggles, gradually gaining insight through shared exploration.

Issues Expressed During the Consultation Process

The consultation process revealed several key themes among participants:

- Mental health struggles: depression, lack of motivation, personality disorders, and distrust of oneself and others.
- Trauma and loss: childhood trauma, experiences of racism, abuse, loss of loved ones, fleeing war, involvement in armed conflict, and seeking refuge (Silove, 1999; Summerfield, 2001).
- Personal struggles and growth: difficulty forming relationships, introversion, love and celibacy, growing up without parents, and self-pity.

One patient recounted the aching loneliness of fleeing war, describing nights spent hidden in forests with nothing but fear for company. Another shared the long shadow of childhood abuse and how it quietly eroded trust in everyone around them. These stories did not merely provide background material; they shaped how the group moved and spoke, and how the participants guarded their fragile moments of openness.

Expectations During the Consultation Process

I requested a three-year commitment from the group, aligning with my training requirements, which included managing the same group for at least two years. This time frame aimed to minimise premature departures and the need to restart the process. Long-term consistency is often crucial when working with individuals from displaced or traumatised backgrounds, as the provision of stability and containment can be reparative in its own right (Kareem and Littlewood, 1992).

The Therapist's Feelings Before the First Session

Before the first session, I felt anxious, questioning how best to manage such a diverse group:

- How should I begin the first session?
- Would I be able to establish the therapeutic factors?
- How would traumatised individuals engage with analytic work?
- Would they attend regularly and remain in the room for the full 90 minutes?
- Would they feel comfortable in the converted therapy room?
- How would they assess one another – and me?

Despite these concerns, the patients arrived early, quietly waiting in the reception area. Ten minutes before the session was due to start, the receptionist directed them to the therapy room.

The First Session

As the session began, each participant took their place in the group:

- Horke (Angolan, atheist, male);
- Ortega (South African, Buddhist, male);
- Abdul (Ugandan, Muslim, male);
- Jose Stephan (Congolese, Protestant, male);
- Tamra (Eritrean, Catholic, male);
- Ana (West Indian, atheist, female);
- Maria (Iranian, Muslim, female, changed her name in London);
- Sabira (Ghanaian, female, former nun, conflicted over falling in love);
- Rita (Chilean, communist/Catholic, female).

The diversity of backgrounds and experiences created a unique energy in the room (Fernando, 2010). As I greeted each member warmly, I felt both excitement and apprehension. The men instinctively sat to my right, the women to my left – an unintentional division. I positioned myself where I could see the clock and easily reach the doorbell.

A tense silence settled over the room. The faint scrape of chairs and the distant hum of city life pressed in. Hoping to ease it, I remarked: 'It seems like it's hard to start talking.' The group agreed.

Tamra broke the silence with a firm voice that carried both resolve and weariness: 'We're here for at least three years.' A few nods followed, as if this commitment was both a shield and a chain. The weight of those words hung in the air, thick and undeniable.

After another pause, Sabira shifted in her seat, eyes downcast, and added softly, 'I think we're waiting for you to start first, out of respect.' Her hands fidgeted with a scarf, betraying her quiet tension.

Ortega then turned to me, a hint of complaint in his voice. 'Is that why you didn't answer me before Dilek arrived? I asked for your name, and you didn't respond.' His brow furrowed, and a flicker of impatience broke the fragile calm.

Sensing the tension, Horke quickly shifted the focus: 'My name is Horke. I'm from Angola.' His voice was steady, calm – an anchor amid the unease. The people in the room seemed to relax slightly as introductions were made, with the first small cracks appearing in the silence.

All members of the group came from diverse cultural backgrounds, naturally transforming the space into an intercultural setting. While the therapeutic process was rooted in the analytic model, it was shaped and deepened by the complexities arising from cultural differences. These dynamics brought both challenges and richness, highlighting the need for an approach capable of holding multiple perspectives within a shared analytic framework.

Initially I felt scared and worried. However, when I saw each member individually for assessment, I felt much more confident. Yet facing them all together felt different, and I wondered how I could manage everything.

Group Introductions and Emerging Themes

One by one, the group members introduced themselves, sharing their names, origins, and reasons for joining. A noticeable hesitation lingered, as if no one wanted to take up too much space.

ABDUL: 'I fled my country and sought asylum in England. I have a 16-year-old son, but I haven't seen him for five years. I wonder if he's okay, if he has enough to eat. Sometimes, I feel like I blame myself for everything I've lost. I couldn't be a good father to him.'

JOSE STEPHAN: 'Five years is a long time. It's strange that you're worried about his food.'

Abdul looked at him, visibly shocked, lowering his head to hide his tears.

THERAPIST (ME): 'Maybe you're all worried about starving in this group. But this isn't just about food – it's about your bond with your son and the feelings that come with that.'

HORKE: 'Hunger isn't just physical. Maybe we're also experiencing emotional hunger.'

ABDUL: 'Feeding this many people won't be easy,' he said with a faint smile, though there was a weight behind his words.

The group chuckled softly, sensing the deeper meaning.

TAMRA: 'It's true. We all carry so much with us – burdens we can't share.'
ORTEGA: 'Yes, and sometimes it feels like no matter how much we try to nourish ourselves emotionally, it's never enough.'

The use of metaphor marked a turning point. The group began to express emotions symbolically – not consciously, but instinctively. These comments signalled the start of a deeper connection, as members articulated their internal worlds. Despite their diverse backgrounds, they were beginning to form the bonds necessary for healing (Akhtar, 1999; Yalom and Leszcz, 2020).

The Therapist's Reflections

At that moment, I realised how vital it was for this group to find a 'soul language' – a shared way to voice pain and hope beyond words. The metaphor of hunger captured not only their personal losses but also a collective yearning for belonging and understanding. As a therapist, I felt both humbled and hopeful, knowing that these early moments of symbolic expression could open pathways to profound emotional growth.

Group Dynamics and Emotional States in the First Session

As discussions unfolded, a sense of connection began to emerge.

ABDUL: 'I think it means being there for one another, listening, and understanding. Like a shared meal, we need to feel connected.'
TAMRA: 'We've all lost something – our homes, our families. Maybe that's why it's so hard for us to connect with each other.'

This shared sense of loss fostered empathy, transforming initial apprehension into collective understanding.

JOSE STEPHAN: 'You're not alone in feeling that way. Many of us carry guilt for those we left behind.'
TAMRA: 'It's hard to reconcile those feelings. We all wanted to stay, but circumstances forced us to leave.'
ANA: 'Leaving home was the hardest decision. I still question if I did the right thing.'

The room grew quieter as vulnerability blossomed into mutual support. I recognised that it was essential for the group to express these emotions as the first step towards seeing their experiences not as isolated struggles but as interconnected parts of a shared journey of loss and resilience (Papadopoulos, 2002; Tribe and Thompson, 2009).

Emotional Reactions and Early Group Dynamics

During the first session, the patients' emotional states varied significantly:

- Horke appeared anxious.
- Jose Stephan appeared withdrawn.
- Sabira was fearful.
- Ortega seemed curious.
- Abdul carried a heavy sense of guilt.
- Ana and Rita adopted a rebellious stance.
- Tamra and Maria showed signs of depression.

Their openness was both a sign of trust and a challenge: would they maintain this vulnerability in future sessions? I had seen individuals withdraw after early emotional exposure. Abdul constantly shook his legs, avoiding eye contact, while Ortega sat upright, bracing himself. These contrasting reactions reflected the complexities of their experiences. As their therapist, I felt a deep responsibility to create a safe space in which they could process these emotions.

Testing and Trust

In the early weeks, the group tested its boundaries with questions such as:

- What kind of group is this?
- Can we trust one another?
- Will our experiences remain confidential?
- Will our depression improve?
- Should we continue or discontinue medication?

Depression and repressed anger were central themes during this crucial phase of trust-building, as members managed their fears and uncertainties (Yalom, 2005). I observed and said, 'At least you've found common ground in your shared struggles. How might you work together to overcome these challenges?'

Discussions about coping strategies – such as Buddhism, Islam, prayer, gratitude, and exercise – led the group to explore deeper aspects of identity. Conversations around racial identity also emerged, especially relating to experiences of being Black and facing racial profiling (Crenshaw, 1989).

Further Reflections

As the session progressed, I quietly observed subtle shifts in group dynamics: hesitation gradually giving way to tentative connection. I felt a mixture of hope and apprehension. Could I maintain a delicate balance between empathy and professional distance? How could I support such diverse emotional expressions without becoming overwhelmed? Managing my own immigrant experience alongside theirs added another layer of complexity. Although I appeared strong and confident, I wasn't: inside, I felt unsure of myself. Yet I reminded myself that vulnerability was the gateway to healing – for them and for me.

Group Dynamics and Identity Exploration

The group's focus turned to identity when a member asked, 'Is it really easy to be mixed-race?' This question sparked dialogue about race, identity, and marginalisation. Muslim members shared challenges related to their faith, while Horke expressed frustration: 'Being Black and being Muslim are not the same! Being mixed-race is easy! As far as I'm concerned, you're White!' His anger ignited a powerful discussion about systemic injustice. Horke recounted a distressing encounter with the police that highlighted intersections of race, faith, and discrimination: 'On my way here, they stopped me at Finsbury Park. They set their dogs on me and searched me down to my underwear. They thought I was involved with the IRA … Luckily, I had the letter Dilek sent me.'

This moment fostered raw reflection on race and discrimination, creating a vulnerable space. However, tensions rose when Maria, frustrated, made a comment about Türkiye: 'Don't talk about Türkiye as if you know everything! You're just another fanatic! I changed my name because of people like you!'

As emotional intensity increased, I intervened, encouraging the group to reflect on personal emotions rather than conflict. I reminded them that the goal was not to convince each other but to understand how these topics affected their internal experiences: 'Let's take a step back. What do we feel when we hear comments about our identities? How do those comments resonate with our personal experiences?'

The atmosphere shifted as the group explored the complexities of identity and belonging, revealing both shared and individual struggles. Discussions about race and skin tone, especially among the Black members of the group, stirred strong emotions. As political discourse began to serve as a defensive shield for some participants, I reminded the group: 'This is not a platform for political propaganda. It is a space to explore the emotional impact of your struggles.'

Managing Conflict

Abdul's frustration boiled over. 'Empty words!' he snapped, his voice rising with fury. 'You talk as if politics can be separated from life! Can anyone here escape it? Isn't it politics that forced us into this room in the first place?' His anger was directed squarely at me. I knew a direct response was necessary. 'You're absolutely right', I responded calmly. 'Politics has profoundly shaped your journey, and it's valid to feel its deep connection to your pain. But here, we're creating a space to explore how these emotions live in your body, your heart, and your relationships.'

The group was frozen for a moment. Abdul stared at me, his chest still heaving. The sharpness in his eyes showed his anger had not fully settled, yet my calm tone seemed to slow his outburst. He lowered his voice, although the tension lingered in the room. I paused, allowing time for reflection. 'How does this frustration feel for you right now?' I asked gently, encouraging connection to present emotions. My intention was to shift the group from blame to personal exploration. 'Rather than blaming each other', I continued, 'let's consider how our experiences have shaped us. How have they made us who we are today?'

The group fell silent, absorbing the invitation. Abdul shifted in his seat, his gaze softening slightly. 'I'm not trying to defend myself,' he said quietly. 'I just feel torn apart by so many things. I don't even know who I am anymore. It's all political, all the time. Without politics, I feel empty – like I've lost something to hold onto.' His vulnerability opened the group to a moment of shared reflection.

However, tensions returned when Abdul repeatedly questioned Maria about her Muslim name – a name she had changed and chosen not to discuss. Despite clear boundaries, he persisted in raising the issue, session after session. Horke intervened firmly but compassionately: 'Do you understand the impact of what you're asking? Maria doesn't want to share her Muslim name. She came here to find belonging, like the rest of us. By questioning her name and faith, you're pushing her away.'

A heavy silence followed. Sensing the group's need for grounding, I asked: 'What makes a space feel truly safe for each of you? How can we ensure no one feels judged or excluded here?' The question hung in the air. Abdul shifted uneasily. 'I just thought ... she needed to be called out', he said defensively. 'We're supposed to be honest with each other, right?'

I saw an opportunity for deeper exploration. Rita spoke, steadily but gently: 'Yes, but honesty shouldn't come at the expense of someone's identity. We're all carrying burdens. Let's build each other up, not tear each other down.' The group sat in silence, Rita's words settling over them. 'How can we balance honesty and respect in this space?' I asked.

Later, tensions rose again when Abdul accused Maria of not being a good Muslim. His sharp words rippled through the group, and Maria flushed with hurt. Horke responded: 'Abdul, that's not for you to decide. We're not here to judge each other's faith or actions. Our purpose is to support one another as we manage our struggles.' Abdul replied: 'I just want her to be honest, to embrace her faith fully.' Rita added: 'Faith is personal. It's not about how someone else thinks it should look. It's about respecting each other's journey, even when we don't fully understand it.'

The room fell quiet. Horke glanced at me, signalling trust. I stepped in: 'In this space, no one should feel judged for who they are. Let's reflect on how we can build a supportive environment where everyone feels heard and respected.' There was a softening in the group – a small but meaningful shift. Yet the tension remained.

In a subsequent session, the conflict escalated again. Abdul again accused Maria of not being a good Muslim, prompting her to stand up and leave the room, visibly shaken. A stunned silence followed. Horke confronted Abdul: 'Do you realise what you've done? Maria left because of your comments. She came seeking support, not judgement.' Abdul looked down, fidgeting. 'I didn't mean to push her away. I thought I was helping her reconnect with her faith.' Horke replied: 'It's not about faith. It's about respect and understanding. We all come from different experiences and beliefs. This group is meant to be a safe space, not a battleground.'

Rita said: 'We need to focus on lifting each other up. We're all carrying traumas. Instead of criticising, we should ask how we can offer support.' The room grew still. I guided them back to empathy and growth: 'Let's take a step back. How has Maria's absence affected you – individually and as a group?' Horke shared her helplessness; Abdul admitted that his words had caused pain. I observed: 'It's important to share feelings, but equally it's crucial to listen without judgement. That's how we build trust.' The discussion deepened. Although tensions remained, the group engaged with greater awareness, laying a foundation for further understanding. I acknowledged the possibility that some might be angry with me for allowing Maria to leave and invited them to reflect on their feelings towards me and my role. I wanted to bring unspoken anger into the open. But my words seemed to drift past them. No one responded. As I sat with these reflections, I realised how unresolved tensions could undermine the group's cohesion. Abdul's admission marked a turning point, yet it exposed the fragility of the safe space we had worked so hard to cultivate. The group sat in silence, absorbing the weight of these reflections. Abdul, still frustrated, initially resisted but eventually acknowledged the difficulty of facing the consequences of his impulsive outbursts.

Maria didn't return the following week. I wrote her a thoughtful letter, expressing how much she was missed and emphasising the importance of her presence in our shared journey. She returned one week later, quiet and withdrawn, and avoided making eye contact with Abdul.

Abdul broke the tense silence with a sincere apology, acknowledging the impact of his actions and taking full responsibility. Then, turning inward, he shared his own struggles – revealing that his wife had left him and taken their son, possibly due to his behaviour. This revelation surprised the group, who had assumed that the separation was due to his asylum-seeking journey.

Inspired by Abdul's honesty, Maria apologised to the group. She admitted that leaving abruptly had been unhelpful for everyone and shared how difficult she found it to face challenging situations. She also expressed how much she had missed the group during her absence. The session became a profound moment of mutual understanding and reconciliation. Vulnerability paved the way for connection, allowing the group to move closer to the safe, supportive environment they all sought. Maria then shared that her mother was an anxious, almost childlike woman, and she feared that she was becoming like her. She also revealed that her name, Amina, was her grandmother's. She despised her grandmother, who had treated her mother cruelly, and out of fear she had changed her own name.

After these confessions, the group felt a sense of relief. A new atmosphere of closeness and openness began to emerge. The group, which had long been in emotional denial, was now in a very different place. Horke would sometimes cry silently while someone else was speaking, although he couldn't articulate why. Maria supported him, while Rita gently asked: 'Why are you crying?' Horke replied, 'I don't know. Oh, if only I knew. For some reason, every time I come to this group, I feel like crying.' 'Maybe you miss your family, the ones you've left behind', Rita suggested, her insight cutting to the core.

The group began to share their experiences: racism, homelessness, poverty, the pain of being a foreigner, the trauma of immigration, the heartbreak of separation from children, harassment, and the lasting impact of torture. Many expressed their suffering physically, through gestures or visible marks, as a way of seeking recognition and understanding, believing that demonstrating their experiences might make them more credible to the authorities or the UK Home Office.

During the first six months, the group scrutinised me intensely – questioning my identity, profession, methods, and personality. As the key authority figure, I was under constant observation. Over time, this authoritative role softened, although moments of regression occasionally emerged during their struggles. At times, the participants idealised me; at others, they criticised me.

Through consistent effort, however, the group dynamics gradually began to shift. Members started forming meaningful connections with one another. Gradually, I stepped back, allowing these connections to flourish – a transformation noticed and appreciated by my classmates and supervisors. Trust, which had initially been a significant challenge, eventually developed; group members were ultimately able to openly express and share their trust.

One day, during a supervision session, someone asked: 'Dilek, how do you cope with such a difficult group and all these emotions? How do you manage?' I had to admit that I wasn't managing well. In fact, I was struggling. In that moment, I realised how overwhelming it was to carry so much emotional weight. Yet Lennox Thomas, the clinical director at the time, always trusted me and listened when I felt overwhelmed. Professor Roland Littlewood, the institution's psychiatrist and adviser to the centre – who remains in contact with Nafsiyat – was also incredibly supportive.

Intense group work can evoke profound emotional strain in therapists, particularly when working with patients whose experiences resonate deeply with their own unresolved wounds. In such moments, doubts about one's capacity to cope may arise, sometimes accompanied by thoughts of seeking medical solutions for what is essentially emotional and relational labour. Clinical supervision and ongoing personal analysis play a crucial role in these situations, offering containment, perspective, and reassurance. Over time, repeated exposure to emotional intensity, when held within a supportive supervisory framework, strengthens the therapist's emotional resilience. The capacity to remain present, calm, and reflective in the group often develops alongside an internal professional stance shaped by earlier clinical training, allowing therapists to tolerate discomfort while offering carefully timed interventions that may initially unsettle but ultimately support therapeutic change.

During those intense sessions, I often sat calmly, listening intently – even when I was deeply affected. At times, I felt like a theatre actress: performing through pain, continuing the role despite personal loss. Yet the calm I had developed during my nursing career, even if only on the surface, served me well. In the most difficult moments, I pictured myself as an operating room nurse – stitching up the group's emotional wounds and bandaging their pain. Sometimes, my words acted like a salve – causing discomfort, but also offering healing.

In supervisory and experiential group settings, expressions of grief and emotional openness can be received and interpreted differently across cultural contexts. Openly sharing grief may be experienced as necessary and relieving for some, while in other contexts it can raise concerns about emotional containment or coping. Such moments often reveal unspoken cultural assumptions about resilience, vulnerability, and appropriate emotional expression. These differences can influence how group members respond to loss, including feelings of discomfort, guilt, or self-questioning, and highlight the importance of cultural sensitivity when working with grief in group and supervisory settings.

This became especially relevant in the group's dynamics. During one session, for instance, Horke shared his harrowing escape from Angola with raw honesty. As he described struggling to breathe in the airless crate of a truck, his tears flowed freely, and he gasped as though reliving the moment. The group's silence was palpable, filled with empathy. Horke's vulnerability inspired the others to open up, leading to a wave of shared stories.

However, at times these exchanges became competitive, with each member trying to assert the importance of their own experience. Their bickering often resembled that of children and tested my patience.

Such dynamics were not uncommon. In another session, Sabira spoke of her time in a monastery and her background as a nurse. Jose Stephan, who frequently complained of back and chest pain, began consulting Sabira about his symptoms – turning the group room into a makeshift clinic. Ana, known for her rebellious spirit, interjected: 'Enough already! Are we going to discuss this here? Why don't you want to understand what's being said? Sabira is trying to share something, and you're fixated on nursing!' Ana's comment prompted the group to reflect on their tendency to create distractions, their difficulty in truly listening, and their failure to hear one another. These patterns occasionally led to hurtful arguments, especially when I remained silent.

Interestingly, Ana and Horke, both staunch atheists, began to show a shift in perspective as their inner conflicts unfolded. One day, Horke admitted: 'Maybe we should believe. I envy those who have faith.' Ana responded, 'But what should I believe in?' Maria added, 'I believe in this group. I've been to the mosque and the church. This group room is my place of worship, and you are my congregation.'

These evolving dynamics highlighted the group's journey towards mutual understanding, revealing both the power and challenge of connecting across diverse beliefs and backgrounds.

'Here, I don't feel the need to hide myself. This is my sanctuary. Others go to the priest to confess; my confessions happen here', Maria said. She paused, then added, 'But when I go to a priest, he listens but doesn't push me. This group is different – it challenges me. It makes me reflect on myself, and I change. That difference matters.'

Tamra agreed with Maria and added, 'But there's a difference. In the mosque or church, believers don't question their faith. In this group, our task is to question and analyse. Sometimes that means letting go of certain beliefs and behaviours.'

Deepening Engagement and Emotional Openings

Through such conversations, I gained a more nuanced understanding of how the group was engaging with the therapeutic process. Positive feelings began to emerge, gradually breaking through their initial defensiveness. Ana, in particular, started to open up about her childhood. She described her mother as emotionally overwhelming and constantly tearful, noting how exhausting it was to care for her own mother while silently yearning for care and understanding herself.

In a rare moment of vulnerability, Ana reflected on my presence in the group:

> Dilek is not like my mother. She doesn't cry; she's very strong! My childhood was filled with my mother's laments. She would sit by the window and cry. Why, I wonder? Maybe she was unhappy with my father. Who knows? But Dilek doesn't cry – isn't that nice?

Laughter rippled through the group. 'Well, she's a therapist. Who knows, she might have her own problems … But she's not going to be like us!' another member added, prompting more laughter. These light-hearted exchanges offered a rare moment of connection, as the group found a way to bond through humour amid pain.

Group Dynamics and Personal Transformations

Despite occasional tensions, the group made significant progress over time. Moments of vulnerability – such as Horke's account of his escape – had a ripple effect. His raw honesty left a lasting impression. The group's attentive silence, filled with empathy, encouraged others to share more deeply, enriching our collective understanding.

A Shift in Structure

After two years, I announced a major change: the group would shift to an open-ended format. Initial anxiety soon gave way to relief. The previous three-year limit had created a sense of pressure, with many fearing that they wouldn't be able to resolve their issues in time. Once the time constraint was lifted, some found the courage to make significant life changes.

New Perspectives, Shared Histories

Over the following five years, the group developed greater self-awareness. Three members left, and two newcomers brought fresh perspectives. One was a young woman who had fled Albania, and spoke of the impact of religious repression under communism:

> I come from a Muslim family. Religion was forbidden, but we prayed in secret. I used to love fasting as a child, although we had to hide it. If the inspectors found out, we'd be punished. We pretended to eat, hiding pumpkin seeds and walnut shells in our pockets. Once, they forced my brother to eat bread in front of them. He cried so much. I'll never forget that.

She paused. 'Look at me now. Everything is free here. You can fast or not. But I don't want to fast anymore ... Am I losing my beliefs?' Her trembling voice revealed deep guilt and confusion, prompting collective introspection.

Another member, a former communist who had fled a right-wing regime, shared his conflicted feelings:

> In my country, people were imprisoned for making a single statement. Oppression only fuels desire. When I arrived here and saw men at Victoria Station selling communist magazines, I couldn't believe it. I spent months in prison for one statement. Now, I don't know what's right or wrong. Sometimes, I wish I hadn't come here.

These vivid stories invited the group to reflect more deeply on their personal and collective histories. As experiences were shared, new layers of meaning gradually unfolded.

Departures and Emotional Crossroads

As members came and went, those who remained in the group often wrestled with feelings of abandonment. Each departure stirred a complex mix of pride, sadness, and uncertainty. The question, 'Should I go, or should I stay?' became a recurring theme. At times, frustrations were projected onto me as the group's therapist. Rita's departure, in particular, was emotionally charged. She confided:

> When I got out of prison, I felt strange emotions – and I still do. I carry a deep guilt for leaving my comrades behind, and now, as I think about leaving this group, I feel something similar. I don't know whether to stay or go, but I've been offered a great job. I feel good. I've shared more here than with my family or closest friends. I want to leave all this here and move forward. I'll definitely write. Dilek, will you share my letters with the others?

Her absence left a noticeable void. In the weeks that followed, the remaining group members spoke of her with a mixture of admiration and envy. 'She's reached a turning point in her life. What about us?' they asked, giving voice to their own uncertainties.

Vignette: Building Trust

One afternoon, during a particularly intense session at Nafsiyat, a letter from Rita was handed to me. I mentioned it to the group, and Maria asked if she could read it aloud. She sat quietly, clutching a worn notebook, hesitating for a moment before beginning. As she read, the room fell silent – Rita's words unfolding as a blend of hope, fear, and determination. Tears welled in some eyes, while others nodded slowly, as if hearing their own struggles echoed back. In that moment, the group felt connected – not just by shared pain, but by shared resilience. The question of staying or leaving seemed less daunting, transformed into a journey they would face together.

In another session, during a cold winter afternoon in the dimly lit room, I noticed that Joseph's nose was bleeding, although he seemed unaware of it. This highlighted the connection between emotional distress and physical reactions. I had to draw on my nursing skills in that moment: calmly pointing out the bleeding and helping him to manage it. The immediate panic in the group subsided, and my composed approach provided the participants with a sense of safety. His subsequent tears, revealing grief over his son in Eritrea, suggested that the bleeding had been linked to suppressed emotion. A fellow group member's comment – 'Now your tears are coming; this is why your nose bleed stopped' – underscored how emotional release can relieve physical tension. This moment also reflected the growing trust within the group, as participants witnessed vulnerability, care, and mutual support in action.

Eighth Year of the Group

In its eighth year, the group's dynamics shifted with the arrival of new members. Longstanding members, feeling territorial, often challenged the newcomers, creating familial tensions. I found myself taking on a maternal role, trying to balance their competing needs without fully satisfying anyone. Some original members felt sidelined, believing that my attention had shifted away from them. I encouraged exploration of these feelings, inviting reflection on how exclusion and resentment might be shaping their personal journeys and the group's cohesion.

During this time, Amina, a young Somali woman, joined the group and shared a painful secret: she was a lesbian, and was hiding this fact from her family and community out of fear. 'If they find out, they'll reject me – or even kill me', she said, trembling. Another member, whose father was Somali and their mother Portuguese, resonated with her struggle and offered support. By now, the group had matured into a space where members listened deeply, questioned without judgement, and shared emotional insights while honouring differences.

Ninth Year of the Group

In the ninth year, Ortega, a practising Buddhist, announced his plan to spend six months in silence at a monastery. 'I will live without speaking', he said, sparking a discussion about the role of silence in personal growth. He explained that silence was not merely the absence of words but a path to confront his inner world. Through this, he sought clarity, healing, and deeper self-awareness. Amina responded with confusion: 'That's strange. In therapy, we need to talk. Why would you go to a monastery where you can't speak?' Sonya, a newer member, challenged Ortega's need for reassurance: 'You're just like my ex-boyfriend – always needing guarantees. Life is full of risks. Make a decision and stick with it. If you can't, don't leave.'

Her words triggered strong reactions, with some criticising her for being harsh. Surprisingly, Ortega defended her, acknowledging the validity of her statements. He shared his fears about leaving, his dependency on the group, and his uncertainty about the monastery. Saying goodbye was emotional. In his final sessions, he spoke at length, as if preparing himself for the silence ahead. When he expressed his gratitude – blending humour with poetry – the group laughed through tears, offering a heartfelt farewell.

The Group's Journey Over the Years

The group's journey was marked by significant milestones:

1 Tamra's marriage: Tamra married his Ethiopian partner, symbolising the strength of cross-cultural connections.

2 Horke's move to a new country: After completing computer training, Horke married his Irish partner and moved to Ireland, illustrating how therapy can support personal growth.
3 Rita's integration: Rita reconciled her dual identity, started a family with a younger Colombian partner, and divided her time between Chile and London.
4 Abdul's resilience: Reunited with his family through the Red Cross, Abdul was struggling with an HIV diagnosis. Through therapy, he regained his resilience and began speaking openly in the group.
5 Sabire's transition and motherhood: Sabire embraced motherhood while living with her Greek partner. Her pregnancy, initially met with mixed reactions, soon became a shared experience within the group. When she returned with her baby, the child's presence symbolised continuity and intergenerational connection, prompting deep reflections on childhood and strengthening the group's emotional bonds.
6 Ana and Maria's journeys: Inspired by their experiences in the group, Ana and Maria pursued careers in psychology and art therapy. They later returned to share their progress, thereby contributing to the group's evolving narrative.
7 Elias's personal growth and inspiration: Elias found strength in the group's support, channelling his experiences into art that reflected hope and healing. Although he wasn't completely healed, he managed his struggles better and became a source of calm and encouragement, inspiring others as he prepared to move forward with renewed confidence.
8 Leyla's new path: Leyla discovered a passion for physical fitness during her time in the group. She trained as a sports instructor, using movement and exercise to support both her own wellbeing and that of others. Leyla's energy and dedication brought a fresh dynamic to the group, showing how physical health can complement emotional healing.

A total of 23 patients benefited from the group therapy, and each eventually moved on to new chapters in their lives. Over a period of fourteen years, the group experienced remarkable personal and collective growth.

As the group's facilitator, I too evolved: I completed my studies, graduated, and later joined Nafsiyat as a professional therapist. This journey was one of mutual transformation, where members supported one another, contributed to the wider community, and forged lasting connections.

Institutional Impact on Marginalised Communities

In group therapy settings, sudden institutional changes can be experienced by participants as a loss of continuity and stability. This is particularly significant when working with individuals from diverse ethnic and cultural backgrounds, highlighting the importance of trust and connection within the group.

While practical and financial considerations may shape such changes, their impact on routines and relationships cannot be overlooked. Participants' responses often reflect the depth of established connections and trust. From a theoretical perspective, systemic and institutional dynamics can unintentionally affect the emotional needs of marginalised groups (Fernando, 2017).

Observations across healthcare, social services, and voluntary sector organisations indicate that tensions between institutional priorities and participant wellbeing are common. Within this context, experiences in group therapy provide a valuable learning opportunity for understanding therapeutic practice in multicultural settings.

Ethical practice requires that services are delivered with attention to consistency, respect, and sensitivity to participants' histories and needs (Banks, 2012; Bolman and Deal, 2017). When institutional changes occur, careful planning and preparation help to ensure that the emotional impact on participants is recognised and addressed.

Although initially potentially unsettling, such changes can contribute to a deeper understanding of the therapeutic process for both participants and therapists and offer opportunities for reflection and learning.

Vignette: A Patient's Farewell

During the final group session, after the closure had been announced, one member, Fatima – a Somali woman who had been attending for over eight years – shared her feelings:

> When I first came here, I was lost – fearful of my past and uncertain about my future. This group became my family, a place where I could be myself without hiding. Now, I feel like I'm being abandoned again, just when I thought I had found stability. Leaving feels like leaving my community behind, like being sent back to a place where no one understands me. How can they decide this without asking us?

Her voice trembled, tears falling silently. The room grew heavy with shared pain and disbelief. For many, this was not merely the end of a group – it was the loss of a lifeline, a rupture in the fragile web of trust that had been carefully woven over the years. There was an unconscious communication at play. As Fatima gave voice to her feeling of abandonment, I sensed that the group was also carrying my own unspoken anger and frustration. I later brought this to supervision, where I explored how to support the group in moving forward without allowing my unresolved emotions to intrude on their process.

As I step away, I reflect on the many experiences that have shaped my work in group therapy. Endings, though often challenging, naturally bring feelings of sadness for participants and therapists alike. These moments also provide opportunities for learning, growth, and deeper understanding of the needs of those we serve. My hope is that the lessons drawn from these experiences – about consistency, thoughtful planning, and the importance of supportive structures – will continue to guide future practice and foster environments that are resilient, inclusive, and nurturing for both participants and therapists.

3 Lived Experience and Clinical Practice: Group Therapy with Survivors of Honour-Based Violence and Political Torture

Honour-based violence, including honour killings, remains a severe violation of human rights worldwide. Rooted in patriarchal and cultural norms that link family honour to women's behaviour, this form of violence disproportionately affects women and girls. It is often driven by intense social pressure to conform to rigid gender expectations (Gill, 2009; Sen, 2005). Despite increasing international condemnation, honour killings continue in many regions, frequently facilitated by legal gaps and varying levels of social tolerance within certain communities (Amnesty International, 2008; UNFPA, 2000; Amnesty International, 2023; UN Women, 2022). Understanding the social and cultural pressures that underpin honour-based violence is essential in therapeutic settings, as it enables practitioners to provide culturally sensitive support and to create safe spaces in which survivors can to process their experiences.

Political torture represents another form of severe trauma experienced by many women globally (Burnett and Peel, 2001). In working with survivors of both honour-related violence and political torture, I encountered narratives marked by profound suffering. At times, these accounts resonated with elements of my own history of political persecution. Although long-term psychoanalytic work had helped me to process much of this experience, the emotional weight of the women's stories remained deeply affecting. This work demanded a careful balance; I needed to remain emotionally available and responsive without becoming overwhelmed. It served as a reminder that these are not theoretical concerns, but ongoing, lived realities for many.

The short-term group therapy programme was developed to support survivors of torture and honour-based violence, with particular attention to the context of asylum and immigration. Its primary aim was to explore how participants engaged with therapeutic work and their readiness to express emotion. As newly arrived individuals, the women were encouraged to shift from acting out through destructive behaviours to articulating their experiences, thoughts, and feelings (WHO, 2025).

Foulkes (1964) proposed that non-verbal, destructive behaviours – often described as 'acting out' – reflect difficulties in communication. This view echoes Freud's (1914) observation that patients do not consciously remember what has been forgotten and repressed but instead express it through actions. In group settings, such behaviours can be reframed as openings for verbal exploration (Foulkes, 1975). Interpreting these actions with sensitivity is crucial, as individuals may unconsciously distort or struggle to verbalise what they have endured. Thoughtful therapeutic intervention can support both the individual and the group in making sense of such expressions and in disrupting unhelpful patterns.

Following initial discussions with 12 women, I offered to conduct an eight-week psychoeducational group. Six chose to participate. The shared intention was to assess – by the end of the pilot programme – whether to extend the group for a longer period or bring it to a close.

Why This Group?

The group was developed to address a clear gap in psychological services for women affected by gender-based violence and political persecution – traumas often overlooked or insufficiently addressed in mainstream mental health settings. Many participants were recently arrived asylum seekers facing multiple layers of vulnerability: forced displacement, cultural dislocation, legal precarity, and unresolved trauma. Standard therapeutic models frequently proved inadequate in responding to such intersecting complexities. Referring professionals often conveyed a sense of helplessness, as these patients' needs extended beyond the reach of conventional clinical approaches.

The group model offered a culturally responsive and therapeutic alternative – an environment in which trust, emotional expression, and relational repair could gradually emerge among women with shared experiences. It was also envisaged as a pilot for potential future service development.

Formation of the Group

Referrals came from doctors, ESOL (English for Speakers of Other Languages) teachers, link workers, social workers, and nurses. While our team had a strong theoretical awareness of the challenges faced by asylum seekers, we had limited practical experience in clinical work with this population. Most of the team consisted of White European professionals – doctors, nurses, link workers, and therapists. I was the only non-European therapist and worked alongside an Argentine colleague. This position shaped my clinical approach, particularly in relation to cultural and emotional sensitivity.

Following a series of clinical discussions, team roles were agreed. I proposed offering a short-term therapy group for immigrant women, many of whom had been waiting for psychological support. The proposal was met with support. Some colleagues appeared relieved, as if I had taken on a particularly complex task. A parallel group for men, led by another therapist, later developed into a 40-week programme. Both groups met for 75 minutes per session, allowing time for meaningful therapeutic work.

One significant challenge was the uncertainty surrounding participants' immigration status. Some women with rejected asylum claims faced the possibility of detention or deportation by the Home Office. As a team, we remained alert to these broader social and political conditions (Summerfield, 2001). At times, professionals unfamiliar with such complexities mistakenly judged these women as unsuitable for therapy. In contrast, I have often found that those with profound experiences of adversity can benefit greatly from therapeutic support (Tribe and Thompson, 2008). Our work often extended beyond the consulting room, including writing psychological reports for solicitors and the Home Office. Balancing these clinical and administrative responsibilities was demanding, yet it offered a deeper insight into the challenges these women faced and the care required to support them effectively.

The precarious nature of immigration status – together with housing instability, financial hardship, and ongoing health concerns – had a clear impact on the women's engagement (Silove et al., 1997). As this was a pilot group, I felt a strong ethical and professional responsibility to offer the programme with care and cultural sensitivity. I hoped that it might serve as a reference point for future work and drew upon my social, cultural, and clinical understanding to facilitate and support the process.

Group Composition and Pre-Group Reflections

The group ultimately included six women, selected from an initial pool of 12 individuals. The other six declined the invitation, explaining that the emotional strain of beginning group therapy felt too intense. The following descriptions provide a summary of key background details and early impressions from the first four and the final sessions of this 40-week programme.

- Jane: A 51-year-old Eritrean woman of Black descent and mother of three. After separating from her husband, she worked as a guerrilla health worker in Eritrea and was later imprisoned. She had a law degree and had been living in England for four months when the group started. Her asylum application had been accepted.
- Roza: A 41-year-old Congolese woman of Black descent who became a mother at the age of 16. Her son had died the previous year. Roza had a grandchild whom she brought to the UK. She was awaiting an asylum decision and relied on support from her church and immigration charities, as she received no public assistance.
- Joanna: A 37-year-old Ugandan woman with a 13-year-old daughter. She fled to the UK with financial help from her husband to ensure her safety. At the time of the group's formation, she had been waiting seven months for an asylum decision.
- Amina: A 34-year-old Iranian woman who fled her country to avoid an honour killing. She was previously married to her cousin and had escaped from an abusive relationship. Her husband had custody of their three-year-old son. Amina faced death threats from her family if she returned to

Iran. Her initial asylum application had been denied, and she was appealing against the decision.

- Amelia: A 23-year-old Russian woman with features typical of the region. She fled Russia after being sexually abused by her stepfather – an experience her mother refused to acknowledge. She lived with her Iraqi boyfriend and was awaiting an asylum decision.
- Zainab: A 29-year-old Somali woman of Black descent. She fled her family at the age of 13 to escape female genital mutilation (FGM) and sought asylum in the UK. Anger was a central theme in her therapy, and often surfaced in early sessions.

Concerns Raised in Pre-Group Meetings

During the pre-group meetings, the women expressed a range of practical concerns but were initially reluctant to engage with their emotions. I clarified that, while I could not directly resolve their practical problems, I could refer them to relevant legal or advisory organisations. I also used an educational approach to explain the purpose and structure of group therapy, emphasising its boundaries and limitations.

Despite initial reservations, all six women agreed to participate – an unexpected and encouraging outcome. Most lived in isolation, except for Amelia, who was in a relationship but felt frustrated that her boyfriend did not understand her. She joined the group to avoid overburdening him. My primary aim during these meetings was to assess their readiness for the emotional work that group therapy would require.

Their early concerns revealed uncertainty, hesitation, and differing expectations:

JANE: 'What if I share my troubles? Will others understand me?'
AMELIA: 'Well, I'd like to give it a try. Maybe it will help.'
AMINA: 'I have no other choice. So long as there are no other Iraqis in the group, I'll come.'
ZAINAB: 'Are there any Muslims? If there are no Somalis in the group, I'll join.'
JOANNA: 'I'm very lonely; I really need to talk.'
ROZA: 'It can't be worse than where I came from. I'll see if others share their feelings – then I will too.'

These statements reflected identity-based anxieties, fears of judgement, and intergroup tensions. Amina and Zainab's remarks, in particular, highlighted ethnic and religious boundaries, pointing to broader social divisions that could challenge group cohesion. These dynamics required careful facilitation to foster trust and psychological safety.

Therapeutic Progress Across Four Sessions

The eight-week psychoeducation phase acted as a bridge between initial resistance and deeper emotional work. These sessions introduced core concepts of group dynamics and gradually encouraged emotional engagement. By the time formal therapy began, the women had developed trust in the process and started sharing more openly.

This preparatory phase helped to normalise the therapeutic setting and provided a scaffold for emotional safety, both essential conditions for refugee women coping with trauma and managing complex cultural transitions.

Tenth Session: Cultural Norms and Group Tensions

Jane arrived ten minutes late to the tenth session and offered a quiet apology. Roza voiced her frustration:

ROZA: 'Jane, I'm sorry, but I have to say this. You're always late. It bothers me. A bit more respect would be appreciated.'
JANE: 'I'm really sorry. I lost track of time.'
ROZA: 'I understand, but it feels like a pattern. This makes me sad.'
JANE: 'I'll try to do better.'Although the exchange introduced tension, others saw value in addressing it directly:
AMELIA: 'We all have struggles. Let's support each other.'
ZAINAB: 'Yes, we're here to help one another.'

Jane explained that in her culture, arriving exactly on time – or early – might be considered disrespectful. This opened a wider conversation about cultural differences in punctuality. Roza responded sharply: 'This is London, not Africa. You need to adapt. Being on time matters here.' Her comment revealed deeper cultural discomfort. I gently intervened: 'Jane, how do you feel about these cultural differences? Do they make you uncomfortable?' Before Jane could respond, another member opined: 'What a strange custom.' Jane fell silent but promised to arrive on time the following week.

This moment illustrated how conflicting cultural norms can generate friction. It highlighted the need for cultural humility in group therapy and showed how cultural conflict could become an opportunity for growth. In later sessions, these tensions opened discussions about identity, belonging, and adaptation. Members increasingly acknowledged the challenge of honouring their cultural backgrounds while adjusting to life in a new society. Many also voiced a quiet but firm rejection of being undermined, especially in ways they felt were normalised within their own cultural contexts.

The group provided
a space in which frustrations could be voiced without fear of rejection, enabling members to practise empathy, negotiate differences, and develop skills

essential for both group cohesion and broader integration. These moments helped to reduce isolation and nurtured a sense of shared resilience among women who had often felt misunderstood or judged.

Emotional Atmosphere and Group Dynamics

Tears flowed freely during sessions, filling the room with sorrow, rage, and grief. Each woman carried her own burden, yet they were united by shared struggles. The emotional intensity revealed both the depth of trauma and the group's capacity for collective healing.

Group Cohesion and Cultural Boundaries

From the outset, identity-based fears and intergroup tensions were evident:

- Amina said she would only attend if no Iraqis were present.
- Zainab insisted that no Somalis should be part of the group.

These statements highlighted the group's fears and past experiences of trauma. They provided an entry point for dialogue about trust, cultural differences, and intergroup misunderstandings. By exploring the reasons behind these preferences, participants gradually became more aware of shared struggles and vulnerabilities. Over time, this process fostered empathy, encouraged negotiation of differences, and laid the groundwork for building cohesion across cultural and ethnic lines.

- Joanna expressed deep loneliness.
- Roza maintained a cautiously open stance.

Cultural Practices and Survival

Zainab shared her experience of escaping FGM: 'This is our culture ... I stood against it. My sister helped me to escape.' Her disclosure stunned the group and prompted a complex discussion. Reactions ranged from solidarity to discomfort. At times, Zainab appeared to defend the practice, revealing internal conflict. Joanna, comparing her own experiences, said, 'Your situation is worse than mine.' The conversation moved on to divorce, domestic abuse, and death threats, thereby uncovering further layers of trauma and survival strategies.

Zainab's story exposed the intersection of cultural identity, gender-based violence, and migration trauma. Her expressions of guilt and regret revealed the emotional complexity survivors often carry, shaped by deeply internalised cultural expectations.

Facilitating such conversations required a careful balance, validating personal experiences while encouraging critical reflection on harmful traditions, without imposing external judgement. These moments created powerful openings for healing, mutual understanding, and shared growth.

High-Stakes Emotional Moments

At one point, Amina disclosed her fear of family violence following her divorce. The group responded with empathy, recognising the serious risks faced by women confronting honour-based violence. Their support became a crucial source of safety and emotional healing.

Key Observations

This section illustrates the complexity of intercultural group therapy with refugee women. Key themes include cultural conflict, poverty, homelessness, trauma, trust-building, and the therapist's delicate task of acknowledging cultural differences while supporting adaptation to the host country's expectations.

The group's evolution – from guarded hesitation to emotionally open sharing – demonstrates the transformative potential of culturally sensitive group psychotherapy. This phase marked a significant turning point: collective grief, sorrow, and anger became vehicles for mutual recognition and the development of resilience. Despite cultural and ethnic differences, the women's shared struggles created unity, revealing the profound therapeutic possibilities of group work with displaced and traumatised women.

Beyond Survival: Stories of Resilience and Change

Long-term group therapy with refugee women offers unique opportunities for healing, resilience, and transformation. Research shows that culturally sensitive group psychotherapy provides a safe space where displaced women can share traumatic experiences, build mutual support, and regain a sense of agency (Schweitzer et al., 2006; Miller and Rasmussen, 2010). These groups support a journey beyond survival, helping women to rebuild their identities and to regain hope despite ongoing adversity (Herman, 1992).

Jane, her voice thick with emotion, spoke through tears: 'I sent my son away when he was eight to become a guerrilla and save my country. Now I can't even recognise him.' Roza, her words sharp with truth, replied: 'But how could you recognise him? He's not eight anymore. He's not the same person.' In subsequent sessions, Jane looked at the group with pleading eyes. Her voice was raw as she said: 'I won't visit my son in the rehabilitation centre anymore. He hates me, and I hate him. I'm already a bad mother. I couldn't protect my country or my children. My family and my life are ruined.' The group sat in stunned silence, each member struggling to offer comfort. The helplessness in their eyes mirrored the weight of Jane's words. There were no easy answers –

no words to undo the pain she carried. One member, her voice soft but steady, said: 'He's your son. You shouldn't give up on him.' Another added: 'What else could you have done?' Jane's grief poured out:

> I feel so helpless and terrible. I've lost not just my son, but my country too. My battles were for nothing. My country is in chaos, and here I am. What did we fight for? Coming here, I see how meaningless my battles were. No one knows each other here. Everyone seems happy … I wish I could enjoy life like the English people, drinking in pubs.

Consumed by guilt and shame, Jane confided: 'I can't live without medication.' At first, there were concerns that Jane might not remain in the group, but like the others she continued to attend despite her struggles.

As a team, we decided to transfer the group to Rebecca, an Argentine therapist committed to working long-term with immigrant communities. I had been assigned to other projects, and Rebecca, a research assistant, needed clinical experience with an established group. We believed continuity would best serve the women's therapeutic needs.

Four weeks before the transition, I informed the group of the upcoming change. I explained the situation openly and honestly, believing that they had the right to know the truth. The group would either conclude or continue their journey with Rebecca in a long-term setting. The women agreed that continuing was the best option, although they had questions and concerns.

Roza, in particular, was deeply affected. She expressed her attachment to me with both hurt and curiosity: 'Why aren't you continuing with us?' she asked. Then, her voice heavy, she added: 'Well, who can bear what we're talking about?'

During the final four weeks, we focused on coping with change, managing feelings of rejection, and facing life's challenges. As the transition approached, Rebecca joined our sessions. The group openly discussed how they would handle my departure. Another box of tissues was used; the bin overflowed. I took deep breaths, struggling to hold back tears. Even Rebecca, despite her experience, found it difficult to contain her emotions.

After the transition, I continued to meet with Rebecca regularly to discuss the group and share reflections. Rebecca had spent seven months in prison in Argentina due to her political beliefs. Despite this, she completed her doctoral studies and remained deeply committed to her work.

The group continued for six years, maintaining the same six members throughout. It was the only long-term group of which I was aware that started and ended with the same participants. Rebecca kept me updated on the women's lives, which continued to unfold with both pain and resilience.

Jane, the Eritrean woman, experienced a series of profound losses. Her son, who lived in the UK, died from a drug overdose. Another son, who remained in Eritrea, emigrated to Canada through Amnesty International, while a third joined her in London. Jane herself was diagnosed with breast cancer, which required a break from therapy. She underwent surgery and began chemotherapy. Yet Rebecca described her as content. Jane, reflecting on her life, said: 'Life is testing me. This illness is my bill.' Now a regular churchgoer, she added: 'I lived through war. I fought with myself and others, but at least maybe I'll die in peace.'

Roza stopped taking her medication and found part-time work in a fashion house, living with her granddaughter. Amelia ended her relationship with her Iranian fiancé and was planning to marry an Englishman. Amina, still separated from her son, studied sociology at a prestigious university and begun working as a research assistant while continuing therapy locally. Joanna was travelling between Uganda and the UK, starting a business and reconnecting with a childhood friend, whom she planned to marry. All the women had received their immigration appointments, and their British passports had arrived.

Zainab, however, was considering settling in Germany. Unbothered by the group's remarks – 'What's this? You keep moving. Change yourself' – Zainab remained firm in her decision.

These brief snapshots cannot fully capture the depth of their experiences. Yet I felt that it was vital to show how, despite the varied traumas they endured, these individuals continue to strive for a happy life and good health.

It is important to challenge the common misconception that migrants and survivors of torture are incapable of standing on their own. While their histories are painful, they possess remarkable resilience, strength of character, and determination (Herman, 1992). They lead full lives – marked by both joy and hardship – and deserve to be seen beyond their victimhood.

The courage to enter therapy signals a desire for growth and change. Within the group, sharing stories became more than recounting trauma; it was a way of making sense of feelings and experiences, facilitating transformation (Mollica, 2006).

Understanding the Therapeutic Journey: The Therapist's Perspective

This section highlights the transformative potential of group therapy and the resilience of migrant women who, despite profound trauma and ongoing challenges, demonstrate remarkable strength and determination. Their journey is not solely about survival but involves active engagement in rebuilding their lives.

The transition from one therapist to another marked a moment of emotional intensity and uncertainty. Roza's attachment to me, the group's shared sorrow, and their decision to continue under new leadership reflected a deep commitment to their therapeutic journey. Despite war, displacement, and loss, these women embodied resilience and hope. Their choice to remain engaged during this transition suggests a strong desire for emotional growth and mutual support (Herman, 1992; Papadopoulos, 2002).

Each woman's journey offered unique insights – Jane's struggle with illness and grief, Zainab's reflections on settlement, Roza's growing independence. While their narratives were distinct, threads of courage, perseverance, and a pursuit of peace ran through them all. This challenges the misconception that trauma survivors – particularly migrants – are passive or dependent. Instead, it reveals them as individuals shaped not only by their histories but also by their personalities, strengths, and aspirations (Summerfield, 2001; Tribe and Raval, 2003).

This perspective underscores the importance of recognising not only suffering but also agency. While their pasts remain significant, these women are equally defined by their efforts to heal and move forward. Ultimately, the message is one of hope: despite profound pain, they continue to seek peace, understanding, and new beginnings. For practitioners working with trauma survivors and migrants, it is essential to acknowledge their strength, potential, and the central role of relational support in recovery (Mollica, 2006; Silove, 1999). It is also important not to view them solely through the lens of victimhood, even when they are identified as survivors. Above all, they are individuals who, like anyone else, aspire to live fully and find meaning and enjoyment in life.

Group Support

Despite initial fears and cultural hesitations, the group gradually became a cohesive and supportive community. Women like Roza, who initially focused on practical concerns, began to show greater emotional depth and care for the group's unity. Their growing awareness of how their behaviours affected the emotional wellbeing of others marked a significant step in their development. This was not merely a gathering of women with shared migration experiences; it developed into a community in which each member brought her own fears, hopes, and history. Their solidarity arose from a shared sense of humanity and mutual recognition (Mondragón et al., 2023).

Emotional Vulnerability

Roza's emotional reaction to Jane's tardiness revealed deeper internal struggles. Her openness and expression of feeling overwhelmed highlighted the importance of creating a therapeutic space in which emotional vulnerability is welcomed and honoured. This shift helped the group to see one another not only through the lens of trauma but also as emotionally complex individuals capable of connection and transformation (Winnicott, 1965; Schlapobersky, 2016).

Holding the Group

As the therapist, my role involved gently managing and holding the group dynamics, especially during moments of tension. When Roza's sharp response threatened to silence Jane's vulnerability, I intervened to maintain a respectful and emotionally safe space. Balancing clear boundaries with empathy was essential in creating an environment where each member felt heard and valued. Over a period of 40 weeks, the group gradually shifted from a structured psychoeducational format to deeper emotional engagement, highlighting the importance of being attuned to both group dynamics and cultural meanings in facilitating meaningful change (Schlapobersky, 2016; Bateman and Fonagy, 2006).

The eventual change in facilitation marked a significant turning point. After I facilitated the group for 40 weeks, the responsibility was passed to Rebecca. This transition was carefully considered, as Rebecca was pursuing her PhD and was able to commit to continuing the group for a longer, potentially open-ended period, due to her research focus and dedication. Although emotionally difficult, the group's decision to continue under her care reflected the strength they had developed. Rebecca's calm presence and attuned manner provided much-needed continuity. Without knowing the details of her background, the women instinctively recognised and trusted her depth and commitment.

Each woman's experience – Jane's endurance through illness, Roza's growing independence, Amelia's evolving relationships, Amina's vocational progress, and Zainab's ongoing perseverance – testifies to the possibility of profound growth even after trauma. These changes unfolded gradually, shaped by years of therapeutic engagement and mutual support.

The broader message is this: trauma survivors cannot be defined solely by their suffering. They are whole individuals – resilient, hopeful, and capable of recovery. Their experiences of trauma and healing are deeply shaped by their cultural backgrounds, which influence how they perceive, express, and cope with distress (Kirmayer et al., 2011). Equally important is recognising their agency and complex identities to avoid reducing them to mere victims (Hook et al., 2016). For practitioners working with survivors, it is essential to approach them as whole individuals, respecting both their personal narratives and cultural identities – acknowledging pain while also recognising strength. In group therapy, recovery extends beyond confronting the past; it involves embracing the future with hope and determination within a culturally meaningful and community-oriented framework.

Managing the Challenges of Transitioning to New Therapeutic Leadership

I have always felt somewhat classless – even within my own family. I chose a career in nursing, which they had initially not approved of, but ultimately, they supported my decision. I grew up in a relatively privileged middle-class family in Türkiye, yet class in the UK functions in a markedly different and more layered way. In many parts of Europe, including the UK, class – like race – remains a powerful but often unspoken force, quietly shaping social belonging, professional perception, and interpersonal dynamics. While my background in

Türkiye afforded me stability and social recognition, in the UK that positioning felt ambiguous, and at times, irrelevant.

Although I initially believed that I could relate to the group through shared middle-class values, I soon recognised the limitations of this assumption. Feeling classless, paradoxically, offered a sense of freedom – a capacity to relate across differences – yet it also left me vulnerable to subtle hierarchies hidden beneath polite exchanges. These interactions often carried an unspoken air of superiority, condescension, or quiet dismissal – never explicitly voiced, yet deeply felt. In therapeutic settings, such distinctions are rarely acknowledged, but their presence is undeniable, particularly when layered with cultural and racial differences. It became essential for me to draw on my professional values – curiosity, openness, and respect – to engage with the group beyond the confines of social class.

At this stage in my practice, I was invited to take over an existing long-term therapy group – a role that challenged not only my clinical skills but also my sense of identity and belonging. The group consisted of eight middle-class professionals from diverse European backgrounds: three English, and one each from Switzerland, France, Ireland, Austria, and the Czech Republic. All were White, representing different genders, with English as the common language. The group had been formed six years earlier by a married couple who had co-facilitated it consistently in a private, fee-paying setting.

This couple had decided to emigrate to Australia for health reasons and to embrace a slower pace of life. Wanting to ensure continuity, they invited me to take over the group. After six months of discussions to assess the group's readiness, I agreed. The transition was finalised, and all relevant information was clearly communicated to the members.

Two concerns weighed on my mind:

1 Would the group accept me as their new therapist, given their previous experience with two therapists?
2 As a Turkish-speaking immigrant psychotherapist with an accent, how would I be received by a group of White, middle-class Europeans?

Underlying these questions was a more personal struggle: I found it difficult to see them purely as patients. Their established professional identities, cultural familiarity with the setting, and subtle group dynamics made it harder for me to inhabit the authority of the therapist role with ease. This hesitation raised further doubts about my place in the room and how I might be perceived.

While I felt confident managing some of the group's dynamics through shared middle-class values, I was also aware of the subtle distinctions between being middle class in Türkiye and in Europe. When I shared these concerns with colleagues, they reassured me that such differences would not pose a problem. Although their confidence was somewhat comforting, I still felt the need to acknowledge the disparities. My colleagues reminded me that the previous therapist, an Australian woman, had also been a foreigner. However, her marriage to an Englishman appeared to ease her cultural assimilation. She was often described as 'more English than the English themselves' – a remark that, despite its kind intent, overlooked the complexities of my own identity and the anxieties I carried.

My colleagues tended to emphasise similarities while overlooking differences – an approach I observed not only in professional contexts but also in their personal relationships, where commonality often served as the foundation of connection. I believe that meaningful understanding, in therapy as in life, requires recognising both similarities and differences.

I met the group four weeks before my colleague's departure. During this introductory session, Mark, one of the members, asked me to repeat my name three times and inquired about my origin, commenting on my accent. The comment about my accent, though seemingly minor, triggered feelings of otherness. In fact, all the participants – including the British members of the group – had their own accents, yet somehow mine was the most visible and remarked upon. Being a minority therapist in a group composed entirely of White members added another layer of complexity. My cultural background, accent, and outsider status made me acutely aware of subtle hierarchies and unspoken norms, highlighting the contrast between my experience and that of the majority group members. It led me to question whether my background and identity would always be perceived as external to the group, despite my professional competence. Before I could respond, my colleague Jane interjected with 'Turkish', pre-empting my answer. As I concluded the session with, 'See you in September', I left with a deep sense of frustration.

Reflecting on this experience, I recognised the challenges ahead – not only in managing the group's dynamics but also in attending to my own emotional responses. While I had anticipated cultural differences, I had underestimated the weight of personal and collective perceptions on my integration into the group. Being an ethnic minority therapist in a predominantly White group added a further layer of complexity, offering both challenges and unique insights into group dynamics. Over time, I came to view these early tensions, however uncomfortable, as valuable learning opportunities – for both myself and the group. They offered a space to examine my own assumptions and emotional responses as part of the therapeutic process, while also considering how best to support the group in moving beyond surface-level differences towards a deeper mutual understanding.

First Group Session

The group arrived punctually – a promising start. I greeted them and took my seat, but they continued their conversation as if I wasn't there. The topic: foreigners in England.

JOHN: 'I just don't understand how they leave their countries and come all the way here. How do they manage it? Even going to south London amazes me. I've given up on the people; even the nature is different.'

BERTHA: 'There are no natives in London. Everyone's a foreigner. My boss is Colombian. I can't even understand her – her accent is so hard. To be fair, she's smart and strong, but I don't know how she manages such a huge company. And since she arrived, the number of Latinos has grown. During coffee breaks, it's always them. Soon, we'll be outnumbered.'

The group continued to voice their frustrations, often characterising immigrants as 'lucky' relative to their difficulties they themselves faced. Jack said: 'Well, if they worked, that would be one thing. Most live off government aid. Everything's handed to them. Meanwhile, my housing benefit was cut off this week. Luckily, I have savings. If I were an immigrant, things would be easier.'

My presence seemed to amplify their frustrations, reflecting an unconscious discomfort with difference – what Sue and Sue (2016) describe as culturally based countertransference, where therapists of colour often become recipients of unresolved racial tensions. I remarked: 'I think my presence is stirring some strong feelings in you and is having an impact.' Instead of engaging with my comment, the group shifted the conversation in a different direction. A silence followed, then a series of questions:

- 'Which school did you graduate from?'
- 'Will you be able to handle this group on your own?'
- 'Have you trained on LGBTQ issues?'

The scrutiny was intense. Rather than responding directly, I offered a reflective comment: 'You've already experienced the loss of two therapists, and I come from a culture that may be unfamiliar to you. I'm curious how this might be affecting you.' Before I could finish speaking, Janet, a member from Prague, interrupted me. 'This group cannot tolerate novelty and difference. Narrow-mindedness!'

Her reaction seemed tied to her own past experiences of exclusion and abuse. In that moment, I became a maternal figure she felt the need to defend – a dynamic Foulkes (1964) recognised as part of the group matrix, where past relational patterns are re-enacted within the group setting. Hopper (2003) further suggests that groups often operate under the influence of the social unconscious, which may manifest as a collective intolerance toward difference or 'otherness'. Such reactions can serve as defences against deeper anxieties, including fragmentation or loss of identity. Janet's outburst, therefore, could be understood both as a personal expression and as a reflection of the group's unconscious resistance to difference.

Another long silence followed.

JOHN: 'What does that have to do with anything?'
JANET: 'Of course it matters. You've caused me pain too.'

Ongoing Challenges

In the early stages, the group expressed doubt and scepticism. Questions arose such as:

- Should we continue with this group?
- Is Dilek a competent therapist?
- I wish our former therapists were still here.
- Why are we discussing differences now? We never did before.

These concerns were often voiced as if my presence were incidental. The group repeatedly tested both the boundaries of the therapy and my role as therapist. At times, sessions felt like a prolonged assessment of my capability – shaped by the group's anger, sense of abandonment, and unconscious biases (Sue and Sue, 2016). These dynamics stirred moments of self-questioning: What am I doing in this country, in this group? Should I return to Türkiye?

I recognise that I take risks easily, both in life and in my professional work. I began to ask myself: Why did I take on this group without thinking it through more carefully? Yet I must also acknowledge that this very aspect of my nature pushed me to engage fully and ultimately helped me to learn and grow.

Aware that these thoughts were emotional and temporary, I remained committed to the process. Over the following eight months, the group's dynamics gradually shifted. My approach – attuned to the emotional undercurrents of resistance and unafraid to name racialised interactions – supported deeper engagement. Although initially met with resistance, and at times mirrored in my own countertransference, an unconscious bond slowly formed. This reshaped the therapeutic alliance over time, reflecting Foulkes' (1982) broader view of the group as a dynamic and interconnected system shaped by shared unconscious life.

Evolution of the Group

Every therapist brings their own culture and personal style to the therapeutic work, subtly shaping the group's evolution. Even therapists trained in the same school or model contribute differences, so change occurs naturally over time, as part of the group's dynamic rather than by deliberate design. Over the next three and a half years, the group underwent structural changes. Two members left, and new participants joined, broadening its demographic composition. What had once been a predominantly White, middle-class European cohort evolved into a more diverse and intellectually dynamic space. The inclusion of a Black man and an Asian woman brought new perspectives, prompting meaningful discussions on discrimination, gender, racism, and socioeconomic issues.

Initially, these changes triggered feelings of jealousy and competition among longstanding members. Rather than suppressing these responses, the group engaged in reflective inquiry, exploring underlying anxieties and reassessing self-perceptions. This process revealed previously unexamined defences, allowing members to move beyond fixed identities of distress, such as identifying primarily as 'depressed'.

As the group matured, creative expression – through writing, painting, and music – emerged as a natural channel for self-exploration. These pursuits deepened self-awareness, helping members to articulate internal conflicts and aspirations. Through active listening, empathetic engagement, and thoughtful challenge, the group fostered an environment of mutual reflection. Over time, these changes unfolded organically, leading to significant shifts in both individual perspectives and collective dynamics. This progression echoes Bion's concept of groups moving beyond unconscious defensive roles towards more productive collaboration (Bion, 1961).

Reflecting on Growth and Transformation

The structural and demographic changes within the group did more than alter its composition; they also offered me, as the therapist, a mirror for my own growth. Witnessing and facilitating this evolution illuminated both the challenges and opportunities inherent in intercultural group work, prompting deep reflection on my assumptions, cultural identity, and approach to the group.

What began as a homogeneous group of White Europeans gradually evolved into an intercultural space, offering rich lessons in resilience, understanding, and human connection. Many of the White patients came to recognise that they too had cultural backgrounds and identities – elements often previously unexamined. This awareness sparked curiosity and openness, enabling engagement with both the challenges and rewards of intercultural work. Today, I continue to work with individuals from diverse backgrounds, deeply grateful to witness and contribute to such meaningful transformation.

When I first took on the responsibility of leading the group, I was filled with doubt about my capabilities and motivations. Managing complex group dynamics – especially within the context of my own cultural identity – left me uncertain. Over time, I became attuned to the group's projections: unconscious expectations about my role, identity, and competence. Recognising these as reflections of their inner struggles, rather than accurate judgements of me, brought clarity and confidence. I also became aware of my own assumptions – particularly how I had unconsciously essentialised White patients, overlooking their individual vulnerabilities. Fernando (2010) warns against this tendency, which risks neglecting unique personal histories and psychological needs. This insight helped me to approach each member of the group with greater openness and empathy.

Over a period of eight years, the group stabilised, becoming a profound learning experience for both the members and myself (Tuckman, 1965).

Managing Resistance and Transformation

In the early stages, distrust and resentment were tangible. At times, it felt as though I faced a wall of silence and resistance. Yet, as the process unfolded, these emotions gradually gave way to mutual respect, trust, and warmth. Occasional anger persisted – often rooted in long-held fears – but was increasingly balanced by the group's shared commitment to open dialogue and reflection.

The group's development mirrored wider social tensions, revealing the interplay between personal growth and cultural expectations. Many members initially struggled with the discomfort of engaging with unfamiliar perspectives. However, as self-reflection deepened, emotional and relational flexibility grew. The group shifted from defensiveness toward collaboration, creating space for vulnerability and shared experience. This transformation was cyclical rather than linear, unfolding through resistance, insight, and adaptation. The group's evolution – from a small, homogeneous unit to a diverse collective – enriched the experience for all involved (Tuckman, 1965).

Throughout the programme, the group confronted their own biases, histories, and fears. Together, we navigated intercultural challenges, facing difficult truths about ourselves and one another. What emerged was not mere tolerance but genuine appreciation of difference – recognising diversity as a source of insight and strength rather than division (Sue and Sue, 2016).

As facilitator, I also examined my own assumptions and learned when to step back and when to intervene, thereby allowing the group to find its voice while providing structure to sustain the work. Just as the group grew, I too evolved as a therapist and an individual. This process became one of mutual transformation, softening the boundaries between therapist and patient and allowing authentic human connection (Yalom, 1995).

What began as a group of individuals grappling with personal challenges became a testament to the power of collaboration, dialogue, and shared psychological growth. Reflecting on this journey, I see it as an ongoing negotiation – between change and stability, vulnerability and resilience. The trust we built was not based on the absence of conflict, but on our capacity to engage with discomfort and disagreement constructively. Through this sustained process, the group became a living example of how growth and healing can emerge from difficult beginnings.

The Closure of the Group

After much reflection, I decided to gradually reduce my professional commitments and eventually retire from certain aspects of my clinical work. The group was informed 18 months in advance, allowing for a shared process of transition. While the announcement initially brought sadness and surprise, the extended time frame enabled members to explore the implications, revisit key moments from our journey, and express their emotions openly. These final months became an integral part of the therapeutic process, facilitating the group toward closure with dignity and mutual respect.

The group's evolution mirrored Tuckman's (1965) stages of development: forming, storming, norming, and performing. Over time, what had begun as a small, homogeneous unit matured into a microcosm of British society, reflecting its complexities, tensions, and potential for growth through diversity and relational depth.

In preparation for the group's closure, I encouraged members to pause reflectively before deciding whether to continue therapy elsewhere. This interval offered the emotional distance needed to integrate our work and clarify individual needs going forward. Many shared that the group had become a meaningful part of their lives, leaving memories, insights, and connections that would continue to shape their personal and relational worlds.

I did not see the closure of the group as a rupture but as a vital developmental stage. By introducing closure gradually, members engaged with the inevitability of endings – both in therapy and in life – beginning to internalise the group's core values and relationships. Ultimately, the conclusion affirmed the significance of our collective work. Rather than representing a loss, it highlighted the transformative potential of human connection. In learning to part with grace and self-awareness, members demonstrated increased resilience, autonomy, and emotional maturity – essential outcomes of long-term therapeutic engagement.

The Therapist's Learning

Reflecting on this experience, I recognise that this group was more than a therapeutic setting; it offered a microcosm of broader societal dynamics – confronting adversity, embracing transformation, and discovering strength in shared experience.

As a therapist, I have become increasingly aware of how negative transference can emerge, particularly with White patients. I now approach feelings of frustration, resistance, or projection as part of the therapeutic process, seeking to respond with empathy and composure rather than assuming I must 'resolve' these dynamics. I have come to recognise that I am reasonably confident in managing negative transference, yet I remain somewhat uncertain when it comes to positive transference. Positive transference – expressed through admiration or warmth – continues to surprise me, serving as a reminder to uphold professional boundaries while acknowledging the human connection inherent in the therapeutic relationship.

Engaging with an intercultural group has deepened my understanding of how cultural identity shapes perception, behaviour, and relational dynamics. I have learned to notice my own assumptions, particularly when working across cultural differences, and to approach each member with curiosity and openness rather than preconceptions.

When processing my feelings about the closure of the group, I initially experienced guilt and uncertainty. Before making the decision, I sought advice from my supervisor, as well as from peer and group supervision, to gain multiple perspectives and ensure that my choice was considered and ethically sound. Through reflection and supervision, I gradually came to understand the decision as aligned with both my personal and professional circumstances. I remain mindful of all the groups I have worked with, and I received feedback, particularly from this group, that they too will carry the group in their reflections. This ongoing reflective practice has been essential in maintaining my effectiveness, humility, and wellbeing as a practitioner, while recognising that learning is never complete and that each group continues to offer new insights.

References

Akhtar, S., 1999. *Comprehensive Dictionary of Psychoanalysis*. London: Routledge.

Al-Issa, I. and Tousignant, M., 1997. *Ethnic Identity and Cultural Adjustment of Immigrants*. Toronto, ON: University of Toronto Press.

Amnesty International, 2008. *The Punishment of 'Honour' Killings: A Global Human Rights Crisis*. London: Amnesty International.

Amnesty International, 2023. *Ending Honour-Based Violence*. Available at https://www.amnesty.org/en/what-we-do/violence-against-women/honour-based-violence/ (accessed 3 August 2025).

Banks, S., 2012. *Ethics in Professional Life: Virtues for Health and Social Care*. Basingstoke: Palgrave Macmillan.

Bateman, A. and Fonagy, P., 2006. *Mentalization-Based Treatment for Borderline Personality Disorder: A Practical Guide*. Oxford: Oxford University Press.

Berry, J.W., 1997. 'Immigration, Acculturation and Adaptation', *Applied Psychology: An International Review*, 46(1), pp. 5–34.

Bhugra, D. and Becker, M.A., 2005. 'Migration, Cultural Bereavement and Cultural Identity', *World Psychiatry*, 4(1), pp. 18–24.

Bion, W.R., 1961. *Experiences in Groups*. London: Tavistock Publications.

Bolman, L.G. and Deal, T.E., 2017. *Reframing Organizations: Artistry, Choice, and Leadership*. 6th edn. Hoboken, NJ: John Wiley & Sons.

Burnett, A. and Peel, M., 2001. 'Health Needs of Asylum Seekers and Refugees', *BMJ*, 322(7285), pp. 544–547.

Çakır, S.G. and Güneri, Y., 2011. 'Exploring the Factors Contributing to the Empowerment of Turkish Migrant Women in the UK', *International Journal of Psychology*, 46(3), pp. 223–233.

Corey, G., 2016. *Theory and Practice of Counseling and Psychotherapy*. 10th edn. Belmont, CA: Cengage Learning.

Crenshaw, K., 1989. 'Demarginalizing the Intersection of Race and Sex: A Black Feminist Critique of Antidiscrimination Doctrine, Feminist Theory and Antiracist Politics', *University of Chicago Legal Forum*, 1, pp. 139–167.

Fernando, S., 2010. *Mental Health, Race and Culture*. 3rd edn. Basingstoke: Palgrave Macmillan.

Fernando, S., 2017. *Institutional Racism in Psychiatry and Clinical Psychology: Race Matters in Mental Health*. Cham: Palgrave Macmillan. doi:doi:10.1007/978-3-319-62728-1.

Foulkes, S.H., 1964. *Therapeutic Group Analysis*. London: George Allen & Unwin.

Foulkes, S.H., 1975. *Group Analysis: Theory and Practice*. London: Tavistock.

Foulkes, S.H., 1982. *Therapeutic Group Analysis*. London: Routledge and Kegan Paul.

Frankl, V.E., 1963. *Man's Search for Meaning: An Introduction to Logotherapy*. 1st edn. New York: Washington Square Press.

Freud, S., 1914. 'Remembering, Repeating and Working-Through (Further Recommendations on the Technique of Psycho-Analysis II)', *Standard Edition*, vol. 12. London: Hogarth Press, pp. 145–156.

Freud, S., 1917. 'Mourning and Melancholia', in J. Strachey (ed.), *The Standard Edition of the Complete Psychological Works of Sigmund Freud*, vol. 14. London: Hogarth Press, pp. 243–258.

Garcia, M. and Sharif, M.Z., 2015. 'The Intersectionality of Race, Ethnicity, and Gender in Health Disparities Research', *Health Education & Behavior*, 42(1 Suppl), pp. 11S–17S.

Gill, A., 2009. *Voices of Victims of Honour Crimes*. London: Routledge.

Hamilton, C.V., 1967. *The Black Family in Slavery and Freedom, 1750–1925*. New York: Vintage Books.

Hays, P.A., 2008. *Addressing Cultural Complexities in Practice: Assessment, Diagnosis, and Therapy*. 2nd ed. Washington, DC: American Psychological Association.

Herman, J.L., 1992. *Trauma and Recovery: The Aftermath of Violence – From Domestic Abuse to Political Terror*. New York: Basic Books.

Hook, J.N., Davis, D.E., Owen, J., Worthington, E.L., and Utsey, S.O., 2016. 'Cultural Humility: Measuring Openness to Culturally Diverse Clients', *Journal of Counseling Psychology*, 63(3), pp. 269–277.

Hopper, E., 2003. *The Social Unconscious: Selected Papers*. London: Jessica Kingsley Publishers.

İnal-İnce, D. and Kaya, A., 2017. 'Family Honour and Gender-Based Violence in Turkey: A Socio-Cultural Perspective', *Journal of Interpersonal Violence*, 32(18), pp. 1–25.

Kağıtçıbaşı, Ç., 2017. *Family, Self, and Human Development across Cultures: Theory and Applications*. London: Routledge.

Kareem, J. and Littlewood, R. (eds), 1992. *Intercultural Therapy*. Oxford: Blackwell Scientific Publications.

Kirmayer, L.J., Narasiah, L., Munoz, M., Rashid, M., Ryder, A.G., Guzder, J., Hassan, G., Rousseau, C., and Pottie, K., 2011. 'Common Mental Health Problems in Immigrants and Refugees: General Approach in Primary Care', *Canadian Medical Association Journal*, 183(12), pp. E959–E967. Available at https://www.cmaj.ca/content/183/12/E959 (accessed 22 August 2025).

Miller, K.E. and Rasmussen, A., 2010. 'War Exposure, Daily Stressors, and Mental Health in Conflict and Post-Conflict Settings: Bridging the Divide between Trauma-Focused and Psychosocial Frameworks', *Social Science & Medicine*, 70(1), pp. 7–16.

Mollica, R.F., 2006. *Healing Invisible Wounds: Paths to Hope and Recovery in a Violent World*. New York: Harcourt.

Mondragón, R., Sánchez, G., Pérez, M., and López, F., 2023. 'Trauma-Informed Care in Multicultural Settings: Lessons from Recent Interventions', *Journal of Community Psychology*, 51(4), pp. 1450–1465.

Nadkarni, A., Velleman, R., Dabholkar, H., Shinde, S., Bhat, B., McCambridge, J., Murthy, P., Wilson, T., Weobong, B., and Patel, V., 2015. 'The Systematic Development and Pilot Randomized Evaluation of Counselling for Alcohol Problems, a Lay Counsellor-Delivered Psychological Treatment for Harmful Drinking in Primary Care in India: The PREMIUM Study', *Alcoholism: Clinical and Experimental Research*, 39(3), pp. 522–531.

Oflaz, F., Ançel, G., and Arslan, F., 2019. 'How to Achieve Effective Teamwork: The View of Mental Health Professionals', *Cyprus Journal of Medical Sciences*, 4(3), pp. 235–241. Available at doi:10.5152/cjms.2019.1009.

Papadopoulos, R.K., 2002. *Therapeutic Care for Refugees: No Place Like Home*. London: Jessica Kingsley Publishers.

Patel, N., Bennett, E., Dennis, M., Dosanjh, N., Mahtani, A., Miller, A., and Nadirshaw, Z., 2000. *Clinical Psychology, 'Race' and Culture: A Resource Pack for Trainers*. Leicester: British Psychological Society.

Rumi, J., 2004. *The Essential Rumi*. Translated by C. Barks. New York: HarperOne.

Rumi, J., 2005. *Özlü Rumi*. Translated by A.K. Özdemir. İstanbul: Yedinci Gün Yayınları.

Rumi, J., 2008. *The Masnavi: Book Six*. Translated by J. Mojaddedi. Oxford: Oxford University Press.

Rumi, J., 2014. *Bütün eserlerinden seçmeler*. İstanbul: Nesil Yayınları. (Original work from the 13th century.)

Rumi, J. [1371] 1992. *Masnavi-ye Ma'navi*. Edited by R.A. Nicholson. İstanbul: Hermes.

Schein, E.H., 2010. *Organizational Culture and Leadership*. 4th edn. San Francisco, CA: Jossey-Bass.

Schlapobersky, J., 2016. *Group Analysis: The Development of Group Psychotherapy*. London: Routledge.

Schweitzer, R., Melville, F., Steel, Z., and Lacherez, P., 2006. 'Trauma, Post-Migration Living Difficulties, and Social Support as Predictors of Psychological Adjustment in Resettled Sudanese Refugees', *Australian & New Zealand Journal of Psychiatry*, 40(2), pp. 179–187.

Sen, P., 2005. '"Crimes of Honour", Value and Meaning', in L. Welchman and S. Hossain (eds), *Honour: Crimes, Paradigms and Violence against Women*. London: Zed Books, pp. 42–63.

Silove, D., 1999. 'The Psychosocial Effects of Torture, Mass Human Rights Violations, and Refugee Trauma: Toward an Integrated Conceptual Framework', *Journal of Nervous and Mental Disease*, 187(4), pp. 200–207. Available at doi:10.1097/00005053-199904000-00002 (accessed 22 August 2025).

Silove, D., Steel, Z., and Watters, C., 1997. 'Policies of Deterrence and the Mental Health of Asylum Seekers', *JAMA*, 278(5), pp. 493–497.

Sue, D.W. and Sue, D., 2013. *Counseling the Culturally Diverse: Theory and Practice*. 6th ed. Hoboken, NJ: John Wiley & Sons.

Sue, D.W. and Sue, D., 2016. *Counseling the Culturally Diverse: Theory and Practice*. 7th ed. Hoboken, NJ: John Wiley & Sons.

Summerfield, D., 2001. 'The Invention of Post-Traumatic Stress Disorder and the Social Usefulness of a Psychiatric Category', *BMJ*, 322(7278), pp. 95–98. Available at doi:10.1136/bmj.322.7278.95 (accessed 22 August 2025).

Tribe, R., 2002. 'Mental Health of Refugees and Asylum-Seekers', *Advances in Psychiatric Treatment*, 8(4), pp. 240–247. Available at doi:10.1192/apt.8.4.240 (accessed 22 August 2025).

Tribe, R., 2007. 'Health Pluralism: A More Appropriate Alternative to Western Models of Therapy in the Context of the Conflict and Natural Disaster in Sri Lanka?' *Journal of Refugee Studies*, 20(1), pp. 21–36.

Tribe, R. and Raval, H. (eds.), 2003. *Working with Interpreters in Mental Health*. London and New York: Routledge.

Tribe, R. and Thompson, K., 2008. *Working with Intercultural and Refugee Trauma: An Overview of Therapeutic Approaches*. London: Routledge.

Tribe, R. and Thompson, K., 2009. 'Exploring the Three-Way Relationship in Therapeutic Work with Interpreters', *International Journal of Migration, Health and Social Care*, 5(2), pp. 13–21.

Tuckman, B.W., 1965. 'Developmental Sequence in Small Groups', *Psychological Bulletin*, 63(6), pp. 384–399.

Tummala Narra, P., 2007. 'Conceptualizing Trauma and Resilience across Diverse Contexts: A Multicultural Perspective', *Journal of Aggression, Maltreatment & Trauma*, 14(1–2), pp. 33–53. doi:doi:10.1300/J146v14n01_03.

United Kingdom Council for Psychotherapy, 2019. *Ethical Principles and Code of Professional Conduct*. London: United Kingdom Council for Psychotherapy.

United Nations Population Fund (UNFPA), 2000. *State of World Population 2000: Lives Together, Worlds Apart*. New York: UNFPA. Available at https://www.unfpa.org/publications/state-world-population-2000 (accessed 22 January 2026).

UN Women, 2022. *Progress on the Sustainable Development Goals: The Gender Snapshot 2022*. New York: United Nations Entity for Gender Equality and the Empowerment of Women. Available at https://www.unwomen.org/en/digital-library/publications/2022/09/progress-on-the-sustainable-development-goals-the-gender-snapshot-2022 (accessed 22 January 2026).

Winnicott, D.W., 1960. 'The Theory of the Parent–Infant Relationship', *International Journal of Psycho-Analysis*, 41, pp. 585–595.

Winnicott, D.W., 1965. *The Maturational Processes and the Facilitating Environment: Studies in the Theory of Emotional Development*. London: Hogarth Press.

Winnicott, D.W., 1971. *Playing and Reality*. London: Tavistock Publications.

World Health Organization (WHO), 2025. *Refugee and Migrant Mental Health*. Geneva: World Health Organization. Available at https://www.who.int/news-room/fact-sheets/detail/refugee-and-migrant-mental-health (accessed 24 January 2026).

Yalom, I.D., 1995. *The Theory and Practice of Group Psychotherapy*. 4th edn. New York: Basic Books.

Yalom, I.D., 2005. *The Theory and Practice of Group Psychotherapy*. 5th edn. New York: Basic Books.

Yalom, I.D. and Leszcz, M., 2020. *The Theory and Practice of Group Psychotherapy*. 6th edn. New York: Basic Books.

Chapter 8

Expectations from the National Health Service in Group Therapy

Understanding the NHS Context

Having worked as a nurse, development worker, and psychotherapist within the National Health Service (NHS) and its former health authority structures prior to subsequent restructuring, and maintaining a professional network within the NHS, I have developed a deep understanding of its organisational culture and challenges. This experience provides insight into how systemic structures shape service delivery, particularly in relation to diversity and inclusion. From this perspective, the book examines whether existing NHS models adequately meet the needs of ethnic minority communities, with particular attention to culturally sensitive group therapy (Bhui et al., 2007; Betancourt et al., 2003; Sue, 1998).

Culturally Sensitive Care

This book argues that the NHS could take proactive steps to improve access for ethnic minorities by offering therapies tailored to diverse populations. The traditional one-size-fits-all approach may not address the complexities of cultural and racial identities. Creating an environment in which patients feel understood, respected, and valued is central to enabling them to express themselves openly without fear, shame, or guilt (Fernando, 2010; Fortuna et al., 2010; NHS England, 2020).

A key step is increasing the recruitment of intercultural therapists, namely clinicians with strong therapeutic skills and cultural competence. These therapists bridge cultural gaps, making therapy more effective and ensuring that patients feel seen and respected (Bhui et al., 2007; Sue, 1998). Incorporating cultural nuances allows individuals to engage fully in their healing (Betancourt et al., 2003; Bhugra, 2004).

Recruitment alone is insufficient. It is advocated that existing staff are given training and resources to address cultural sensitivity and psychological differences. This includes professional development, cultural competence workshops, and access to supervision and peer support, particularly when managing

DOI: 10.4324/9781003726012-9

complex issues of race, identity, and culture (Fernando, 2010; Sue, 1998). Such support empowers therapists to provide care grounded in both emotional intelligence and cultural awareness.

Working with Interpreters

Access to interpreters remains limited in many mental health settings, despite the important role they play in enabling communication and understanding. Patients who are not fluent in English can feel overlooked or misunderstood when interpretation is unavailable, which may affect trust and engagement in therapy.

Working with an interpreter requires careful preparation and ongoing reflection. The therapist must attend not only to the patient but also to the nuances introduced by translation, including cultural context, non-verbal cues, and subtle shifts in meaning. Interpreters need to be well trained, skilled, and able to uphold confidentiality to support the therapeutic process effectively. While access to a suitably qualified interpreter may at times be limited, adherence to professional standards remains essential in safeguarding patient trust and ensuring the quality of communication, both of which are central to successful therapeutic outcomes.

Effective use of interpreters depends on fostering a respectful, collaborative relationship. Briefing the interpreter beforehand and debriefing them afterwards helps to ensure that the patient's voice remains central and that the therapeutic process retains its integrity. Reflecting on these experiences also highlights wider systemic limitations and the ongoing need to advocate for accessible, culturally sensitive care.

During my career, I have facilitated short-term group therapies with the help of interpreters, particularly with Chinese and Somali patients, as well as some individual sessions. While individual work might be assumed to be easier with an interpreter, I found group sessions more manageable. These experiences provided insight into the dynamics of working through an interpreter, a topic which, although beyond the scope of this book, warrants further exploration.

Long-Term Therapeutic Support

Mental healthcare should be seen as an ongoing process rather than a brief intervention. While short-term therapies like CBT can be effective, many patients face deep-rooted issues requiring sustained support (NHS England, 2020). In group therapy, building trust, sharing experiences, and understanding others takes time (Tuckman, 1965). Long-term support is particularly important for ethnic minority patients, who often experience multiple layers of stress related to racism, discrimination, and cultural displacement (Bhui et al., 2007; Bhugra, 2004).

Beyond therapy, the analysis suggests that the NHS needs to foster an environment in which patients feel safe, validated, and empowered. Attention to diversity and inclusion across all aspects of service delivery, from therapists' attitudes to the physical spaces in which therapy occurs, appears central to this process (Bhugra, 2004; Sue, 1998).

Vignette: Managing Cultural Nuances in Therapy

During a group session, a Black British patient expressed frustration about feeling invisible within the NHS mental health system. Despite articulating his distress, his cultural background and the racialised aspects of his experience were often overlooked. Subtle assumptions about his 'toughness' led some clinicians to underestimate the depth of his emotional pain, reflecting everyday microaggressions that can affect therapeutic outcomes (Sue et al., 2007).

As the group therapist, I observed how the group's silence mirrored wider societal discomfort around race. When an intercultural therapist joined the session, their culturally informed approach opened a space for authentic dialogue. The patient's narrative was heard not just as symptoms but as a lived reality shaped by systemic racism and cultural identity (Bhui et al., 2007; Fernando, 2010).

This episode highlighted the need for services to move beyond generic approaches. Therapists with cultural competence can help to bridge gaps in understanding, validating experiences that might otherwise be dismissed – a necessity for healing, especially for patients navigating complex intersections of identity and trauma (Betancourt et al., 2003).

Incorporating Patient Voices

Effective mental health services should prioritise listening to patients through meaningful consultation (NHS England, 2020). Patients, whether from ethnic minority backgrounds or White, should be engaged as active partners in their care. Consulting patients uncovers unique challenges and preferences that standardised models often overlook. By co-creating treatment plans, the NHS can build trust, improve engagement, and deliver person-centred care (Bhui et al., 2007).

Despite efforts to improve accessibility, some NHS practices continue to create barriers. An emphasis on cost-effective therapies, such as cognitive behavioural therapy (CBT), may fail to address the cultural or psychological needs of some patients (Fortuna et al., 2010). Additionally, the use of younger or less experienced practitioners can create a mismatch between therapist expertise and patient expectations, potentially undermining trust and leaving patients feeling misunderstood. In such cases, patients may be more likely to seek support outside the NHS.

Broadening Therapeutic Options

To improve care quality, the analysis suggests that the NHS could benefit from expanding its range of therapies and recruiting skilled, culturally competent therapists. This might include psychodynamic therapy, trauma-informed care, art and music therapy, and mindfulness-based treatments, which may offer long-term benefits for those facing complex issues related to identity, race, and culture (Bhugra, 2004; Sue, 1998).

Equally, patients benefit from being offered meaningful choice in their therapeutic journey. For example, analytic intercultural therapy – grounded in depth work and cultural sensitivity – can be a vital option for those seeking to explore unconscious processes alongside their lived cultural realities. By broadening therapeutic options, the NHS can help to ensure that care is not limited to a narrow set of interventions but is responsive to diverse patient needs.

A culturally sensitive approach to group therapy can help to remove barriers that prevent patients from accessing support. Such environments offer all patients, regardless of background, a sense of belonging and solidarity often missing in more traditional models. Grounded in cultural understanding, these groups provide a space where individuals can explore their experiences safely, be heard, and feel valued, thereby enhancing engagement and supporting meaningful therapeutic progress (Fortuna et al., 2010; Tuckman, 1965).

Conclusion

Mental health services should not be a privilege or an afterthought – they should be accessible, available, and effective for all. With a stronger commitment to cultural competence, the NHS has the opportunity to transform mental healthcare into a more inclusive, empathetic, and effective service, particularly for historically underserved communities (Bhui et al., 2007; NHS England, 2020).

References

Betancourt, J.R., Green, A.R., and Carrillo, J.E., 2003. 'Defining Cultural Competence: A Practical Framework for Addressing Racial/Ethnic Disparities in Health and Health Care', *Public Health Reports*, 118(4), pp. 293–302.

Bernal, G. and Domenech Rodríguez, M.M., 2012. *Cultural Adaptations: Tools for Evidence-Based Practice with Diverse Populations*. Washington, DC: American Psychological Association.

Bhugra, D., 2004. 'Migration, Distress and Cultural Identity', *British Medical Bulletin*, 69(1), pp. 129–141. doi:doi:10.1093/bmb/ldh007.

Bhui, K., Warfa, N., and Jones, E., 2007. 'Mental Illness in Black and Asian Ethnic Minorities: Pathways to Care and Outcomes', *Advances in Psychiatric Treatment*, 13 (6), pp. 270–277.

Fernando, S., 2010. *Mental Health, Race and Culture*. 3rd edn. Basingstoke: Palgrave Macmillan.

Fortuna, L.R., Alegría, M., and Gao, S., 2010. 'Preventive Mental Health Interventions for Ethnic Minority Populations', *Annual Review of Clinical Psychology*, 6, pp. 143–174.

NHS England, 2020. *The NHS Long Term Plan*. London: NHS England. Available at https://www.longtermplan.nhs.uk/ (accessed 26 August 2025).

Papadopoulos, R.K., 2007. 'Refugees, Trauma and Adversity-Activated Development', *European Journal of Psychotherapy & Counselling*, 9(3), pp. 301–312.

Sue, D.W., 1998. *Multicultural Counselling Competencies: Individual and Organizational Development*. Thousand Oaks, CA: Sage.

Sue, D.W., Capodilupo, C.M., Torino, G.C., Bucceri, J.M., Holder, A.M.B., Nadal, K. L., and Esquilin, M., 2007. 'Racial Microaggressions in Everyday Life: Implications for Clinical Practice', *American Psychologist*, 62(4), pp. 271–286. doi:doi:10.1037/0003-066X.62.4.271.

Tuckman, B.W., 1965. 'Developmental Sequence in Small Groups', *Psychological Bulletin*, 63(6), pp. 384–399.

Yalom, I.D. and Leszcz, M., 2020. *The Theory and Practice of Group Psychotherapy*. 6th edn. New York: Basic Books.

Chapter 9

Reflections at the Journey's End

The journey of writing this book has been long, intricate, and deeply transformative. Over the years, I have collected countless notes – fragments of thought – only to rediscover them later, often surprised by their enduring consistency. Each rediscovery has offered a quiet moment of self-appreciation.

This project has unfolded over more than a decade, with pauses – sometimes lasting years – when the manuscript lay untouched. During those times, I questioned its worth, occasionally believing it was ready for publication but choosing to let it rest. That space allowed me to reflect on clinical experiences, gain new perspectives, and refine my thinking.

Writing has always been more than a passion; it has served as a sanctuary – a form of inner restoration. When I write, the noise of the outside world fades, and I become absorbed in the creative process. In earlier years, when words felt unreachable and fear silenced my voice, I turned to painting for expression and renewal. Today, writing is my voice, my refuge, and my way of connecting with others. Through the written word, I express deeper layers of myself – and find solace. Each chapter reflects not only intellectual engagement but also personal and professional growth.

While writing this book, I engaged with a wide range of references, including those grounded in intercultural perspectives that resonate with my professional identity. I also drew on the work of White therapists, whose theories and practices have shaped much of the psychotherapeutic tradition. This inclusive approach has enriched the work, offering a nuanced understanding that honours diversity, complexity, and the evolving landscape of therapy (Bernal and Domenech Rodríguez, 2012; Bhugra and Becker, 2005).

I hope that this book offers insight and thoughtful provocation. It is intended as a resource for students, therapists, and psychological counsellors interested in psychotherapy. Within these pages, I invite the reader to explore the principles and practice of group therapy – its dynamics and challenges, especially those shaped by bias, racism, and the interplay of identity. Group therapy offers a space in which to confront assumptions, reflect on behaviour, and foster growth in relationships. It nurtures self-awareness and mutual respect – healing unfolds through shared experience.

DOI: 10.4324/9781003726012-10

This book also engages with questions many practitioners ask: Why did we choose this path? What draws us to group therapy? These are deeply personal as well as professional questions. I have explored distinctions between individual and group therapy, differing techniques, and the relational experiences that emerge between therapists and group members. To bring theory into practice, I include personal narratives and anonymized clinical examples drawn from my journey as a Turkish-speaking psychotherapist and group analyst based in London.

S.H. Foulkes, a pioneer of group analysis in England, recognised that the therapist's personality significantly shapes group dynamics. In *Therapeutic Group Analysis* (1964), he emphasised that the conductor – the group therapist – is not a neutral figure but an integral part of the group matrix: 'The conductor is part of the group and his personality inevitably influences the process. His training, experience, and personal qualities all play a role in how the group functions' (Foulkes, 1964, p. 39).

I am grateful to S.H. Foulkes and Jafar Kareem, whose work has shaped my understanding and practice of group therapy. Although both are no longer living, their insights continue to guide me, allowing me to integrate their approaches into my work. Their legacies live on through the groups I facilitate and the patients I accompany on their therapeutic journeys.

This insight remains highly relevant in intercultural psychoanalytic therapy, where the individuality of both the therapist and the group members enhances the process. Each session becomes an opportunity to explore cultural and personal complexities – a collective space where differences are embraced. Such differences remind us that while each of us is unique, we are connected in our shared humanity.

Intercultural therapy – whether individual or group – offers no simple solutions. A well-facilitated group provides a flexible structure, free from rigid dogma, guided by a trained professional. To use a metaphor: group therapy does not serve a pre-prepared meal; rather, it encourages each participant to learn how to cook – to experiment with ingredients, discover personal preferences, and create something personally meaningful. This approach enriches Western psychotherapy by offering enduring models for engaging with patients from diverse cultural identities (Bernal and Domenech Rodríguez, 2012).

Thus, therapy becomes a means not only of healing but also of recognising and honouring difference. The experiences shared in this book reflect my professional path – traversing nursing, teaching, management, community development, and psychotherapy across Türkiye (formerly Turkey), the United Kingdom, Europe, and Asia. These encounters have shaped my understanding of psychotherapy's cultural dimensions. I see therapy not solely as a science but also as an art – one requiring empathy, patience, and a willingness to embrace uncertainty. It is through this openness that healing becomes possible, and by embracing our differences, we strengthen our communities (Papadopoulos, 2007).

A continued adherence to ideals of 'Whiteness', 'sameness', and Western norms may risk neglecting the richness of Blackness, other languages, spiritual beliefs, and cultural rituals – practices that challenge dominant ideologies. When these cultural ways of being go unrecognised, they risk being reduced to superficial traits or filtered through narrow theoretical lenses. Our work must be rooted in culturally informed practice – engaging with and learning from diverse traditions while honouring individual, familial, and communal values.

Over the past 30 years, I have witnessed psychotherapy's power to transform lives. Yet I have also seen individuals who might have benefited from talking therapies turn instead to medication – often because of stigma, limited access to services, or societal pressure for quick solutions. For instance, a young refugee struggling with anxiety and grief relied solely on medication. While it alleviated immediate distress, it did not address the deeper layers of trauma or the relational difficulties that affected their everyday life and relationships. This example highlights the limits of a purely pharmacological approach and the potential missed opportunities for healing and self-understanding that psychotherapy can offer.

As a psychotherapist and group therapist, I hold my patients' stories and emotions with deep respect. These stories will accompany me throughout my life, informing my practice and perspective (Papadopoulos, 2007).

If this book has illuminated the enduring value of talking therapies, I consider it a privilege. To contribute to the field and share these reflections is something I deeply appreciate. Words hold power – through them, we understand, connect, and move towards healing.

The clinical examples here – from the 1990s to the present day – blend personal and professional insights drawn from 50 years of practice. While names, locations, and details have been altered for confidentiality, the emotional and therapeutic essence remains intact. This collection reflects a rich tapestry of learning and growth accumulated over decades.

In closing, I hope that this book has offered space for reflection, sparked curiosity, and encouraged new ways of thinking about therapy's role in understanding and healing the human condition. We stand at a crucial moment in psychotherapy when cultural competence is not an optional enhancement but an essential part of ethical and effective practice. The therapeutic space needs to evolve in order to reflect the diversity it serves. I hope that this work contributes to that evolution and inspires meaningful change within our field and society.

Ultimately, this book celebrates the resilience and richness within us all. It reminds us that therapy is not only about mending what has been broken but also about embracing the full complexity of human connection, growth, and difference. I invite you to continue exploring, keep learning, and never lose faith in the transformative potential of words.

References

Bernal, G. and Domenech Rodríguez, M.M., 2012. *Cultural Adaptations: Tools for Evidence-Based Practice with Diverse Populations*. Washington, DC: American Psychological Association.

Bhugra, D. and Becker, M.A., 2005. 'Migration, Cultural Bereavement and Cultural Identity', *World Psychiatry*, 4(1), pp. 18–24.

Foulkes, S.H., 1964. *Therapeutic Group Analysis*. London: Routledge & Kegan Paul.

Papadopoulos, R.K., 2007. 'Refugees, Trauma and Adversity-Activated Development', *European Journal of Psychotherapy & Counselling*, 9(3), pp. 301–312.

Chapter 10

Glossary of Psychoanalytic Terms

General Acknowledgement

This glossary draws primarily on classical psychoanalytic literature. Several definitions are informed by *The Language of Psychoanalysis* by Laplanche and Pontalis (1973), alongside the work of Freud and later psychoanalytic and group-analytic theorists. Where concepts are closely associated with particular authors or works, individual references are provided. More widely accepted psychoanalytic terms are not individually cited, as they form part of the shared theoretical foundation of the field.

Glossary of Terms

Abreaction	A process in which repressed emotions linked to past experiences are released, often through recalling or reliving those experiences. Freud and Breuer (1895) described abreaction in Studies on Hysteria, noting that patients experienced relief when unexpressed affect was discharged. In contemporary therapy, abreaction is understood as part of integrating unconscious material into conscious awareness.
Acting out	A defence mechanism involving the expression of unconscious wishes, impulses, or conflicts through actions rather than words. Freud (1914) observed that patients may not remember repressed material but instead 'act it out'. In therapy, acting out is often seen as non-verbal communication of unresolved emotional conflicts. In group therapy, such behaviours – whether disruptive, silent, or provocative – can facilitate insight and change when carefully interpreted by the therapist.

DOI: 10.4324/9781003726012-11

Aggression	Aggression refers to tendencies expressed through real or fantasy behaviour aimed at harming, intimidating, or constraining others – physically, verbally, or emotionally. In psychoanalysis, aggression is understood in the context of unconscious conflicts, repressed impulses, and early relational experiences (Klein, 1946).
Ambivalence	The simultaneous presence of opposing emotions – such as love and hate – towards the same person, object, or idea. Freud (1910) considered ambivalence fundamental to human relationships, especially within the parent–child bond. In group settings, ambivalence may appear when patients both desire closeness and fear dependency.
Anna Freud's defence mechanisms	According to Anna Freud (1936), the following mechanisms protect the ego from anxiety:
•	Denial: Refusing to accept reality.
•	Displacement: Shifting emotions to a safer target.
•	Introjection: Absorbing others' beliefs or values.
•	Isolation: Separating thoughts from feelings.
•	Projection: Attributing one's own feelings to others.
•	Reaction formation: Expressing the opposite of true feelings.
•	Regression: Reverting to earlier behaviour.
•	Repression: Blocking distressing thoughts from awareness.
•	Reversal: Turning an emotion into its opposite.
•	Splitting: Seeing things as all good or all bad.
•	Sublimation: Redirecting impulses into acceptable activities.
•	Turning against the self: Directing hostility inward.
•	Undoing: Trying to cancel out guilt through action.
Anxiety	A psychological state triggered by perceived threats to one's wellbeing. In Freud's psychoanalytic theory, anxiety arises from internal conflicts between the id, the ego, and the superego, often rooted in early childhood experiences (Freud, 1926).
Attachment	Developed outside classical psychoanalysis but influential in psychodynamic practice, John

	Bowlby's attachment theory emphasises the emotional bond between infant and caregiver, shaping patterns of security, anxiety, or avoidance in later relationships (Bowlby, 1969). In group therapy, attachment dynamics emerge in how members relate to the therapist and one another.
Authoritarian personality	A personality structure marked by rigid thinking, submission to authority, hostility towards outgroups, and intolerance of difference. Developed by Adorno et al. (1950), it links unconscious conflicts and strict early parenting to prejudice and discriminatory behaviour. In group therapy, authoritarian traits may appear as dominance, resistance to ambiguity, or reliance on rigid hierarchies.
Autonomy	The capacity for self-regulation and independence, achieved through differentiation from primary caregivers while maintaining meaningful connections. In psychoanalytic thought, autonomy develops gradually alongside ego strength. In groups, it appears when members take responsibility for their contributions without withdrawing from the collective process (Winnicott, 1960).
Consciousness	In Freudian theory, consciousness refers to the part of the mind containing thoughts, perceptions, and feelings of which a person is currently aware. Freud distinguished consciousness from the preconscious and the unconscious, which contains repressed material influencing behaviour without awareness (Freud, 1915).
Containment	Introduced by Wilfred Bion, containment describes the therapist's capacity to receive, hold, and process a patient's intense emotions without becoming overwhelmed, returning them in a manageable form (Bion, 1962). This supports emotional regulation and integration.
Countertransference	Originally introduced by Freud as the therapist's unconscious emotional reactions to the patient, often seen as an obstacle. Later psychoanalysts recognised countertransference as a valuable source of insight when the therapist becomes aware of and manages these feelings (Heimann, 1950; Gabbard, 2014).

Defence mechanisms	Unconscious strategies used to reduce anxiety by managing internal conflict. First introduced by Freud (1894) and systematically classified by Anna Freud (1936). While protective, overuse can cause difficulties.
Depressive position	Introduced by Melanie Klein, this is an early developmental stage where the infant perceives the mother as a whole, separate person rather than split into 'all good' or 'all bad'. Acceptance of ambivalence and concern for others' wellbeing are key to emotional growth (Klein, 1946).
Displacement	A defence mechanism redirecting emotions from a threatening source to a safer substitute, often unconsciously. Forms include emotional, behavioural, and symbolic displacement (Freud, 1894).
Ego	The part of the psyche that mediates between the instinctual demands of the id, the moral constraints of the superego, and the realities of the external world. Governed by the reality principle, the ego enables the individual to delay gratification, manage anxiety, and navigate social expectations. It develops with maturity and operates across conscious, preconscious, and unconscious levels (Freud, 1923).
Envy	A complex and powerful emotion described by Melanie Klein as the expression of destructive feelings towards another's perceived good or pleasurable qualities. Envy emerges in early development and reflects frustration at not being able to possess or share in what the other has. It differs from jealousy and can involve an unconscious wish to diminish the object of envy. In therapy, exploring envy helps patients to recognise unconscious dynamics and form more constructive relational patterns (Klein, 1946).
Free association	A psychoanalytic technique developed by Freud in which the patient speaks freely without censorship. This process reveals unconscious conflicts, desires, and patterns underlying psychological distress, remaining a foundational method in classical psychoanalysis (Freud, 1900).
Gay	A term describing individuals, particularly men, who are emotionally, romantically, or sexually

	attracted to others of the same gender. It also functions as an inclusive identity within the LGBTQ+ community, carrying cultural and political significance associated with self-acceptance and visibility (APA, 2022).
Group analyst	A psychotherapist trained in group analysis, focusing on understanding and working with group dynamics. The group analyst facilitates communication, fosters insight, and attends to conscious and unconscious processes that emerge within the group setting (Foulkes, 1964).
Holding environment	Introduced by Donald Winnicott, the term describes the emotional and relational space provided by a caregiver or therapist that offers safety, consistency, and reliability. This environment allows the individual to explore difficult emotions and early relational experiences without fear of rejection, supporting the development of a cohesive sense of self (Winnicott, 1960).
Id	The most primitive part of the psyche, present from birth, operating entirely in the unconscious. Driven by the pleasure principle, the id seeks immediate gratification of instinctual desires, such as hunger, aggression, and sexuality, without moral considerations (Freud, 1923).
Insight	The conscious understanding of unconscious motivations or conflicts underlying psychological symptoms. Gaining insight is considered essential for emotional growth and therapeutic progress (Freud, 1910).
Introjection	A defence mechanism in which a person unconsciously adopts the attitudes, values, or feelings of another. Introjection helps to integrate external influences but can also perpetuate unresolved conflicts (Freud, 1923).
Jealousy	A complex emotional response involving fear of losing a valued relationship or object to a rival. Unlike envy, which focuses on wanting what another has, jealousy centres on anxiety about potential loss. Klein linked jealousy to early developmental experiences and object relations, affecting interpersonal behaviour. Exploring jealousy in therapy reveals unconscious fears and attachment dynamics (Klein, 1946).

Lesbian	A term describing a woman who is romantically or sexually attracted to other women. It also functions as an identity within the LGBTQ+ community, connected to cultural, social, and political dimensions of self-acceptance and pride (APA, 2022).
Masochist	An individual deriving gratification from experiencing pain, humiliation, or suffering. First introduced by Krafft-Ebing (1886), Freud later explored masochism psychoanalytically (Freud, 1924), linking it to unconscious guilt, early relational experiences, and internalised aggression.
Mirror phase	A concept developed by Lacan describing a developmental stage (from the age of six to 18 months) when a child recognises their reflection in a mirror. This stage is critical for forming self-identity and distinguishing self from others (Lacan, 1949).
Mirroring	The reflection of another person's emotions, behaviours, or attitudes. Introduced by Winnicott in early mother-infant attachment, mirroring supports self-development. Kohut later highlighted its role in fostering empathy, validation, and a cohesive sense of self (Winnicott, 1960; Kohut, 1971).
Neurosis	A psychological condition marked by persistent distress (e.g. anxiety, obsessive thoughts, phobias) without loss of reality testing or major personality disruption. Often linked to unresolved unconscious conflicts (Freud, 1894, 1926).
Neurotic symptoms	Psychological or physical symptoms caused by unconscious conflict, such as anxiety or intense emotional reactions, often addressed in therapy (Freud, 1926).
Patient	An individual engaged in therapy to explore psychological, emotional, or relational difficulties. In psychoanalysis, the patient actively uncovers unconscious processes rather than being a passive recipient (Freud, 1910, 1923).
Post-Traumatic Stress Disorder (PTSD)	A mental health condition triggered by severe trauma, marked by flashbacks, nightmares, hyperarousal, and avoidance. Psychoanalytically,

	trauma disrupts the self's coherence and integration of experience (Herman, 1992).
Preconscious	A level of the mind between conscious and unconscious, holding thoughts, memories, and feelings accessible to awareness. Associations, slips, and forgotten material often surface here before deeper unconscious content is explored (Freud, 1915).
Pre-Oedipal	The early developmental stage (from birth to three years of age) preceding the Oedipus complex, shaped primarily by relationships with primary caregivers. Expanded upon by post-Freudian analysts (Klein, 1932).
Projection	A defence mechanism where unacceptable thoughts or feelings are unconsciously attributed to others to avoid internal conflict (Freud, 1894).
Psychoeducation	The process of educating individuals about psychological concepts, mental health conditions, and coping strategies, clarifying how therapeutic dialogue differs from everyday conversation (Lukens and McFarlane, 2004).
Psychosis	A severe mental condition marked by disturbances in thought, perception, and reality testing, often including delusions or hallucinations (Freud, 1911; Bleuler, 1911).
Psychosomatic symptoms	Physical symptoms caused by psychological distress rather than medical conditions, often improving with psychotherapy (Alexander, 1946; Lipowski, 1988).
Psychotherapist	A trained professional specialising in treating emotional, psychological, and behavioural difficulties. Psychoanalytic work focuses on uncovering unconscious patterns and relational dynamics (Fonagy et al., 2002).
Psychotic	Describing symptoms such as delusions or hallucinations indicating a significant disconnection from reality (APA, 2013).
Resistance	Unconscious processes that hinder therapeutic progress by avoiding distressing emotions, insights, or memories. Resistance may appear as silence, intellectualisation, or deflection in therapy (Freud, 1912).
Sadist	An individual who derives pleasure, often sexual, from inflicting pain, suffering, or humiliation on

	others. In psychoanalysis, sadism can reflect aggression, unconscious conflicts, or certain personality structures (Freud, 1905).
Sadomasochism	A relational dynamic where individuals derive pleasure from both inflicting and receiving pain, typically within consensual contexts. It may represent internal conflicts between aggression and guilt or struggles with power and vulnerability (Freud, 1905; Glick and Meyers 1993).
Sibling rivalry	Feelings of competition and jealousy between siblings, shaped by early family dynamics. In group therapy, similar relational patterns may emerge, providing insight into interpersonal behaviour (Adler, 1927; Bowen, 1978).
Splitting	A defence mechanism in which individuals perceive others or situations in extreme, black-and-white terms – entirely good or entirely bad. This rigid perception can lead to unstable relationships and emotional distress (Klein, 1946).
Superego	The internalised moral authority formed through parental and societal values. Developing later in childhood, it inhibits the impulses of the id, guides the ego toward moral decisions, and fosters guilt or pride. In some individuals, the superego may become overly rigid or punitive (Freud, 1923).
Therapeutic alliance	The collaborative and trusting relationship between patient and therapist, essential for effective therapy. A strong alliance supports exploration of unconscious material and helps patients to feel safe expressing emotions (Bordin, 1979).
Transference	The unconscious redirection of emotions from past relationships onto present ones, often onto the therapist. Freud first systematically described this phenomenon, which can reveal unresolved conflicts from early relationships (Freud, 1912).
Transference-countertransference	A combined concept describing the mutual influence of a patient's transference and a therapist's countertransference. Recognising this dynamic helps therapists to understand unconscious relational patterns and manage emotional reactions (Heimann, 1950).

Trauma	A psychological response to deeply distressing or life-altering events, often resulting in long-term emotional, cognitive, and sometimes physical difficulties. Psychoanalytic perspectives emphasise how unprocessed trauma affects the unconscious and relational patterns (Herman, 1992).
Triangulation	A relational pattern in which two people involve a third person to manage conflict, anxiety, or tension. Commonly observed in family therapy, triangulation reflects unresolved emotional issues from earlier attachments (Bowen, 1978).
Unconscious	A central concept in Freudian theory, referring to the hidden aspects of the mind outside conscious awareness. It contains repressed memories, emotions, and desires that continue to influence behaviour, thoughts, and experiences (Freud, 1915).
Unconscious communication	Ways in which unconscious feelings and thoughts are expressed indirectly, for example through dreams, slips of the tongue, body language, or behaviour (Freud, 1901).
Undoing	A defence mechanism where an individual attempts to reverse or negate an unacceptable thought, feeling, or action, often through a symbolic or compensatory act (A. Freud, 1936).
Unfinished business	A Gestalt therapy concept referring to unresolved emotional issues or conflicts from the past that continue to affect present behaviour and relationships (Perls et al., 1951).
Unformulated experience	A psychoanalytic concept, usually associated with Donnel Stern, referring to implicit, often preverbal experiences not yet symbolised or brought into conscious awareness (Stern, 1985).
Unintegration	A state in which experiences, thoughts, or emotions remain fragmented and are not fully incorporated into the psyche, leading to psychological tension or distress (Kernberg, 1975; Bollas, 1987; Ogden, 1989).
Unrepresented states	Introduced by Christopher Bollas, these are emotional experiences that have not been processed or symbolised in the mind and are expressed somatically or behaviourally. They often stem from early developmental trauma and failures in attunement (Bollas, 1987).

Unrepressed impulses	Impulses or desires that are present but are not fully controlled by the ego, sometimes manifesting in behaviour, fantasies, or creative expression (Freud, 1915, 1923).
Unthought known	A term by Christopher Bollas describing knowledge or experience that is felt or acted upon but not consciously articulated, often originating from early relational experiences (Bollas, 1987).

References

Adler, A., 1927. *Understanding Human Nature*. London: George Allen & Unwin.

Adorno, T.W., Frenkel-Brunswik, E., Levinson, D.J., and Sanford, R.N., 1950. *The Authoritarian Personality*. New York: Harper.

Alexander, F., 1946. *Psychosomatic Medicine: Its Principles and Applications*. New York: W.W. Norton.

American Psychiatric Association (APA), 2013. *Diagnostic and Statistical Manual of Mental Disorders*, 5th edn. Arlington, VA: American Psychiatric Publishing.

American Psychiatric Association (APA), 2022. *APA Dictionary of Psychology*. Available at https://dictionary.apa.org (accessed 27 January 2026).

Bion, W.R., 1962. *Learning from Experience*. London: Heinemann.

Bollas, C., 1987. *The Shadow of the Object: Psychoanalysis of the Unthought Known*. London: Free Association Books.

Bordin, E.S., 1979. 'The Generalizability of the Psychoanalytic Concept of the Working Alliance', *Psychotherapy: Theory, Research & Practice*, 16(3), pp. 252–260.

Bowen, M., 1978. *Family Therapy in Clinical Practice*. New York: Jason Aronson.

Bleuler, E., 1911. *Dementia Praecox or the Group of Schizophrenias*. New York: International Universities Press.

Bowlby, J., 1969. *Attachment and Loss*, vol. 1: *Attachment*. London: Hogarth Press.

Fonagy, P., Gergely, G., Jurist, E.L., and Target, M., 2002. *Affect Regulation, Mentalization, and the Development of the Self*. London: Karnac Books.

Freud, A., 1936. *The Ego and the Mechanisms of Defence*. London: Hogarth Press.

Freud, S., 1894. 'The Neuro-Psychoses of Defence', in *Collected Papers*. London: Hogarth Press.

Freud, S., 1900. *The Interpretation of Dreams*. London: Hogarth Press.

Freud, S., 1901. *The Psychopathology of Everyday Life*. London: Hogarth Press.

Freud, S., 1905. *Three Essays on the Theory of Sexuality*. London: Hogarth Press.

Freud, S., 1910. 'The Future Prospects of Psycho-Analytic Therapy', *The International Journal of Psychoanalysis*, 1, pp. 1–20.

Freud, S., 1911. 'Formulations on the Two Principles of Mental Functioning', *The Standard Edition of the Complete Psychological Works of Sigmund Freud*, vol. 12, London: Hogarth Press, pp. 213–226.

Freud, S., 1912. 'The Dynamics of Transference', *The Standard Edition of the Complete Psychological Works of Sigmund Freud*, vol. 12, London: Hogarth Press, pp. 99–108.

Freud, S., 1914. 'Remembering, Repeating and Working-Through', *The Standard Edition of the Complete Psychological Works of Sigmund Freud*, vol. 12, London: Hogarth Press, pp. 147–156.

Freud, S., 1915. 'The Unconscious', in *The Standard Edition of the Complete Psychological Works of Sigmund Freud*, vol. 14. London: Hogarth Press, pp. 159–215.
Freud, S., 1923. *The Ego and the Id*. London: Hogarth Press.
Freud, S., 1924. 'Some Psychical Consequences of the Anatomical Distinction between the Sexes', *The Standard Edition of the Complete Psychological Works of Sigmund Freud*, vol. 19, London: Hogarth Press pp. 248–258.
Freud, S., 1926. *Inhibitions, Symptoms and Anxiety*. London: Hogarth Press.
Freud, S., and Breuer, J., 1895. *Studies on Hysteria*. London: Hogarth Press.
Foulkes, S.H., 1964. *Therapeutic Group Analysis*. London: Allen & Unwin.
Gabbard, G.O., 2014. *Psychodynamic Psychiatry in Clinical Practice*. 5th edn. Washington, DC: American Psychiatric Publishing.
Heimann, P., 1950. 'On Counter-Transference', *International Journal of Psychoanalysis*, 31, pp. 81–84.
Herman, J.L., 1992. *Trauma and Recovery*. New York: Basic Books.
Klein, M., 1932. 'The Psycho-Analytic Play Technique in the Treatment of Children', *International Journal of Psychoanalysis*, 13, pp. 395–409.
Klein, M., 1946. *Notes on Some Schizoid Mechanisms*. London: Hogarth Press.
Kohut, H., 1971. *The Analysis of the Self: A Systematic Approach to the Psychoanalytic Treatment of Narcissistic Personality Disorders*. Chicago: University of Chicago Press.
Lacan, J., 1949. *The Mirror Stage as Formative of the I Function as Revealed in Psychoanalytic Experience*. Available at https://www.lacan.com/lacan_mirror_stage.htm (accessed 27 January 2026).
Laplanche, J. and Pontalis, J.-B., 1973. *The Language of Psychoanalysis*. London: Hogarth Press.
Lipowski, Z.J., 1988. *Psychosomatic Medicine: Past and Present*. Cambridge: Cambridge University Press.
Lukens, E.P. and McFarlane, W.R., 2004. *Psychoeducation in Mental Health Care*. Arlington, VA: American Psychiatric Publishing.
Ogden, T.H., 1989. *The Primitive Edge of Experience*. Northvale, NJ: Jason Aronson.
Perls, F., Hefferline, R., and Goodman, P., 1951. *Gestalt Therapy: Excitement and Growth in the Human Personality*. New York: Julian Press.
Winnicott, D.W., 1960. 'The Theory of the Parent-Infant Relationship', *International Journal of Psychoanalysis*, 41, pp. 585–595.

Index

For Product Safety Concerns and Information please contact our EU
representative GPSR@taylorandfrancis.com
Taylor & Francis Verlag GmbH, Kaufingerstraße 24, 80331 München, Germany

www.ingramcontent.com/pod-product-compliance
Ingram Content Group UK Ltd.
Pitfield, Milton Keynes, MK11 3LW, UK
UKHW020008200926
475702UK00015B/2540
* 9 7 8 1 0 4 1 2 1 1 8 9 1 *